WITHDRAWN

Total Lobbying

WHAT LOBBYISTS WANT
(AND HOW THEY TRY TO GET IT)

Anthony J. Nownes
University of Tennessee, Knoxville

CAMBRIDGE UNIVERSITY PRESS
Cambridge, New York, Melbourne, Madrid, Cape Town, Singapore, São Paulo

Cambridge University Press
32 Avenue of the Americas, New York, NY 10013-2473, USA

www.cambridge.org
Information on this title: www.cambridge.org/9780521838177

First published 2006

Printed in the United States of America

A catalog record for this publication is available from the British Library.

Library of Congress Cataloging in Publication Data

Nownes, Anthony J.
Total lobbying : what lobbyists want (and how they try to get it) / Anthony J. Nownes.
   p. cm.
Includes bibliographical references and index.
ISBN 0-521-83817-7 (hardback) – ISBN 0-521-54711-3 (pbk.)
1. Lobbying – United States. 2. Lobbyists – United States. I. Title.
JK1118.N693 2006
328.73'078–dc22   2006002229

ISBN-13   978-0-521-83817-7 hardback
ISBN-10   0-521-83817-7 hardback

ISBN-13   978-0-521-54711-6 paperback
ISBN-10   0-521-54711-3 paperback

Contents

Preface

This book is about lobbying in the United States. What separates it from most books on lobbying is its broad focus. As you will see, the book examines two types of lobbying – land use lobbying and procurement lobbying – that are seldom mentioned, much less studied, by scholars of lobbying and lobbyists. Of course, the book also takes an extensive look at public policy lobbying – the type of lobbying that *is* the focus of most studies of lobbying and lobbyists. This book is also unique in that it uses the words of actual lobbyists to illuminate the process of lobbying.

As much as possible, in the pages that follow I attempt to eschew jargon and make the book accessible to a broad audience of undergraduates and graduate students studying lobbying and/or interest groups in the United States, as well as interested laypeople. My hope is that by the time you are finished reading this book, you will have a thorough understanding of who lobbyists are, where they operate, what they want, what they do, and how influential they are.

Before moving on, I must acknowledge my debts to the many people who have helped make this book a reality. First, I would like to thank Ed Parsons, the magnificent editor who shepherded this book through the writing and production process. Ed's instincts are excellent, and his patience seems to know no bounds. Second, I would like to thank Rogan Kersh, who introduced me to Ed. Professor Kersh is a fine scholar (whose work provided inspiration for much of this book) and a good man, and I appreciate his graciousness and magnanimity. Third, I would like to thank my academic gurus, Allan J. Cigler and Paul E. Johnson. It is not in jest that I refer to Dr. Cigler as my "faculty dad." As for Professor Johnson, both personally and professionally he has proven to be a fine lodestar over the years. Fourth, I would like to thank my wife, Elsa, who listened far more than should have been required to stories about zoning variances, government procurement practices, and the pitfalls of elite interviewing as a research method.

Intellectually, I owe debts to literally dozens of people, including the following: Robert M. Alexander, Jeffrey Berejikian, Regis F. Boyle, Clint Cantrell, William K. "Bubba" Cheek, Christopher Cooper, David Elkins, R. Kenneth Godwin, David J. Houston, Frankie Sue Howerton, Jeffrey G. Johnson, Debra P. McCauley, Emil Nagengast, Gregory Neddenriep, Lilliard Richardson, Bryan Schmiedeler, and Marc Schwerdt. Finally, for inspiration, I would like to thank Jason Falkner, Roger Joseph Manning, Jr., and Luke Steele.

1 Studying Lobbyists and Lobbying

Anne Dooley[1] is an accomplished land use attorney and lobbyist based in one of America's largest cities. Anne is the president of Land Use Policy Advocates, a firm that specializes in getting local government approval for controversial land use projects. Among her recent clients is a firm seeking to build a massive development of single-family homes, office buildings, and commercial space on a largely undeveloped tract of more than 5,000 acres; another firm is seeking government approval to build several low-income housing units in a high-income neighborhood. Anne's work often includes grassroots lobbying efforts designed to demobilize public opposition to potentially controversial development projects. She also has regular face-to-face meetings with city legislators.

Erica Nowitzki is deputy legislative director for a well-regarded Washington, DC-based senior citizens' advocacy group that focuses on Social Security and Medicare. Though the group is no AARP (the 35,000,000-member organization formerly known as the American Association of Retired Persons), it is impressive in its own right. It boasts hundreds of thousands of members and has a multimillion-dollar budget. Erica works almost exclusively on Capitol Hill (i.e., Congress). She came to the profession from a staff position on "the Hill" and spends a lot of time doing the things that the archetypal lobbyist does – testifying at congressional committee hearings and meeting with legislators and their aides.

Across the country in a sprawling sunbelt city, John Hodges works for a high-profile "full service" public affairs firm. The firm offers a variety of services to clients, including what it calls "advocacy," which it defines broadly as "representing clients before local, state, and federal governmental bodies." The firm also provides its clients with "government procurement services." What this means is that John and his firm help clients identify and secure government contracts. John's clients are not interested in public

policy decisions per se. Rather, they are interested in procurement decisions – government purchasing decisions worth hundreds of thousands of
dollars to his clients that "sell to government." John helps them understand and navigate complex and arcane procurement rules, and he also
meets personally with legislators and executive agency personnel.

Finally, in the capital city of a large western state, Kenneth Brady heads
up the government relations division of a massive "peak" trade association (i.e., a trade association that represents business firms in various
industries). On behalf of the group's more than 10,000 member firms,
Kenneth works on a wide assortment of issues that concern businesses in
his state. Because he is based in the state capital, he is in the thick of a
great deal of political action. Very few high-profile state issues escape his
attention. Kenneth uses practically every lobbying technique in the book.
For example, he meets personally with legislators and their aides and with
executive agency personnel, uses several grassroots lobbying techniques,
and makes monetary contributions to candidates for office.

LOBBYING: A COMPLEX PHENOMENON

These four brief case studies, which are based on interviews I conducted for
this book, demonstrate that lobbying is not a simple and straightforward
phenomenon. The case studies illustrate, for example, the following:

1. *Lobbying occurs at all three levels of government – state, local, and national.*
   Anne lobbies local officials exclusively. In contrast, Erica lobbies only
   national government officials. Kenneth lobbies state government
   officials primarily. John lobbies both state and local officials.
2. *Lobbying occurs in all three branches of government.* Anne lobbies
   city council members (i.e., legislators) primarily, but executive
   agency officials as well. Similarly, John lobbies both legislators and
   bureaucrats.[2] In contrast, Erica focuses her lobbying efforts almost
   exclusively on the legislature. Finally, when Kenneth lobbies officials of state government, he does so across all three branches of
   government.
3. *Lobbying takes a variety of forms.* Lobbyists use a large array of techniques. Anne meets personally with local legislators on a regular
   basis, testifies at city council hearings, and engages in grassroots lobbying. Erica meets personally with legislators and their aides, testifies before legislative committees, helps draft legislation, and makes
   monetary contributions to candidates. John testifies at executive
   (bureaucratic) agency hearings, submits written reports to agency

officials, helps draft rules and regulations, and meets personally with executive agency personnel. Finally, Kenneth meets personally with legislators and executive agency personnel, socializes with legislators, contributes money to legislators' campaigns, testifies before legislative committees, and engages in grassroots mobilization.

4. *Lobbying is practiced by a wide variety of organizations.* Anne works mostly on behalf of business firms (e.g., development companies), but also occasionally represents nonprofit groups such as charities and governmental entities (e.g., states, cities, counties). Erica works for a mass membership citizen group (i.e., a group that is open to any citizen), John works exclusively for business firms, and Kenneth works for a trade association (an organized group of business firms).

5. *Lobbying is practiced in virtually every issue area imaginable.* Erica focuses on Social Security and Medicare, while Kenneth works on a broad assortment of issues, including business taxation, health care, tort reform (i.e., lawsuit reform), and workers' compensation. For their part, Anne and John do not really work on "issues" at all. Rather, Anne seeks permission from local governments for her clients to develop land, while John tries to convince government officials to buy what his clients' companies are selling.

6. *Lobbying sometimes produces results and sometimes does not.* Anne recently received permission from a local government for one of her clients to develop a huge tract of land outside a major city. In contrast, Erica was recently disappointed when Congress refused to increase the cost-of-living allowance (COLA) for Social Security recipients. John has had better luck recently, having just won for one of his clients a government contract to provide architectural services for the construction of a new library in a major city. Finally, Kenneth lost a battle recently when the state assembly voted to increase the state's minimum wage.

My point here is this: *Lobbying is a complex and heterogeneous phenomenon.* Understanding lobbying requires understanding the varying behavior of a plethora of individual lobbyists; working at different levels of government, for several different types of organizations, on a seemingly endless variety of issues; using a wide array of techniques; and achieving various levels of success. This is not easy.

The Need for This Book
My purpose in writing this book is to demystify lobbying and lobbyists. The topic cries out for such treatment because as I point out here (and

will continue to do throughout the chapters that follow), it is a complex
phenomenon that is not easy to comprehend in its entirety. To be sure,
scholars and journalists alike have written literally volumes about this
topic, but the extant literature is not always accessible to a broad audience.
Much of it, unfortunately, is aimed either at insiders directly involved in
lobbying or at scholars who already know a great deal about lobbying.
This book is different. Here, I try hard to make the world of lobbying
comprehensible to a wide audience of undergraduates and nonexperts. To
this end, I eschew jargon whenever possible and focus on the basic *facts*
of lobbying, rather than on any theory or framework designed to explain
it. Ultimately, my goal is to provide a balanced look at the full range of
lobbying and lobbyists in America in the hope that you will be interested
in learning more about the subject. In sum, I wrote this book to provide
a solid foundation of knowledge on which the student of lobbying can
build.

My Approach

Because lobbying is such a complex phenomenon, I believe the best way
to proceed is to divide it into easily digestible chunks.[3] Thus, in this book,
instead of trying to describe every possible manifestation of lobbying,
I assume that there are three basic kinds: (1) *public policy lobbying*, (2) *land
use lobbying*, and (3) *procurement lobbying*. *Public policy lobbying* is *the lobbying that accompanies government decisions (e.g., laws, rules, regulations, court
decisions) made in response to societal demands for action on important issues of
the day.* For example, the lobbying that surrounds government decisions
about such high-profile public policy issues as abortion, gay rights, gun
control, immigration, taxes, trade, and war is public policy lobbying. *Land
use lobbying* is *the lobbying that accompanies government decisions rendered in
response to specific requests for permission to utilize land in a certain way.* For
example, the lobbying that surrounds a city's decision whether or not to
allow Wal-Mart to build and open a new superstore on a prize piece of
land within the city's boundaries is land use lobbying. *Procurement lobbying*
is *the lobbying that accompanies government decisions concerning which specific
goods and/or services the government will purchase.* For example, the lobbying
that is aimed at convincing a government entity (Congress, for example)
to purchase something (say, a new aircraft carrier) is procurement lobbying. Lobbying that is designed to convince a government entity (for
example, an executive agency) to purchase one brand of product or service (say, a copy machine or janitorial services) over another brand is also
procurement lobbying.

I believe that once you understand these three basic kinds of lobbying, you will be in a good position to understand lobbying in its totality. Of course, I am not saying that after you read this book you will know everything there is to know about lobbying. But it is hoped that this book will provide you with good, simple, and straightforward information about who lobbyists are, what interests they represent, what they want, what they do, and the extent to which they affect government decisions.

SOME IMPORTANT TERMS

For the chapters that follow, you will need to know precisely what we are talking about when we use the terms *lobbying* and *lobbyist*. In this section, I define these two terms, as well as one other – *organized interest*. These three terms are absolutely critical for a full understanding of lobbying.

Lobbying

You would think that such a well-known and well-traveled term would be well defined. This, however, is not the case. In their panoramic overview of the literature on interest groups and lobbying in the United States, political scientists Frank R. Baumgartner and Beth L. Leech note that "[t]he word *lobbying* has seldom been used the same way twice by those studying the topic."[4] Other scholars of lobbying have reached the same conclusion.[5] After considering many definitions of lobbying that have been offered over the years, Baumgartner and Leech ultimately settle on this basic definition: Lobbying, they say, is "an effort to influence the policy process."[6] This is a good definition. It is not, however, ideal. Unfortunately, including "policy process" in the definition of lobbying introduces a bit of confusion. As policy scholar Paul Sabatier notes, the policy process "involves an extremely complex set of interacting elements over time."[7] Neither I nor anyone else can fully enumerate all these elements. Thankfully, if we modify Baumgartner and Leech's definition only slightly, we do not have to grapple with the thorny question of precisely how to define the policy process. Here then is my slightly modified version of Baumgartner and Leech's definition: *Lobbying* is *an effort designed to affect what the government does*. As you can see, the key difference between this definition and theirs is that I have substituted the phrase "what the government does" for the phrase "the policy process." This definition of lobbying is exceedingly broad – by design. As you will see in the next chapter, scholars have discovered that lobbying can take a wide variety of forms.

At this point it is important to note that lobbying is a *process* rather than a single *activity*.[8] Another way to put this is as follows: When attempting to affect what the government does, a lobbyist seldom does only one specific thing at one specific time. Rather, he or she typically does multiple things over a period of time. A hypothetical example can help illustrate what I mean. Let us assume for a moment that there is a vacancy on the United States Supreme Court. A women's rights group wishes to affect what the federal government does about this vacancy. That is, the group wishes to influence the choice. What the federal government decides in this case will be embodied in a final authoritative decision made by the Senate when it votes either to accept or to reject the president's nominee for the post. However, the Senate's vote is not the only relevant decision here. Many government decisions will precede this one, including the president's regarding whom to consider and then nominate, and those of various senators and presidential aides about whom to recommend to the president. Because what the government ultimately decides in this case is a function of several decisions made by several political actors, rather than one decision made by one political actor, the lobbying effort of the women's rights group targets many different individuals (including the president, presidential aides, senators, and legislative staffers) across two different branches of government (the legislative and the executive), and encompasses a variety of lobbying techniques.

In short, lobbying is not one discrete activity, such as testifying before a congressional committee or meeting with a legislator. Rather, it is a *process* that comprises several discrete activities. Thus, when I define lobbying as "an effort designed to affect what the government does," I am necessarily defining the term "effort" broadly to encompass several distinct but related lobbying activities.

Organized Interest

Lobbying is by far the most important term I use in this book. However, the term *organized interest* is also important here primarily because by definition, lobbyists represent organized interests when they lobby. Here, I define an *organized interest* as *an organization that engages in political activity – that is, activity designed to affect what the government does.*[9]

Most treatments of lobbying and lobbyists eschew this term in favor of the more common *interest group*. I believe this is a mistake. An interest group is generally defined as a voluntary association of "joiners who share a common characteristic" and "have a public policy focus."[10] Organizations that fit this definition include mass membership groups, such as the National Education Association (NEA), National Rifle Association (NRA), and AARP. Clearly, groups like these are important players in American politics. Nonetheless, they comprise only a fraction of the U.S. organizations that lobby. Approximately 25 years ago, political scientists Kay Lehman Schlozman and John T. Tierney surveyed lobbyists working in Washington, DC, and found that many of them represented not interest groups like the NEA, NRA, or AARP but nonmembership organizations such as business firms.[11] They concluded that "interest group" simply does not accurately represent the universe of organizations that hire lobbyists in the United States. Subsequent empirical studies confirmed that interest groups comprise only a small fraction of politically active organizations in the United States.[12] To reflect the fact that many (if not most) lobbyists work not for interest groups but for other types of politically active organizations, Schlozman and Tierney coined the term *organized interest* to denote organizations that lobby government. This term is broad enough to encompass the entire range of organizations that lobby in the United States, including traditional membership-based organizations like the NEA, NRA, and AARP and such nonmembership organizations as business firms, think tanks, and universities and colleges. (In Chapter 2 I describe the broad range of organizations that comprise the universe of organized interests.)

Lobbyist

This term is also important here. It is tempting to define a lobbyist simply as "someone who lobbies." However, because I define lobbying so broadly, this definition would encompass any citizen who votes, belongs to a membership-based organized interest, or writes a letter to his or her member of Congress. Since not all of us are lobbyists, this simple definition will not do. We generally reserve the term *lobbyist* for an individual who lobbies on behalf of an organized interest.[13] Thus, here I adopt the following definition of lobbyist: *a person who lobbies on behalf of an organized interest (or numerous organized interests)*. This definition is broad enough to encompass the entire range of lobbyists, but narrow enough to exclude ordinary citizens who make appeals to government officials on their own behalf.

Summary

In the chapters that follow I use three terms repeatedly: *lobbying, organized interest*, and *lobbyist. Lobbying* is defined as *an effort designed to affect what the government does*. An organized interest is defined as *an organization that engages in political activity*. A *lobbyist* is defined as *a person who lobbies on behalf of an organized interest (or numerous organized interests)*. From time to time as you read the chapters, it may be necessary to revisit these definitions.

DATA AND METHODS

As you will see from the scores of footnotes in the chapters that follow, some of the information I present comes from previous studies of lobbying and lobbyists. Over the past 50 years, political scientists have undertaken extensive studies of lobbying and lobbyists in the United States, and this book attempts to summarize what they have learned. A great deal of the information, however, comes from original interviews I conducted with lobbyists. I began this project with the firm conviction that the best way to gain a clear understanding of lobbying was to go directly to the source – to speak with lobbyists themselves.

The Interviews

Chapters 3–6 describe and analyze the three types of lobbying I have identified – public policy lobbying, land use lobbying, and procurement lobbying. These chapters are informed by previous studies of lobbying and lobbyists, but also draw upon data I gathered from interviews with 34 lobbyists across the United States. You can find details about these interviews in Appendix B.

Table 1 contains basic information about the lobbyists I interviewed for this book. For each lobbyist, there is an identification number (that I will use in subsequent chapters to identify who says what), an indicator of the primary level of government at which the lobbyist works, the type of organization that employs the lobbyist, and the lobbying classification (or classifications) in which the lobbyist fits. Realistically, I cannot provide more information about my respondents because I promised them complete anonymity and confidentiality. Table 1 shows that 16 sample lobbyists lobby the national government primarily, while 9 lobbyists concentrate on state government and 9 concentrate on local government. As for the employers of the sample lobbyists, 20 lobbyists are employed by consulting, law, lobbying, or public relations firms, 2 by trade associations, 2 by business firms, 2 by professional associations, 1 by a private university, 1 by a labor union, 1 by an educational accrediting commission, 1 by a coalition of trade and professional associations, 1 by a coalition of government entities, 1 by a citizen group, and 1 by a "think tank." (I discuss the universe of organized interests in Chapter 2). One of my respondents is an independent contract lobbyist. Finally, 20 are public policy lobbyists, 15 procurement lobbyists, and 8 land use lobbyists. While my sample is clearly not representative of all lobbyists in the United States, I believe it is acceptable for my purposes.

TABLE 1. Sample lobbyists

ID	Primary level of government lobbyist lobbies (and location)[a]	Employer[b]	Classification[c]
1.	State	"voluntary association" of cities and towns	public policy
2.	City (San Diego)	"advocacy and government affairs consulting firm"	land use
3.	National	"accrediting commission" for vocational schools	public policy
4.	National	"large law firm"	public policy
5.	National	"architecture, engineering, and consulting firm"	procurement
6.	State (Tennessee)	law firm	public policy
7.	State	"holding company" that controls a freight railroad	public policy
8.	State	"state architectural" professional association	procurement, public policy
9.	State	peak trade association	public policy
10.	National	"public relations firm"	procurement, public policy
11.	National	"research and education institute"	public policy
12.	National	full-service consulting firm	procurement
13.	City (Chicago)	"multi-service law firm"	procurement
14.	City (Orlando, FL)	"law firm"	land use
15.	State (California)	"public affairs advocacy firm"	procurement, land use
16.	National	"lobbying, public relations, and business consulting firm"	procurement
17.	National	citizen group that lobbies "to protect senior citizens' benefits"	public policy
18.	State (Connecticut)	law firm	public policy
19.	National	"independent coalition of trade and professional associations"	public policy
20.	City	labor union consisting of "sworn law enforcement officers"	public policy

(*continued*)

TABLE 1 (*continued*)

ID	Primary level of government lobbyist lobbies (and location)[a]	Employer[b]	Classification[c]
21.	State (Texas)	"national law firm"	procurement, public policy
22.	City (Orlando, FL)	"law firm"	land use
23.	National	professional association of physicians (specialists)	public policy
24.	National	trade association of building materials manufacturers	procurement
25.	National	"government relations and marketing firm"	procurement
26.	National	freelance contract lobbyist	procurement, public policy
27.	State (California)	"government relations firm"	public policy
28.	City (Los Angeles)	"consulting firm"	land use, public policy
29.	City	private university	land use, public policy
30.	City (San Francisco)	"public relations and public affairs firm"	land use
31.	City (Los Angeles)	"public affairs consulting firm"	land use, procurement
32.	National	"consulting firm"	public policy, procurement
33.	National	"consulting firm"	procurement
34.	National	"lobbying firm"	procurement

[a]Specific city or state is denoted in parentheses, but only for lobbyists who specifically gave me permission to mention their state or city.

[b]Quotation marks are used to denote a direct quote from respondent or from respondent's Internet Web page.

[c]For lobbyists with more than one specialty, primary specialty is listed first.

Summary

To gather information for this book, I read much of the extant research on lobbying and lobbyists and also interviewed 34 lobbyists in depth. I asked each lobbyist a standard set of background questions, as well as questions concerning his or her lobbying specialty or specialties. In all, I compiled 248 single-spaced pages of interview data.

THE PLAN OF THE BOOK

Chapter 1 was designed primarily to do three things: (1) explain why I wrote this book, (2) define a few key terms that recur throughout the chapters, and (3) describe my data and methods. I began by making the case that lobbying is an extremely complex and multifaceted phenomenon. I then explained that the way I approach this phenomenon here is by dividing it into three distinct subtypes. After defining the three kinds of lobbying, I defined three important terms that recur throughout the book. Finally, I briefly described the data and the methods I have used.

What's Next?

Most of the remainder of the book is dedicated to exploring the lobbying process. Before I get to these analyses, however, Chapter 2 will offer an overview of what political scientists have learned about lobbying and lobbyists. This chapter is essentially a primer on lobbying for newcomers to the subject.

Chapters 3 and 4, which examine public policy lobbying, begin my investigation of lobbying processes. Chapter 3 examines who public policy lobbyists are and what they do in addition to lobbying. Chapter 4 focuses upon what public policy lobbyists actually do when they lobby. These chapters describe in detail what public policy lobbyists do and where they fit into the policymaking process. They also examine how public policy lobbying differs from other kinds of lobbying.

Chapter 5 examines land use lobbying. Local governments do many things, but none are more important than regulating land use. Not surprisingly, lobbyists are key players in land use politics. This chapter examines what land use lobbyists do and how land use lobbying differs from other types of lobbying.

Chapter 6 explores procurement lobbying. Every year, governments across the United States purchase hundreds of millions of dollars worth of goods and services. This chapter examines the role that lobbyists play in determining what governments buy. It also examines what procurement lobbyists do and how procurement lobbying differs from other types of lobbying.

Finally, Chapter 7 sums up the major findings of this book and makes an argument about the role of lobbyists in American democracy.

2 Lobbying and Lobbyists in the United States: A Primer

This book is not intended to be simply a rehash of old information on lobbying. Instead, it draws upon new information (in the form of direct quotes from lobbyists themselves) to paint a broad picture of lobbying and lobbyists in America. Before proceeding, however, I provide a brief overview of what we know about lobbying and lobbyists in the United States in order to provide you with the background information needed to understand subsequent chapters.

AN OVERVIEW OF NINE FINDINGS

In this section is a discussion of nine well-documented findings that together comprise a sort of "conventional wisdom" on lobbyists and lobbying in America. This conventional wisdom does not include everything there is to know about lobbying, but it does represent a broad introductory overview.

1. Many Types of Organized Interests Engage in Lobbying

Recent estimates suggest that between 10,000 and 90,000 lobbyists operate in Washington, DC.[1] Many more lobbyists (perhaps as many as 200,000) operate in states and localities throughout the country.[2] The presence of this many lobbyists begs the following question: What kinds of organizations engage in lobbying? The short answer to this question is: *all kinds.* More specifically, political scientists have found that 12 basic types of organized interests engage in lobbying.

First, large numbers of *business firms* lobby government. Business firms are *commercial enterprises (e.g., corporations) "that exist primarily to make money."*[3] Many of the world's largest companies, including Citigroup,

ExxonMobil, Microsoft, and Wal-Mart lobby extensively.[4] Many medium-sized and small business firms lobby as well.

Second, large numbers of *trade associations* lobby government. Trade associations are *organized groups of business firms*.[5] Among the most prominent trade associations in the United States are the Chamber of Commerce of the United States (an umbrella trade association that represents more than 3 million businesses of all types and sizes) and the National Association of Manufacturers (a trade association of more than 14,000 manufacturing firms).[6] There are a number of more specialized trade associations as well, such as the Association of American Railroads and the Illinois Manufacturers' Association. Many business firms that have their own lobbyists also belong to trade associations. In this way, their interests are "double-represented" before government.[7]

Third, many *professional associations* lobby government. Professional associations are *organizations that represent "the interests of people in a specific profession."*[8] Professional associations represent high-status professionals such as doctors, lawyers, and dentists. Two of the most prominent professional associations in the United States are the American Bar Association (the ABA, which represents lawyers and has more than 400,000 members) and the American Medical Association (the AMA, which represents medical students and doctors).[9] There are hundreds of professional associations in the United States, including more obscure groups, such as the Professional Association of Innkeepers (which represents, you guessed it, innkeepers) and the Association of Professional Chaplains (which represents thousands of chaplains involved in pastoral care).[10]

Fourth, *citizen groups* lobby. Citizen groups are *membership-organized interests that are open to virtually anyone who wants to join them*.[11] Examples of such organizations include the AARP (the lobbying behemoth that boasts approximately 35 million members and had revenues in excess of $750 million in 2005), the NRA (the well-known citizen group that represents gun enthusiasts), the Sierra Club (one of the premiere environmental groups in the United States, with a membership of 750,000), and the manifold neighborhood associations that operate in localities throughout the country.[12] Citizen groups are active on a large variety of public policy issues including abortion, the environment, gay and lesbian rights, gun control, and women's rights. Citizen groups (more specifically, neighborhood associations) are also very active in land use politics.

Fifth, *labor unions* lobby government. Labor unions are *organized groups of workers joined together for collective bargaining purposes*.[13] Among the most prominent labor unions in the United States are the International

Brotherhood of Teamsters (which represents 1.4 million workers in a variety of industries, including transportation), and the American Federation of State, County and Municipal Employees (AFSCME, which represents more than 1 million government employees).[14] It is interesting to note that perhaps the best-known labor union in the United States is not really a labor union at all. The AFL-CIO, which many people think is a labor union, is actually a *conglomeration* of labor unions – a sort of trade association of labor unions.[15]

Sixth, many *governmental entities* lobby. Governmental entities are *organized interests that lobby one government or part of government on behalf of another government or part of government*.[16] For example, many states regularly lobby the national government, as do many cities, counties, towns, public utilities, regional authorities, and foreign governments.[17]

Seventh, many *think tanks* lobby. A think tank is an *institution that conducts and disseminates research designed to affect government decisions*.[18] It is essentially an organized group of smart people (usually academics and/or former government officials) who study things and issue research reports. Many think tanks do not have members per se, but rather are comprised of researchers, called "fellows" or "scholars," and supporters (i.e., institutions and/or individuals that donate money to the organization). Among the best-known think tanks in the United States are the American Enterprise Institute for Public Policy Research (a conservative group that produces research reports designed to serve its goal of "preserving and strengthening the foundations of freedom – limited government, private enterprise, vital cultural and political institutions, and a strong foreign policy and national defense")[19] and the Heritage Foundation (another conservative group that disseminates research intended to "promote conservative public policies").[20] As these two examples suggest, many think tanks are overtly partial to a specific political ideology and conduct research that supports this ideology.

Eighth, many *charities* lobby. Charities are *organizations that exist primarily to help those in need (e.g., the sick, the poor, the hungry, the mentally ill)*.[21] Charities work primarily to help people, but many charities also lobby extensively. The Alzheimer's Association, for example, has long pushed for more federal funding for Alzheimer's research.[22] Similarly, the American Cancer Society lobbies for cancer research funding and tighter regulations on tobacco products.[23]

Ninth, many *universities and colleges* lobby. Universities and colleges are *institutions of higher learning*.[24] Many universities and colleges (state universities, for example) are government entities that rely heavily upon government funding to stay in business, and are thus very interested in government decisions. Private universities and colleges also benefit from government-funded student loans and research support. Many major universities and colleges have full-time lobbyists on staff, and many smaller institutions hire lobbyists as well.

Tenth, many *coalitions* lobby. A coalition is *"a loose collection of organizations" and/or individuals "that cooperates to accomplish common objectives."*[25] Among the prominent coalitions actively lobbying today are the Tax Relief Coalition (a national alliance of more than 1,000 business firms and trade associations that advocates for business tax relief) and the Sustainable Energy Coalition (a national alliance of business, consumer, and environmental groups that advocates federal support for "clean energy").[26] Many coalitions are temporary, and are designed to act on a specific proposal before government.

Eleventh, some *hospitals* lobby. Hospitals are *nonprofit or for-profit institutions that provide medical care*. Because the federal government and state governments are actively involved in the health care industry, hospitals of all kinds lobby to ensure that their interests are represented before government.

Finally, many *churches* lobby. Churches are *organized groups of believers and/or worshippers*.[27] Many local churches, for example, lobby on social issues (often using volunteer "citizen lobbyists"). Moreover, many large religious denominations have their own church organizations (e.g., the United States Conference of Catholic Bishops, the Southern Baptist Convention) that attempt to influence government decisions. Like charities, churches and church organizations do not exist primarily to lobby government. Nonetheless, many churches and church organizations engage in lobbying.

In sum, many types of organized interests lobby government. You may have noticed that I have said nothing about the numerous consulting firms, law firms, lobbying firms, public relations firms, and government relations firms that operate across the country and employ thousands of lobbyists. This is the case because most of these firms do not operate as organized interests per se. Instead, they are for-profit business organizations that employ lobbyists on a "for hire" basis.[28] The lobbyists who work for such organizations generally represent the organized interests that hire them, rather than the organizations that technically employ them when they lobby.[29]

2. Lobbying Takes Place at All Three Levels of Government (National, State, and Local)

People who study lobbying tend to focus on Washington. There are two good reasons for this "Washington-centric" focus. First, the federal government has taken the lead in addressing the most contentious and important public policy issues of the past hundred years, including civil rights, environmental regulation, national defense, and terrorism. Second, information on Washington lobbying is more readily available than information on state and local lobbying. Most large-circulation newspapers and magazines, including the *New York Times, Newsweek, Time* magazine, *USA Today* the *Wall Street Journal,* and the *Washington Post,* cover national politics much more than local and state politics. Similarly, the most widely watched television news outlets – Fox News, CNN, and the broadcast networks – cover national politics much more than local or state politics. In addition, the federal government is more transparent than many (though not all) state and local governments; it requires lobbyists to register and report their activities, and makes lobbyist registration and activity documents available to the public.[30]

Despite the disproportionate attention given to Washington, lobbying is ubiquitous "across the board" in America.[31] Just how ubiquitous? A clue lies in the sheer number of lobbyists plying their trade outside of Washington, DC. A few examples are in order. In 2004, 3,842 people registered to lobby New York State government, while 542 lobbyists registered in Tennessee and 1,159 in Michigan.[32] One recent study estimates that there are approximately 44,000 lobbyists operating at the state level today.[33] Lobbyists are plentiful in localities as well. In 2004, for example, 218 lobbyists registered to lobby in the city of Los Angeles,[34] while 215 registered to lobby in the county of Los Angeles.[35] Not all localities have this many lobbyists. For example, in 2004, only 16 lobbyists registered with the city of Anchorage, Alaska, while 52 lobbyists registered to lobby the Metropolitan Government of Nashville, Tennessee.[36] In sum, no matter what town, city, village, or state you live in, you can be sure that there are lobbyists there trying to influence government decisions.

3. Lobbyists Have a Wide Variety of Lobbying Techniques at Their Disposal

As I mentioned in the last chapter, lobbying is defined as an effort designed to affect what the government does. As this broad definition implies, lobbying takes many forms. Surveys of lobbyists, for example, show that lobbyists have a huge variety of techniques to choose from.[37] Table 2 presents a list of some of the most common techniques that lobbyists use, as well as a crude indicator of how often they use each of these techniques. This list – with a few changes – is adapted from several surveys of lobbyist activity.[38]

Legislative Lobbying Techniques. At all three levels of government the legislature attracts a lot of lobbying attention, primarily because that's where the action is. Legislatures have the power to make decisions that affect organized interests.

Lobbyists lobby legislatures in several ways.[39] First, lobbyists testify at legislative hearings. At the national and state levels of government, many pieces of legislation (bills) begin in committees that engage in "markup," which is the process of reviewing and revising a bill before it is considered by the full legislature. Typically, committees hold hearings during the markup process. At the local level, some legislatures have committee hearings akin to those at the state and national level, while many others hold hearings as a body. Legislative hearings are somewhat akin to court hearings – witnesses appear before legislators to speak for or against a particular proposal. Not surprisingly, many of the witnesses at legislative hearings are lobbyists. Legislative hearings are ideal forums for lobbyists to present their views to legislators. In some cases, legislators ask lobbyists to testify at hearings, and in other cases, lobbyists implore legislators to let them testify.[40]

Second, lobbyists meet personally with legislators and/or their aides. Lobbyists meet with legislators in many different places, including their personal offices, meeting rooms in government buildings, and informal venues such as bars and restaurants. Personal meetings give lobbyists a chance to present relevant information directly to the decision makers. Because legislators are generally busy, lobbyists often meet with their aides instead. When lobbyists meet with legislators or legislative aides, they often emphasize how a proposed bill will affect a legislator's constituents. In some cases, lobbyists work with legislators to formulate strategies and tactics designed to ensure that a proposed bill will succeed (or fail). Moreover, on some occasions, legislators actually introduce bills written by lobbyists or ask lobbyists to help them revise bills during the markup process. Legislators and their aides often call upon lobbyists for such help because many are experts in their field of specialization.

Third, lobbyists lobby the legislature by doing favors and/or providing gifts for legislators. The laws concerning the types and value of favors and gifts that lobbyists are allowed to provide vary from place to place. But in Washington and elsewhere, lobbyists and the organized interests they

TABLE 2. Lobbying techniques

Specific technique	Frequency of use
Legislative branch[a]	
Doing favors and/or providing gifts for legislators	–
Meeting personally with legislators and/or their aides	very often
Testifying at legislative hearings	very often
Executive branch[b]	
Interacting with special agencies that advise the chief executive	–
Interacting with special liaison offices within chief executive's office	–
Meeting personally with chief executive and/or aides	seldom
Meeting personally with executive agency personnel	very often
Serving on executive agency advisory boards or committees	occasionally
Submitting written comments on proposed rules or regulations	very often
Testifying at executive agency hearings	–
Judicial branch[c]	
Attempting to influence judicial selections	–
Engaging in litigation	occasionally
Submitting amicus curiae briefs	occasionally
Grassroots/indirect[d]	
Arranging face-to-face meetings between group members/supporters and government officials	–
Dispatching a spokesperson to the media	–
Engaging in e-mail, letter, telegram, or telephone campaigns	very often
Engaging in demonstrations or protests	seldom
Running advertisements in media	seldom
Direct democracy	
Attempting to place an initiative or referendum on the ballot	–
Campaigning for or against an initiative or referendum	–
Electoral	
Campaigning for or against candidates	seldom
Endorsing candidates	seldom
Engaging in election issue advocacy	seldom
Making in-kind contributions to candidates	seldom
Making monetary contributions to political parties	seldom
Making monetary contributions to candidates	occasionally
Mobilizing activists to work on a candidate's behalf	–
Issuing voter guides	seldom
Other	
Joining coalitions with other organizations and/or lobbyists	very often

represent are known to provide gifts and favors considered desirable yet negligible in value, such as catered food, flowers, candy, free baby-sitting, rides to work, tickets to athletic events, and discounted rides on corporate jets.[41]

Executive Branch Techniques. The executive branch of government consists of the chief executive (e.g., the president, the governor, the mayor) and the executive bureaucracy.[42] Because the executive branch wields considerable decision-making power, it is often the target of lobbying.[43]

There are two principal ways that lobbyists lobby the chief executive.[44] First, they meet personally with the chief executive and/or his or her aides. Because chief executives are typically busy, lobbyists often have more access to their aides. Second, lobbyists lobby the chief executive by interacting with special liaison, outreach, or advisory offices located within the chief executive's office.[45] At the federal level, for example, lobbyists lobby the president by interacting with the Office of Public Liaison (OPL),

---

Notes and Sources for Table 2:

Note: Coding for frequency of use was done by me, based on the studies cited in this table. I also drew upon Table 8.1 in Baumgartner and Leech, *Basic Interests,* p. 152. Categories are very often, occasionally, and seldom. A dash indicates that there is little basis on which to judge the frequency of use of the technique in question.

[a] Some of the surveys on which this category is based included alerting legislators to the effect of a bill on their district, consulting with legislators to plan legislative strategy, helping to draft legislation, and wining, dining, or entertaining legislators or their aides as separate lobbying techniques. For the sake of parsimony and because these activities take place during personal meetings with legislators, I have subsumed them under the broader technique meeting personally with legislators and/or their aides.

[b] Some of the surveys on which this category is based included attempting to shape policy implementation and helping to draft regulations or rules as separate lobbying techniques. For the sake of parsimony and because these activities take place during personal meetings with executive agency personnel, I have subsumed them under the broader technique meeting personally with executive agency personnel.

[c] In truth, attempting to influence judicial selections is a legislative branch and/or executive branch and/or electoral lobbying technique. But most surveys of lobbying label it a judicial lobbying technique.

[d] Some of the surveys on which this category is based include attempting to set the government's agenda and mounting grassroots lobbying efforts as separate lobbying techniques. However, I have included neither on this list. The first "technique" is a goal rather than a technique, and the second is too general to be of much use here.

Sources: Cooper and Nownes, "Citizen Groups in Big City Politics," p. 107; Heinz et al., *The Hollow Core,* p. 65; David Knoke and James R. Wood, *Organizing for Collective Action: The Political Economies of Associations* (Hawthorne, NY: Aldine de Gruyter, 1990), p. 208; Kollman, *Outside Lobbying,* Chapter 2; Nownes and Freeman, "Interest Group Activity in the States," p. 92; Rosenthal, *The Third House*; Schlozman and Tierney, *Organized Interests and American Democracy,* p. 150.

the Office of Legislative Affairs, the Office of Political Affairs, and other special offices.[46]

The executive bureaucracy also attracts a great deal of lobbying attention. The primary task of the executive bureaucracy (which is broadly defined as the set of agencies, bureaus, and departments that implements government decisions) is to implement decisions made by the other branches and parts of government. For example, at the federal level, the Environmental Protection Agency (EPA) enforces and implements environmental laws made by Congress and the president. Many bureaucratic agencies, however, have the power to *make* important decisions as well as implement decisions made elsewhere. For example, though the primary power to regulate food in this country lies with Congress and the president (who are empowered to pass regulatory legislation), the Food and Drug Administration (FDA) also has broad powers to issue new regulations and rules concerning food.

One way that lobbyists lobby bureaucratic agencies is by meeting personally with agency personnel. They do so in order to try to affect how decisions are implemented and to assist bureaucrats in drafting new rules and regulations.[47] Another way that lobbyists lobby bureaucratic agencies is by testifying at agency hearings. Some executive agencies (especially at the federal and state levels) hold hearings when they are considering new rules or regulations. During these hearings, witnesses of all kinds comment upon pending rules or regulations. Lobbyists use executive agency hearings to present information to bureaucrats about how pending rules and regulations will affect them. Lobbyists may also present information on proposed rules and regulations via written comments that are submitted to agency personnel.

Lobbyists also lobby bureaucratic agencies by serving on agency advisory committees. Many state, local, and federal agencies have special advisory boards or committees that are set up (by the chief executive, the legislature, or the agency itself) to provide complex technical information to agency personnel (about proposed regulations and rules) and to "serve as sounding boards for testing agency proposals."[48] Because advisory committees have the ear of agency personnel, lobbyists value advisory committee assignments. The rules concerning how people get appointed to advisory committees vary from agency to agency and place to place. But whatever the rules, lobbyists see advisory committees as important vehicles for making their views known to executive agency personnel.

Somewhere in between the chief executive's office and the executive bureaucracy are agencies that advise chief executives on bureaucratic proposals. For example, at the federal level, the president is advised by the Office of Management and Budget and other agencies under direct control of the Executive Office of the President. Many governors have similar agencies that often review proposals proffered by other agencies and keep the chief executive abreast of what they are doing. Lobbyists often meet personally with bureaucrats within these agencies to "say their piece."[49]

Judicial Branch Lobbying. Like the other two branches of government, the judicial branch attracts lobbying attention. Organized interests and their lobbyists "lobby the courts" in three principal ways.[50] First, they engage in litigation.[51] The precise ways they do so are complicated, and they vary across levels of government and jurisdictions. In essence, engaging in litigation entails bringing a suit or suits before the courts in an attempt "to seek a policy change or to stop a change from taking place."[52] Organized interests can, for example, sue bureaucratic agencies to stop them from adopting regulations or rules. They can also sponsor litigation. Perhaps the most famous organized-interest sponsor of litigation is the National Association for the Advancement of Colored People (NAACP), which essentially sued state and local governments in the 1940s and 1950s on the grounds that they were violating the constitutional rights of African American citizens. In one of the most important judicial victories in American history, the NAACP prevailed in the case of *Brown v. Board of Education* (1954), which declared "separate but equal" educational facilities unconstitutional.[53]

Second, organized interests lobby the courts by submitting amicus curiae ("friend of the court") briefs. Courts are often asked to render decisions on important matters (e.g., abortion, affirmative action, gay rights, immigration), and in some cases organized interests file amicus briefs that "inform the Court of their views on the possible implications of its decision and urge adoption of the resolution they favor of the legal dispute."[54] An amicus brief is essentially a memo that presents an organized interest's views on an active case to the court that is deciding the case.

Finally, organized interests engage in judicial lobbying by attempting to influence judicial selections. At the federal level, the chief executive makes judicial appointments with the approval of the Senate. States use a variety of judicial selection methods, including chief executive appointments, chief executive appointments with legislative approval, and elections. No matter the method, organized interests try to affect judicial selection. They are especially active in battles over Supreme Court nominations, during

which they lobby the president (in an attempt to influence his appoint-
ment) and/or senators (in an attempt to influence how they vote on the
president's nominee).

Grassroots/Indirect Lobbying. Grassroots lobbying (also known as "indirect," or "outside" lobbying) is is aimed at ordinary citizens, rather than
government decision makers. The goal of grassroots lobbying is to mobilize citizens to "participate in some way so their [voices] will be heard"
by government decision makers.[55] The idea behind grassroots lobbying is
simple: to demonstrate to government officials that lots of people have
a certain view and that officials should heed this view when they make
decisions. Grassroots lobbying campaigns are generally designed either to
get government officials to pay attention to an issue or topic (i.e., to "set
the agenda") or to pressure government officials "to support the group's
agenda" (e.g., vote "yes" on a proposal the group favors).[56]

Organized interests use a variety of grassroots techniques. First, they
engage in e-mail, letter, telegram, or telephone campaigns. For example, an evangelical Christian citizen group in opposition to a bill before
the state legislature that would allow gays and lesbians to enter into civil
unions may urge its members and supporters (personally, or by telephone,
e-mail, or letter) to e-mail, telephone, or write letters to state legislators
expressing their opposition. Second, organized interests arrange face-to-
face meetings between group members or supporters and government
officials.[57] For example, many organized interests have annual "lobby
days" on which they transport large numbers of group members and
supporters to Washington, the state capitol, or city hall to meet personally
with government officials (usually legislators). Third, organized interests
run advertisements in media. Returning to the hypothetical example of
the evangelical Christian citizen group, it may run an advertisement in
the newspaper, on the Internet, or on television or radio urging people
to express their opposition to gay civil unions. Fourth, organized interests may engage in demonstrations or protests. Again returning to our
hypothetical example, the Christian citizen group may invite thousands
of members and supporters to participate in a march on the state capitol to wave signs, shout slogans, and attempt to garner media attention.
Fifth, an organized interest may dispatch a spokesperson to the media in
an attempt to whip up public support for its position. An environmental
citizen group that opposes a new proposal to allow increased logging in
national parks, for example, may appear on a television news program
decrying the proposal.

Direct Democratic Techniques. In several states and cities in the United States, citizens are given the right directly to make authoritative decisions through initiatives and/or referenda. An *initiative* or *referendum* is defined as *a proposed law or constitutional amendment that is placed on a ballot for citizen approval.*[58] Organized interests and their lobbyists use two main direct democratic lobbying techniques. First, organized interests may attempt to place an initiative or referendum on the ballot. States and localities have different rules about how it gets on the ballot, but in many places, an initiative can be placed on a ballot if a sponsor (e.g., an organized interest, a private citizen, a politician) collects a certain number of signatures. In some places, referenda work this way as well. Second, after an initiative or a referendum is placed on the ballot, organized interests may campaign for or against it. For example, an organized interest that favors passage of an initiative or referendum may run advertisements urging people to vote "yes" on election day.[59]

Electoral Lobbying. Many government officials, including legislators (i.e., members of Congress, state legislators, county commissioners, city council members), chief executives (i.e., the president, mayors, governors), and other assorted officials (e.g., sheriffs) get their jobs by winning elections. Not surprisingly, organized interests are active in election campaigns. The primary way that organized interests "lobby" during election campaigns is by making monetary contributions to candidates. In many places, organized interests are forbidden to contribute money directly to candidates. Instead, they must form special affiliated organizations called political action committees (PACs) to do so. The rules that govern how organized interests can raise and spend campaign money are quite complicated.[60] For now, suffice it to say that in federal elections as well as elections in many states and localities, organized interests, usually through PACs, are allowed under the law to contribute money to candidates for public office. Though the amounts they can give are generally limited, this does not stop organized interests from being heavily involved in election campaigns. They can also support candidates for office by making in-kind contributions (that is, contributions of goods and/or services) to candidates. Examples of in-kind contributions include advertising services, consulting services, printing services, and office supplies.[61]

Organized interests engage in electoral lobbying in six additional ways. First, they campaign for or against candidates. For example, at the federal level, the law allows organized interests (again, through their PACs) to campaign directly for or against candidates by using "radio, television, direct mail, and telephone communications that *expressly* call for the election or defeat of a candidate for a federal office."[62] In a closely related technique, organized interests (usually through their PACs) campaign for or against candidates indirectly by highlighting their strengths or weaknesses, but not expressly calling for the election or defeat of a specific candidate. This is a practice known as election issue advocacy, and it is highly controversial.[63] Third, organized interests mobilize activists to work on a candidate's behalf. Since the 1990s, for example, the Christian Coalition and other right-leaning groups have mobilized their members and other like-minded activists to pound the pavement for conservative Republican candidates.[64] Fourth, organized interests (again, usually through their PACs) endorse candidates for public office. For example, in 2004 the Sierra Club openly endorsed John Kerry for president, while a number of right-leaning organizations endorsed George W. Bush.[65] Fifth, organized interests issue voter guides, which are essentially brief publications that present candidates' positions on issues of concern to the organized interest.[66] A typical voter guide presents two candidates' stances on a variety of issues, tacitly urging voters to choose one candidate over the other. For example, in 2004 the Christian Coalition distributed a voter guide (and placed the guide on its Internet site) that compared George W. Bush to John Kerry. The guide contrasted the candidates' views on such issues as "unrestricted abortion on demand," "adoption of children by homosexuals," and "permanent elimination of the marriage penalty tax."[67] Bush, the guide reported, opposes the first two of these and favors the last. Kerry, in contrast, was said to have "no response" on the first and third issues, and was listed as opposing the last. Sixth, organized interests engage in electoral lobbying by making monetary contributions to political parties. Although the laws governing how organized interests can support political parties are complicated, they essentially allow organized interests (again, generally through their PACs) to contribute money to party organizations that in turn can use it for various activities to help candidates.[68]

Other: Joining Coalitions. Finally, one common lobbying technique is forming coalitions with other organized interests because of a belief that there is strength in numbers. In other words, organized interests believe (and there is some evidence that they are correct) that they are more likely to get what they want from government if they have lots of other organized interests on their side.[69] Once a coalition is formed, it can engage in a variety of lobbying techniques.

Lobbying Techniques: Two Important Points. Two facts in particular stand out from Table 2. First, lobbyists target government officials in all three branches of government. The term "lobbyist" was originally coined to describe people who hung around the lobbies of the legislature waiting to buttonhole legislators and ask them for favors. To this day, the prototypical lobbyist – the one who shows up in American government textbooks and on the evening news – is someone who spends a great deal of time trying to influence legislative decisions. Nonetheless, as this section and Table 2 attest, scholars have learned that lobbyists at all three levels of government are active across all three branches of government.

Second, lobbyists target ordinary citizens as well as government officials. Many people assume that lobbyists lobby only government officials and their aides – the powerful people who actually make government decisions. However, studies show that lobbyists and the organized interests they represent often try to influence *our* opinions – the opinions of ordinary citizens – in their quest ultimately to affect government decisions. In fact, a number of recent studies suggest that grassroots lobbying is more common than ever before.[70]

Which Techniques Are Most Effective? As Table 2 and this section attest, lobbyists have a wide variety of techniques to choose from. The availability of so many techniques begs the following question: Which techniques are most effective? Surprisingly, few studies have addressed this question directly.[71] One of the few scholars who has done so is political scientist Jeffrey Berry, who in the mid-1970s asked several dozen citizen group lobbyists to indicate whether or not specific lobbying techniques were effective.[72] In a pioneering study published in the 1960s, lobbying scholar Lester Milbrath asked a similar question of a broad range of Washington lobbyists.[73] Both Berry and Milbrath concluded that meeting personally with government officials (though neither specifies which government officials) and engaging in grassroots lobbying are particularly effective lobbying techniques. In perhaps the most ambitious study of lobbying ever conducted, Robert Salisbury and his colleagues also addressed the question of technique effectiveness. After a series of sophisticated quantitative analyses, they could not reach any definitive conclusions specifying the techniques or combinations of techniques that are most effective.

Summing up the literature on lobbyist and organized interest power, political scientist Clive Thomas notes that "scholarly studies are largely inconclusive as to any definitive explanation of group power."[74] In short, the question of which lobbying techniques work (and which do not) remains an open one.

Summary. Lobbyists have an amazing array of techniques at their disposal, and lobbying takes a wide variety of forms. It is important to note at this point that though Table 2 treats lobbying techniques separately, lobbyists seldom do one and only one thing. Rather, the typical lobbyist uses a large assortment of techniques.[75] While lobbyists use some techniques more than others, most do not specialize in one technique or one branch of government. As for the lobbying techniques that are most effective, we are far from having a definitive answer. However, studies suggest that meeting personally with government officials is a singularly effective lobbying technique.

4. Lobbying = Providing Information
Many of the lobbying techniques listed in Table 2 entail the provision of information. Nearly every study of lobbying ever conducted illustrates that the lobbyist's stock in trade is information used in an attempt to convince either government officials or the public that he or she is right. The most eloquent expression of the idea that lobbying is about providing information comes from political scientist John R. Wright, who created what is known as "the communications theory of lobbying."[76] Wright's contribution is important and influential, and it deserves a closer look.

In his book *Interest Groups and Congress: Lobbying, Contributions, and Influence*, Wright, who studies lobbying within Congress, begins with the assumption that members of Congress have three interdependent goals: (1) reelection, (2) good public policy, and (3) influence within Congress.[77] Let's consider the goals one at a time. First, legislators want to be reelected: If they are not in office, they cannot achieve their other goals. Second, legislators want to make good public policy – policy that is good for their constituents. Finally, legislators want to exercise influence within the legislature. Wright notes that legislators cannot achieve their policy goals (i.e., make good public policy) unless they have some measure of power within their branch of government. The best way to exercise power within the legislature is to propose legislation and get it passed. Another way is to help others get legislation passed.

After establishing that members of Congress have three primary goals, Wright notes that members must seek to achieve them in an environment fraught with uncertainty: "The attainment of these goals is complicated by the fact that legislators cannot be certain about how voters will react to their policy decisions, how policies will actually work once implemented, or what kinds of political complications might arise during the legislative process."[78]

In other words, members of Congress are in a bind. On the one hand, they have clear-cut goals. On the other hand, they are unsure of precisely how to achieve these goals. According to Wright, this is where lobbyists come in. Lobbyists are useful to members, he argues, because they provide information to them. In fact, this is their modus operandi – they provide information to government decision makers in the hope that this information will affect their decisions. The information lobbyists provide reduces uncertainty, thereby helping legislators know what they need to do to achieve their goals. Organized interests and their lobbyists, he says, "achieve influence in the legislative process by strategically providing information to change or reinforce legislators' beliefs about legislative outcomes, the operational effects of policies, and the electoral ramifications of their actions."[79]

An Example: Information as a Lobbying Tool. Here's a hypothetical example to demonstrate what Wright means. Let us assume that a member of the House of Representatives is considering whether or not to vote for a bill that decreases taxes on wealthy Americans. Some of the questions the representative is likely to raise before the vote include the following: How do my constituents feel about the bill? If I vote for (or against) it, will my vote haunt me or help me when I stand for reelection? And what about the policy implications of the bill? Will it help or hurt the economy? Will it increase inflation? Will it help create jobs? Will it increase the deficit? And finally, what are the chances that the bill will pass? Will my vote even matter? How are my colleagues going to vote? Will I be able to offer an amendment to the bill if I disagree with some of its provisions? In sum, our hypothetical House member raises a battery of questions before deciding how he or she will vote on this tax bill.

Now into this hypothetical picture, let's inject a lobbyist for a conservative anti-tax group that supports the tax cut. The lobbyist, according to Wright's theory, does his or her job by providing information to help the House member answer these questions. For example, the lobbyist may present poll results showing that the member's constituents overwhelmingly support the bill. Additionally, the lobbyist may present data showing that the tax reduction would create jobs by increasing the amount of money available for economic investment. Finally, the lobbyist might present political information suggesting that House leaders will allow the member to amend the bill on the floor if he or she is not happy with some of its provisions. Of course, it is important to note that while the anti-tax lobbyist is providing information that makes his or her side look good, a pro-tax lobbyist may be providing information that makes *the other side* look good (e.g., poll numbers suggesting that most citizens support a progressive tax system). In either case, however, the idea is the same: A lobbyist attempts to exert influence by providing information to legislators.

The Three Types of Information Provided by Lobbyists. Although Wright considers only legislative lobbying, his basic proposition can be applied more broadly. Specifically, it can be stated more generically as follows: *When lobbyists lobby, they seek to affect government decisions by providing information to the people they lobby.* What kind of information do lobbyists provide? Wright says that the information provided to legislators comes in three forms: (1) political information "about the status and prospect of bills"; (2) electoral information "about the electoral implications of legislators' support for or opposition" to a bill; and (3) policy information about "the likely economic, social, or environmental consequences of proposed policies."[80] While he designed this threefold classification of information to apply only in the legislative context, it can be converted into a more generic classification that applies to all sorts of government contexts. The generic version I use here holds that lobbyists provide three types of information to government actors: (1) *political information* about the status and prospect of a proposed or potential government decision; (2) *career-relevant information* about the implications of a particular course of action for a government official's prospects of keeping and/or advancing in his or her job; and (3) *policy-analytic information* about the potential economic, social, or environmental consequences of a particular course of action.

Wright is not the only person who has asserted that lobbying is largely about providing information. Indeed, study after study illustrates that lobbyists often make their cases by providing information to government decision makers, or to the public (if they are engaging in grassroots lobbying).[81] The information, of course, is generally biased in the lobbyist's favor. Seldom, however, do lobbyists tell unabashed lies. Lying would be detrimental to a lobbyist's ability to retain access to government decision makers.

To summarize, lobbying is often about providing information. Lobbyists generally provide political information, and/or policy information, and/or career-relevant information when they lobby.

5. Institutions – Especially Business Firms – Dominate Lobbying in the United States

Previously I established that there are tens of thousands of lobbyists and tens of thousands of organized interests active in the United States. In fact, the sheer number of lobbyists and organized interests in the United States makes it seem as though lobbyists represent virtually every interest you can imagine. But studies show that this is not the case. It turns out, in fact, that some interests are much better represented before government than are others. Specifically, studies show that institutions – especially business firms – are far better represented before government than are other types of organized interests.

An *institution* is broadly defined as *a nonmembership organized interest*. Examples include business firms, governmental entities, colleges and universities, and hospitals. In one study of Washington, DC, lobbying, political scientists Frank R. Baumgartner and Beth L. Leech concluded that business firms account for a large plurality of lobbyist registrations.[82] Similarly, in an expansive study of organized interests active at the state level, political scientists Virginia Gray and David Lowery found that institutions – again, business firms in particular – comprise the majority of lobbyist registrations at the state level as well.[83] Finally, studies of local politics suggest that institutions – again, especially business firms – are particularly well represented at the local level as well.[84]

The Free-Rider Problem. Studies indicate that institutions, especially business firms, are better represented by lobbyists than are noninstitutions (that is, membership organizations). The reason is that there are substantial barriers to the formation and survival of organized interests (that is, it is not necessarily easy to start and maintain an organized interest), and institutions are uniquely suited to overcoming these barriers.

One barrier to the formation and survival of an organized interest is what political scientists call the *free-rider problem*. To understand this problem, you must first understand that many organized interests seek *collective goods* when they lobby. Collective goods are defined as goods that, *if attained by the organized interest, "can be shared by members and nonmembers alike."*[85] Political scientist Jeffrey M. Berry asks whether it makes sense for someone who supports, say, the goals of the environmental movement to join the Sierra Club to support its lobbying.[86] If the Sierra Club succeeds in, for example, getting Congress to pass a bill that designates a large piece of Utah wilderness a national forest, environmentalists who are not members of the Sierra Club will enjoy the benefits of the new national forest just as much as environmentalists who *are* members of the Sierra Club will. In other words, the new national forest is a collective good – it can be enjoyed by Sierra Club members and nonmembers alike.

Many people faced with the question of "Should I join a group that is lobbying to achieve collective goods that I value?" will answer "No." They realize that they can enjoy the benefits of the group's lobbying even if they do not join. Economist Mancur Olson has called the propensity for people not to join groups that lobby for collective goods they value "free-riding." This label is based on the notion that by not joining the group but trying to enjoy the benefits of joining nonetheless, nonjoiners are free-riding on the efforts of others.[87] The free-rider problem is a substantial barrier to the formation and survival of organized interests because individuals are often inclined not to join organized interests, even those organized interests that lobby for collective goods they value.

The Free-Rider Problem and Institutions. The presence of the free-rider problem helps explain why institutions are so well represented before government. Because institutions *do not face* this problem, they have a much easier time getting the money they need to hire lobbyists than do membership organizations. To illustrate this point, I examine two hypothetical cases. First, let us consider the case of ABC Corporation, a business firm that earned $2 million in profits last year from manufacturing ballpoint pens. Second, let us consider the case of the employees of ABC Corporation. This group consists of 1,000 employees who work at the company's manufacturing facility in Springton, Kansas (a hypothetical place). Now, let's assume that Congress is debating a bill that would raise the minimum wage by $1.15 per hour. The ABC Corporation opposes the bill because it would raise labor costs, thus lowering company profits. Most of the employees of ABC Corp., however, favor the minimum wage increase, thinking that it will mean more money in their pockets. Let us further assume that both the company (an institution) and the workers (a group of individuals) want to hire a lobbyist. The workers face the free-rider problem; why should employees join a group representing their interests when they will reap the benefits of the group's work even if they do not join? Why, in other words, should an employee *not* free-ride off the contributions of others?

In short, the group of workers faces a barrier – the free rider problem – in its attempt to raise enough money to hire a lobbyist. In contrast, the company does *not* face this barrier. The CEO of the company needs only to find the right person and use some of the company's $2 million profits to hire a lobbyist. In fact, if the company *really* wants to make sure the minimum wage bill does not pass, it could hire several lobbyists and even, perhaps, join a trade association or coalition with other business firms.

In sum, institutions, especially business firms, are better represented by lobbyists than are other types of organized interests.[88] This is the case partially because they do not face the free-rider problem that plagues membership-organized interests (e.g. citizen groups, charities, labor unions, professional associations, and churches). The predominance of lobbyists representing institutions (again, especially business firms) does not mean that institutions always get what they want from government. But it does mean that the interests of institutions are almost always well represented before government.

6. Lobbyists Spend Considerable Time on Nonlobbying Activities

Lobbyists are called lobbyists because they lobby. But this is not all they do. Years of research have shown that they spend a great deal of time on non-lobbying activities, two in particular: (1) monitoring and (2) interacting with their clients.

Monitoring. First, lobbyists engage in monitoring.[89] They monitor both the government and the activities of other organized interests and lobby-ists. Monitoring government is important because it helps lobbyists learn what things are in the pipeline that may affect the interests they represent. Political scientist Robert Salisbury has pointed out that the "great expan-sion in the scope of [government] programs since World War II ... has meant that many more elements of the society are far more extensively affected by what the government does" than ever before.[90] Because what government does profoundly affects them and the organizations they rep-resent, lobbyists keep close tabs on what it is up to. As for monitoring other organized interests and lobbyists, it is important for lobbyists to know what their enemies and allies are doing so that they can craft their appeals accordingly and determine how best to utilize their resources and perhaps locate allies who can help them.

More than anything else, monitoring entails sifting through informa-tion. One recent study found that lobbyists "devote several hours on most days to absorbing, discussing with colleagues, and analyzing in writ-ten memos both substantive and political aspects of the issues on their agenda."[91] Lobbyists gather information from many sources, including daily newspapers; specialty political publications (e.g., *National Journal,*

Congressional Quarterly Weekly); government documents (e.g., legislative or executive branch reports); press releases or issue summaries from government officials, lobbyists, or organized interests; and conversations with other lobbyists and government officials.

Interacting with Clients. A second nonlobbying activity in which lobbyists engage is what political scientist Rogan Kersh calls "client interaction."[92] Client interaction comprises several specific activities, including receiving directions from clients (i.e., the supervisors or managers to whom lobbyists report), discussing issues with clients, explaining issues to clients, explaining lobbying strategies to clients, soliciting business, preparing clients for meetings with government officials, and brokering meetings between clients and government officials.[93] Of these activities, Kersh finds that lobbyists spend the most time explaining issues to clients.[94] Most clients who hire lobbyists, he concludes, "know little of Washington activity and decisions, even those directly affecting their interests."[95] As such, lobbyists must spend time "educating and instructing clients" about issues and activities, "often introducing preferences and interests along the way."[96] In addition to explaining and describing issues to clients, lobbyists spend surprising amounts of time seeking new clients – that is, trying to retain business or drum up new business. Kersh found that the typical lobbyist in his study spent 14 percent of his or her client interaction time soliciting business.[97]

To sum up, lobbyists spend considerable time engaging in nonlobbying activities. Two such activities are particularly important – monitoring and interacting with clients. If actually making a case to a government official or to the public is the centerpiece of the lobbyist's job, monitoring and interacting with clients are considered background work.

7. Lobbyists Sometimes Get What They Want

Over the years, scholars have studied the influence of lobbying and lobbyists from many different perspectives. No matter what perspective they use, one overarching finding emerges: *Lobbyists sometimes get what they want.* Political scientists known as "pluralists," for example, who studied organized interests primarily in the 1950s, argued that lobbyists are highly influential actors who exert profound influence over government decisions.[98] Similarly, disparate critics of pluralism who became prominent in the mid-1960s, while finding fault with a number of other aspects of pluralism, agreed that organized interests and their lobbyists wield considerable influence over government decisions.[99] Finally, contemporary scholars of organized interests and lobbying, many of whom are called "neo-pluralists," consistently find that lobbyists, though far from omnipotent, affect government decisions under certain circumstances.[100]

The fact that lobbyists sometimes win and sometimes lose inevitably leads to the following question: What determines whether a lobbyist succeeds or fails in getting what he or she wants from government? I addressed this question partially when I noted that studies show that some lobbying techniques (e.g., meeting personally with government officials) appear to be more effective than others. To this I add two other findings of note. First, it appears that lobbyists with lots of experience and connections are generally more successful than inexperienced lobbyists with few connections. Second, studies suggest that lobbyists who avoid conflict with other lobbyists by focusing narrowly on one small issue or set of issues are more effective than lobbyists who regularly confront other lobbyists and focus broadly.[101] Beyond these three basic findings, we know surprisingly little about what determines whether a lobbyist succeeds or fails. In fact, in arguably the largest study of lobbyist influence ever conducted, Robert Salisbury and his colleagues go so far as to say that the determinants of lobbyist success "are usually situation specific."[102]

8. Lobbyists Are Neither Whores nor Scoundrels

As I pointed out in Chapter 1, what distinguishes ordinary citizens trying to influence what the government does from lobbyists is the fact that when lobbyists try to affect what the government does, they are doing so on behalf of an organized interest rather than on behalf of themselves. Indeed, this is where lobbyists get their bad reputations: People tend to think of them as meretricious "hired guns" who jettison their principles (if they have any), sell themselves to the highest bidders, and then "carry water" for the well-heeled organized interests that hire them.

There are two major problems with the lobbyist-as-whore caricature. First, studies suggest that most lobbyists work for causes they believe in. The most important evidence supporting this assertion is the finding that the large majority of lobbyists work for the organized interests they represent rather than hire themselves out to whoever offers to pay them. Political scientists distinguish between two basic types of lobbyists: *in-house lobbyists*, who work for and are employed by the organized interests they represent, and *contract lobbyists*, who work for themselves (or lobbying firms) and represent whoever hires them. As political scientist Clive Thomas points out, contract lobbyists "constitute only about one-fourth of the federal and state capital lobbying communities."[103]

A second finding that contradicts the negative stereotype of lobbyists is that most lobbyists are honest, ethical, and professional. Occasional scandals notwithstanding, few lobbyists use illegal techniques, such as bribery, blackmail, or extortion. Moreover, studies of both lobbyists and public officials show that honesty and credibility are absolutely essential to successful lobbying.[104] Lobbyists may (and often do) exaggerate, "spin," or leave out important details when they lobby, but they tend not to lie or cheat. Lying and cheating, it turns out, are bad for business, as government officials are loath to listen to, and organized interests are loath to retain, liars and cheaters.

In sum, the research on lobbying and lobbyists shows that lobbyists are neither whores nor scoundrels. There are tens of thousands of lobbyists in America today. Very few of them have ever been arrested for illegal behavior, and it appears that almost all of them behave ethically and professionally most of the time. Moreover, they are not the venal opportunists that many people think they are. Most lobbyists are employed by the organizations for which they lobby, and it is fair to say that most seldom (if ever) actively lobby for causes they do not support.

9. Most Lobbyists Are Well-Educated, Well-Paid, Seasoned, White, Male Professionals

Up until now I have said very little about lobbyists themselves – the individuals who actually comprise the lobbying profession. While this topic is not particularly relevant to this book, I will nonetheless share what scholars have learned about people who lobby for a living. To put it briefly, studies show that the typical lobbyist in America is a well-educated, well-paid, 40- or 50-something, white male with government experience.[105] The not-so-well-educated, the poor, the young, women, ethnic and racial minorities, and people with no government experience are underrepresented among lobbyists. Depending on your point of view, this is either troubling or no big deal. Those in the latter camp observe that lobbyists fit the profile of most high-end, lucrative professions, while critics express concern that large groups of people are underrepresented in lobbying communities.

Summary: The Conventional Wisdom on Lobbyists and Lobbying

Political scientists have studied lobbyists and lobbying for decades. Their research has yielded nine important findings that together comprise a sort

TABLE 3. The conventional wisdom on lobbyists and lobbying in the United States: A summary
1. Many types of organized interests engage in lobbying.
2. Lobbying takes place at all three levels of government (national, state, and local).
3. Lobbyists have a wide variety of lobbying techniques at their disposal.
4. Lobbying = providing information.
5. Institutions – especially business firms – dominate lobbying in the United States.
6. Lobbyists spend considerable time on nonlobbying activities.
7. Lobbyists sometimes get what they want.
8. Lobbyists are neither whores nor scoundrels.
9. Most lobbyists are well-educated, well-paid, seasoned, white, male professionals.

of conventional wisdom about lobbyists and lobbying in America. This conventional wisdom is rendered in Table 3.

CONCLUSION: WHAT WE HAVE LEARNED ABOUT LOBBYING AND LOBBYISTS

This chapter has reviewed and summarized what political scientists have learned about lobbyists and lobbying over the years. To this end, it has presented nine well-documented findings that together comprise a sort of conventional wisdom on lobbyists and lobbying in America. This chapter is not intended to be a definitive and comprehensive overview of everything political scientists have learned on the subject. As the plethora of footnotes accompanying this chapter attest, there are dozens of excellent studies on lobbyists and lobbying, and I could not possibly do them all justice in one chapter of a relatively short book. Nonetheless, the relative newcomer to the topic of lobbying should have a better grasp of the subject.

Needless to say, I believe that we still have a lot to learn about lobbying and lobbyists. Otherwise, I would not have written this book. My discussion of the variety of techniques available to lobbyists, for example, points up the fact that we still do not have a complete understanding of how lobbyists decide which technique(s) to use. Though we have recently made progress in answering this question, we remain a long way from a definitive answer.[106] This discussion also underscores the fact that we still know little about which lobbying techniques are most effective and under what circumstances. In a similar vein, my discussion of the informational basis of lobbying raises the question of whether different types of lobbyists (that is, public policy, land use, and procurement lobbyists) rely upon different types of information when they lobby. In addition, my discussion of the nonlobbying activities of lobbyists raises the question of what other nonlobbying tasks lobbyists perform. For obvious reasons, people who study lobbyists generally focus on what they do when they lobby. Nonetheless, a complete understanding of lobbying and lobbyists requires that we cover the full range of lobbyist activities. Finally, my discussion of the determinants of lobbying success calls attention to the fact that we still know little about what determines whether a lobbyist wins or loses. While this chapter attests to the fact that we know a great deal about lobbying and lobbyists, it also makes plain that we still have a lot to learn.

3 Public Policy Lobbying, Part One

In this chapter and the next, I begin my exploration of lobbying by examining public policy lobbying – that is, the lobbying that accompanies government decisions (e.g., laws, rules, regulations, court decisions) made in response to societal demands for action on important issues of the day. Unfortunately, it is arguably more difficult to reach definitive conclusions about public policy lobbying than it is to reach such conclusions about either procurement or land-use lobbying. This is the case because the range of public policy issues with which governments in the United States deal is exceptionally broad. Governments in this country concern themselves with high-profile issues such as affirmative action, the environment, gay rights, gun control, health care, and taxes, as well as less visible issues such as agriculture price supports, banking regulation, and trade with Peru. Indeed, the range of public policy issues with which governments deal is virtually unbounded. Nonetheless, it is possible to reach some general conclusions about public policy lobbying.

This chapter presents some basic information about how public policy decisions in the United States are made. I examine who public policy lobbyists are and what types of organized interests they represent, concluding with a brief overview. Chapter 4 examines what public policy lobbyists do. You may have noticed that while I devote only one chapter each to land use and procurement lobbying, I devote two chapters to public policy lobbying. Does this mean that I think it is more important than the others? My answer is an emphatic "*No.*" As you will see, public policy lobbying is a more varied phenomenon than either land use or procurement lobbying. It is conducted by a wider variety of organized interests, takes a wider variety of forms, and occurs in more places than other types of lobbying. Therefore, the chapter on public policy lobbying has been divided into Part One and Part Two.

PUBLIC POLICYMAKING IN THE UNITED STATES

Before examining who public policy lobbyists are, what they do, and where they fit into our political system, it is essential for us to understand the rudiments of the process by which public policy decisions are made in this country. What follows is not a definitive treatment of this process but a primer on the subject.

Types of Policy Decisions

Leading policy scholar James Anderson defines public policy as "a relatively stable, purposive course of action followed by an actor or set of actors in dealing with a problem or matter of concern."[1] Anderson notes that public policy comprises "courses or patterns of action taken over time by governmental officials rather than their separate, discrete decisions."[2] Public policy, he concludes, "includes not only the decision to adopt a law or make a rule on some topic but also the subsequent decisions that are intended to enforce or implement the law or rule."[3] In other words, public policy decisions are not separate, distinct government decisions, but rather come in bundles that together comprise government approaches to certain problems. For example, public policy on gun control comprises numerous individual court decisions, legislative decisions (made by Congress, state legislatures, and local legislative bodies), and executive branch decisions. There is no single, discrete government decision that comprises public policy on gun control.

Generally when we talk about public policy, we do so in relation to specific issue areas: There is no such thing as one, comprehensive, overarching public policy. Instead, there is crime policy, economic policy, education policy, environmental policy, health care policy, and so on. Within a given issue area – and the list of areas is quite long – public policy comprises the sum total of all individual public policy decisions. The number of such decisions on any given issue area may be very large. Moreover, public policy decisions may be affirmative – that is, decisions to do something – or negative – that is, decisions to do nothing. Finally, to make matters more complex, when governments decide to *do* something, they have several options. Specifically, affirmative government decisions can take several forms: (1) laws, (2) regulations (or rules) adopted by executive agencies, and (3) court decisions. Let's briefly examine each of these forms to illustrate the types of decisions that public policy lobbyists attempt to influence.

Laws. A *law* is *a formal act of a legislature that sets forth a rule or body of rules governing a particular kind of activity.*[4] Laws are also referred to as resolutions, statutes, acts, ordinances (at the local level), or pieces of legislation. Typically, as the state of Ohio's Web site indicates, laws declare, command, or prohibit something.[5] For example, in this country we have laws that (1) prohibit people from kidnapping and killing each other; (2) command employers to pay their employees a minimum wage; and (3) declare that certain days, weeks, or months will honor certain activities, events, organizations, or people.

Although chief executives tend to get more attention from media than legislatures, legislatures are generally much more powerful in the lawmaking process than are chief executives. For example, the Constitution clearly makes Congress the most powerful branch of the federal government, and state governors also typically exercise far fewer lawmaking powers than state legislatures. In the United States, legislatures at all three levels of government pass laws on a regular basis, and generally have broad powers to tax, spend money, and enact legislation on a wide variety of topics. Each year, for example, Congress passes approximately 300–700 bills and considers hundreds more.[6] State and local legislatures pass thousands of additional laws each year.

Before leaving the topic of laws, it is important to note that chief executives generally play a crucial role in their adoption. At the federal and state levels, as well as in some localities, the chief executive has the veto power, which means that he or she can kill a bill passed by the legislature. While the legislature generally has the power to override a chief executive veto, doing so is generally difficult. President Bill Clinton, for example, vetoed a total of 37 bills during his eight years as president, and Congress managed to override only 2 of them.[7] In short, the chief executive's approval (or at least lack of disapproval) is almost always necessary for a legislature to adopt legislation. Moreover, chief executives often propose legislation. All of this adds up to the fact that chief executives are important parts of the legislative process, even though they are not part of the legislature.[8]

Regulations (or Rules). While many people tend to think that public policy is comprised solely of laws passed by the legislature (and approved by the chief executive), many affirmative public policy decisions come in the form of regulations or rules issued by the bureaucracy, which in this country is huge. The federal bureaucracy alone consists of more than 2,000 agencies and bureaus and employs approximately 3 million people. There are several thousand more bureaucratic agencies at the state and local levels. As mentioned in Chapter 2, the foremost task of bureaucratic agencies is to implement government decisions. Nonetheless (also mentioned in Chapter 2), today bureaucratic agencies *make* public policy decisions in addition to implementing them.[9] This is the case primarily because legislators and chief executives often delegate policymaking power to these agencies.[10] For example, at the federal level, Congress may pass a law that instructs the EPA to provide "fishable and swimmable water, everywhere in the United States" and then leaves it to the agency to adopt regulations that achieve this goal.[11]

A *regulation* (or rule) is defined as *an agency-issued directive designed to make specific a law administered by the agency*.[12] Continuing our example, in an effort to fulfill Congress's wishes to provide fishable and swimmable water, the EPA might adopt a regulation that makes it illegal to dump motor oil or any other petroleum product into a river, a lake, or the ocean. The actual process by which government agencies make regulations is complex. For now, suffice it to say that many government agencies in this country have the power to adopt regulations that have the force of law.

Court Decisions. The main job of the judicial branch of government in the United States is to resolve civil and criminal disputes. Nonetheless, like bureaucratic agencies, though their primary job is not to make public policy decisions, courts often do so. In this country, courts have the power to interpret laws and regulations, but as legislative scholars have noted, seldom do laws cover each eventuality that may occur during implementation. Thus, courts are often called upon to clarify what laws passed by the legislature "really mean." Some states, for example, have adoption laws that neither prohibit nor explicitly allow the adoption of children by homosexual couples, and it is up to the state courts to decide if they can.[13]

Courts also have the power to declare unconstitutional both laws of the legislature and acts of the executive branch. The Supreme Court of the United States can declare laws invalid if it believes they violate the Constitution, as it did in a famous case in the 1980s when it ruled that state laws that ban flag burning are unconstitutional (because they violate the First Amendment right to free speech). Similarly, many state supreme courts can declare state and local laws unconstitutional. Courts have similar powers to declare the actions of executive branch personnel (be they chief executives, bureaucrats, or staff people) unconstitutional.

In sum, court decisions that clarify laws and or mandate certain types of behavior are also public policy decisions.

Nondecisions. Sometimes the government chooses *not* to act. Consider the following example. For years, many scientists have argued that the world is growing warmer as the global climate changes. The result of this global warming, according to these scientists, is increased illness and disease (as rodents and mosquitoes move into new areas), the destruction of beaches and wetlands (as oceans rise), and increased natural disasters (such as droughts and floods and hurricanes), among other things. Thus far, the federal government has done little or nothing to combat global warming. In other words, global warming is a case of *nondecision*.[14]

Other Types of Decisions. Most public policy decisions come in the form of laws, regulations, rules, court decisions, or nondecisions, though not all. For example, at all three levels of government, the chief executive has the power to appoint (often with the approval of the legislature) certain other government officials (such as high-level bureaucrats). Similarly, some legislatures have the power to impeach and remove the chief executive and/or other government officials from office. For example, Congress has the power to remove the president and federal judges. Nonetheless, because most important public policy decisions come in the form of laws, rules or regulations, court decisions, and nondecisions, these are the types that lobbyists generally try to affect.

Two General Observations about the Policy Process

As the previous section attests, public policy decisions come in several forms. This is an important point to make because it highlights the fact that all three branches of government are involved in the public policy-making process. In other words, public policy in many (if not most) policy areas comprises decisions made in all three branches of government. On a related note, this classification of public policy decisions also makes clear that there are many access points in government for the public policy lobbyist. Because these decisions flow from all three branches of government (and for that matter, all three levels of government), there are numerous places that a lobbyist can "plug in" to the process.

There is another crucial point about the public policy process. Public policy decisions are generally made in a two-step process. First, an issue reaches the *governmental agenda*, which policy scholar John Kingdon defines as "the list of subjects that are getting attention" from government officials.[15] At any given time, there is a limited number of items on the governmental agenda. After all, while there are many government actors in this country, governments cannot pay attention to all issues at all times. Instead, they focus on a "short list" of issues. Items reach the governmental agenda in two primary ways: (1) via a dramatic event or crisis (e.g., a plane crash, a terrorist attack); or (2) the hard work of a "policy entrepreneur" (i.e., a political activist or lobbyist) who convinces government officials that a certain issue is worthy of government attention.

The second step in the process by which a public policy decision is made is for governmental actors to choose an *alternative*. An alternative is *a policy proposal that deals with an item on the governmental agenda*. If the issue of welfare reform is on the agenda, for example, government officials might consider a number of alternatives, including dismantling the current welfare program completely, limiting benefits to recipients, or forcing recipients to work in order to receive benefits.

In sum, a public policy decision is comprised of two steps: the decision to include an issue on the governmental agenda, and the decision to choose an alternative course of action on the issue.

Summary

Public policy in a given issue area (e.g., the environment, affirmative action, gun control, abortion) comprises the sum total of individual public policy decisions relevant to that area. The authoritative government decisions that comprise public policy come in a variety of forms, including laws, rules and regulations, court decisions, and nondecisions. Public policy lobbyists lobby to affect these types of decisions and others. The process by which governments in the United States make public policy decisions has two steps. First, the government must consider doing something about an issue: It must reach the governmental agenda. Second, once the issue reaches the agenda, the government must decide precisely what to do, if anything, about it from a number of alternatives.

PUBLIC POLICY LOBBYISTS: BACKGROUND INFORMATION

The data reveal a great deal about who public policy lobbyists are and what types of organized interests they represent. Two findings in particular stand out: (1) Public policy lobbyists represent organized interests of all kinds; and (2) Relatively large numbers of public policy lobbyists are in-house lobbyists. Let's discuss these two findings in turn.

Public Policy Lobbyists Represent Organized Interests of All Kinds

Although my sample is small and perhaps unrepresentative, it nonetheless illustrates the large variety of organized interests engaged in public policy lobbying. Of the 20 public policy lobbyists I interviewed, 2 work for professional associations, 1 works for a trade association, 1 for an accrediting commission for vocational schools (which is essentially a special type of trade association), 1 for a private university, 1 for a labor union, 1 for a coalition of trade and professional associations, 1 for a citizen group, 1 for a think tank, 1 for a business firm, and 1 for a coalition of government entities. The remaining 9 work as contract lobbyists for consulting, law, lobbying, public affairs, or public relations firms.[16] I did not ask these 9 lobbyists specifically what kinds of organizations they represent. But in the course of our conversations I learned that they all represent business firms primarily. However, 4 of these lobbyists told me they regularly represent other types of organized interests as well.

In sum, both my sample and my conversations with public policy lobbyists indicate that a wide variety of organized interests is involved in public policy lobbying. As you will see in Chapters 5 and 6, a rather narrow assortment of organized interests engages in land use and procurement lobbying.

Relatively Large Numbers of Public Policy Lobbyists Are In-House Lobbyists

Although I must again caution that my sample of lobbyists is small, the data indicate that relatively large numbers of public policy lobbyists are in-house lobbyists. Of the 20 public policy lobbyists interviewed, 11 are in-house and 9 are contract lobbyists. In other words, over half of my public policy lobbyist respondents work in-house. As you will see in Chapters 5 and 6, a much smaller proportion of land use lobbyists (13 percent) and procurement lobbyists (20 percent) work in-house. This, of course, begs the following question: Why are so many public policy lobbyists in-house lobbyists? I defer this answer until after we have learned more about land use lobbying and procurement lobbying in Chapters 5 and 6.

Summary

The data illustrate two general points about public policy lobbyists. First, they represent organized interests of all kinds. Second, many are in-house lobbyists. While that data suggest that most procurement and land use lobbyists are contract lobbyists, it appears that most public policy lobbyists are in-house lobbyists.

WHAT PUBLIC POLICY LOBBYISTS DO OTHER THAN LOBBYING

The data show that not all of what public policy lobbyists do is lobbying. There are two things in particular that they do in addition to lobbying.

First, they monitor government. Second, they manage their clients and/or members. In this section, I summarize what public policy lobbyists told me about these two aspects of their work.

Lobbyists Monitor Government

Public policy lobbyists (like land use and procurement lobbyists) spend a great deal of their time monitoring government.[17] I cannot say for certain how much of their time they spend monitoring government, but the data show that it is substantial. The data also show that all monitoring is not the same. Public policy lobbyists engage in two distinct kinds of monitoring: (1) policy monitoring, and (2) compliance monitoring.

Policy Monitoring. I define *policy monitoring* as *monitoring designed to help lobbyists determine the best course of lobbying action.* When public policy lobbyists engage in policy monitoring, they are seeking information that will help them be effective advocates. All 20 of the public policy lobbyists I interviewed told me they engage in policy monitoring.

At the most basic level, policy monitoring entails identifying potential government actions that may affect a lobbyist's client(s) (in the case of a contract lobbyist), or organization (in the case of an in-house lobbyist). A Washington-based in-house lobbyist who works for a labor union, for example, will monitor government to detect any potential changes in labor law. Similarly, a state lobbyist who represents an environmental citizen group will monitor state government to spot any environmental legislation or regulations that may be in the offing. This basic kind of policy monitoring can be tedious, and in large part comprises the tracking of proposed bills (in the legislature) and regulations and rules (in bureaucratic agencies). Lobbyist no. 6, a contract lobbyist in Tennessee, told me:

> The [clients who hire me] want to know what's going down the pipe. They want to be plugged into the system. They want to be able to have a quick response as opposed to finding out too late. We read virtually every bill that is filed, [or] at least a synopsis of them.

Lobbyist no. 18, a contract lobbyist in Connecticut, told a similar story: "Monitoring is underrated and is very important because things happen very quickly." Later, she added:

> We read every proposed bill. We read every single amendment. Not just ones that we think might be [relevant to our client]. And I don't know what the amendment process is for other states, but you can get a title of a bill and if you rule out a bill just based on the title, you've missed so

much because there are things hidden, and deliberately so. And we've done some of the hiding quite honestly! But you have to read everything. . . . You don't have the luxury of picking and choosing [which bills to look at], because things are hidden in big omnibus bills and they're hidden in amendments.

The vast majority of proposed bills, regulations, and rules that a lobbyist identifies will not be relevant to the organized interest(s) that he or she represents. Some, however, will be relevant. After a lobbyist has identified a proposed government action that is relevant, the decision must be made as to where the organized interest stands on the bill. For example, after an environmental citizen group learns that Congress is considering a bill that would change fuel efficiency standards for automobiles, the lobbyist must figure out what position to take on it. To do this, the lobbyist must discover precisely what provisions are in the bill. Does the bill increase or decrease fuel efficiency standards? When do the standards take effect? What vehicles are exempt from the standards? All of these questions must be answered before the decision is made to take a stand on the bill.

Lobbyist no. 18 told me that her clients, which include universities, business firms, labor unions, and citizen groups, ask her to monitor government and then help them decide what lobbying action to take:

Our job is to monitor things on the legislative level – any kind of proposed legislation that is being bandied about. Or on the state agency level we research . . . proposed regulations . . . on behalf of clients. And when we say monitoring, first we monitor it and then we decide what to do.

How do lobbyists decide what to do about proposed government decisions? The data show that contract lobbyists pass the information they receive on to their clients, and then consult with their clients about what to do next. In-house lobbyists consult with officers and executives from the organization they represent and determine a course of action. (Later in this section, I will say more about consultations between lobbyists and their clients and/or managers.) In either case, after the initial information-gathering stage, policy monitoring moves into the discussion phase during which lobbyists decide what to do next.

Several respondents told me that the reason they closely monitor *potential* government actions, rather than simply keeping track of laws, regulations, and rules that have been adopted, is that after a policy decision has been made it is difficult to get rid of it. Lobbyist no. 29, an in-house, big-city lobbyist for a large private university, put it this way: "It is always much easier to stop something than to start something. So much of what we end up doing is playing defense – playing goalkeeper rather than power forward." Lobbyist no. 18 used very similar language:

> [O]ne thing that may be a recurring theme in your research is that we are often on defense more than we are on offense on behalf of our clients. . . . Sometimes in doing defense, the defense is to try to defeat a piece of legislation or change the focus of a proposal or redirect it in a way that might be more helpful.

Lobbyists believe it is better to "get out in front" of proposed policies and attempt to change them or kill them if necessary than it is to react to policies once they are adopted.

In sum, public policy lobbyists monitor government because what government does affects the organized interests they represent. Lobbyists want to have the opportunity to stop or modify potentially *harmful* government policies or to push hard for potentially *helpful* government policy decisions before either are adopted. The failure to identify relevant potential policy decisions can have negative consequences for lobbyists and the groups they represent. Lobbyist no. 8, an in-house state lobbyist who works for a professional association of architects, for example, admitted to me that last year he overlooked a state bill (which eventually became law) that affected some of the architectural firms his organization represents:

> I had to do a major fix this year because of a change in the state law last year that I and really a lot of other people did not catch. Pardon my frank language, but [the change] has screwed some architecture firms. They lost business with public clients because the law changed on them. They did work for the University of California, and then the consulting work led to projects, and the law changed [so] they're no longer eligible for the projects.

Had he been aware of the bill before it passed, Lobbyist no. 8 acknowledged, he certainly would have fought hard against it.

Compliance Monitoring. Public policy lobbyists also engage in what I call *compliance monitoring – monitoring designed to help organized interests comply with government decisions.* When public policy lobbyists engage in compliance lobbying, they are gathering information that can help the organization they represent stay in compliance with government policies.

When the national government, a state government, or a local government makes a public policy decision, the decision invariably affects organized interests. For example, when the national government makes a policy decision to raise the minimum wage, every U.S. organized interest with employees is affected. In order to comply with minimum wage leg-islation, which is usually "big news," organized interests (and citizens) throughout the country must become aware of it. However, many govern-ment policies – especially those that affect few organized interests or that are not particularly newsworthy – attract very little media attention. Thus, it behooves lobbyists to monitor government closely to ensure that the organized interests for which they work are aware of policies by which they must abide. Organized interests that do not comply with government policies can be punished (e.g., fined).

Several respondents told me that an absolutely critical part of a lobby-ist's job is compliance monitoring. For example, Lobbyist no. 18, a contract lobbyist in Connecticut who represents several corporate clients told me: "[W]ell we have some corporate clients and we watch things globally of importance, like worker's compensation legislation...you know, those kinds of things." Clients like to know, Lobbyist no. 18 told me, how new policies affect them and how they can comply with new rules and regula-tions and laws. Lobbyist no. 4, a Washington, DC, contract lobbyist who often represents business firms in the health care industry, told me that he has recently spent a lot of time counseling clients on how to comply with the provisions of the Health Insurance Portability and Accountability Act of 1996 (HIPAA), a sweeping overhaul of the country's health-care-infor-mation privacy laws. The law contains provisions that restrict what infor-mation health care professionals can collect from patients, and what they can do with the information after they collect it. Lobbyist no. 4 told me:

> You...try to give your client advice about how to comply and how to meet the expectations of the regulations. I [have] spent a lot of time in this area, particularly [with companies in] the clinical laboratory indus-try.... One of my areas of specialty is helping them ascertain what they have to do to comply. [I have had] a lot of discussion[s] with clinical labs on [this] issue. It's an area that...we haven't gotten a lot of [guidance] from the federal government, [and] there's still a lot of questions.

Often, Lobbyist no. 4 said, laws are difficult to understand, and business firms need help figuring out how to comply with them: "A lot of [what HIPAA requires] is not evident on the face of the [law]. [Understanding HIPAA] requires an understanding of the [health care] business and the regulations." He concluded his discussion of compliance monitoring by noting that many of his corporate clients place a high value on his counsel concerning how best to abide by federal laws and regulations: "They're asking you for advice and so you're giving them advice."

Lobbyist no. 23, a Washington, DC, in-house lobbyist who works for a professional association that represents doctors who are specialists in a narrow field of medicine, told me that he believes it is absolutely crucial to keep his member doctors up to date on new health care rules: "That's even one of our member services . . . alerting [doctors] to compliance issues. There are a lot of things [coming] out of [various government agencies] – all this regulatory stuff. We feel very strongly that's our obligation to provide that information to members." Lobbyist no. 8, whose group represents professional architects, also told me that compliance monitoring is very important to him and his members:

> I think if someone is going to pay 600 or 700 bucks a year to be a member of an association [and] its stated primary focus is government relations, they should expect at the end of the year a document that says, "These are the changes in the law that occurred that will affect your practice whether it's a business thing, whether its an architecture thing, what have you." I think it's a source of information where they're going to depend on us.

In sum, one of the reasons that lobbyists monitor government is to pass information on to their clients or parent organizations so that they can keep abreast of government policies affecting them. Several respondents told me that it is their responsibility to keep the organizations they represent "out of trouble." Because governments in the United States adopt thousands of new rules, regulations, and laws each year, it is important for the organizations affected by new policies to keep abreast of policy changes so that they can modify their operations (if necessary) to abide by the law.

Where Do Lobbyists Look for Information? The fact that lobbyists engage in so much monitoring begs the following question: Where do lobbyists look when they monitor government? The answer is fourfold. First, they look at media sources. The data suggest that the most important of these media sources are publications. In Washington, DC, for example, lobbyists monitor popular newspapers such as the *New York Times*, the *Washington Post*, and the *Wall Street Journal*, as well as more specialized publications such as *Roll Call* and *Congressional Quarterly Today* (each of which contains more detailed information about congressional goings-on). Lobbyist no. 17, an in-house Washington lobbyist for a citizen group, told me:

> We get *Roll Call*. That has just gone to four days a week, so I read that pretty religiously. I also read *CQ Today*, and again that comes out every

day of the congressional session. It gives highlights of the meetings and what's going on on the floor, and other political insider stuff. [I also read] the *New York Times* [and the] *Washington Post*.

Almost all of the public policy lobbyists I interviewed provided similar accounts of the publications they read daily. None of my respondents mentioned either television or radio as important sources of information.

Second, several respondents told me that they obtain information from tracking services. *Tracking services* are *companies that are hired by lobbyists to provide information on proposed government policies*. Lobbyist no. 27, a state contract lobbyist, told me about the bill tracking service that he uses:

> When I'm looking at bills . . . it's the actual text of the bill. And [I] usually [do that at the beginning] of [a] legislative session when all the new bills are introduced. And then throughout the session [I am] looking for amendments that may somehow affect my client as well. I'm a sole proprietor and so I subscribe to a [computerized] bill tracking service that works very well. It shows all the new introductions. It allows me to categorize the bills – [to] make . . . computer files for bills for all my different clients. The computer has been a wonderful thing. In the past, you had to get hard copies of all the bills, look them over, put them in envelopes [and] send them to clients. Now I can just pass them on electronically to clients and then you get them immediately.

Stateside Associates, a well-known state and local government-monitoring firm based in Virginia, is a good example of a full-service tracking firm. Among the services offered by Stateside Associates are (1) legislative monitoring, whereby the company identifies "and monitor[s] legislation for clients by combining an extensive network of contacts in each state, solid knowledge of a client's issues and an intimate familiarity with the legislative processes"[18]; and (2) regulatory monitoring that "keep[s] clients abreast of new and emerging requirements from the regulatory arenas."[19] Many bill and regulatory tracking services are now computerized, allowing lobbyists to search for pending bills or regulations by keyword or topic. Moreover, most state governments now have Internet sites that allow users to track proposed legislation by keyword, committee, legislator, or issue. Some tracking services allow a lobbyist to name a topic or two and receive daily updates on government activity germane to the topic(s). Lobbyist no. 6, a contract lobbyist in Tennessee, told me that he uses two different services:

> We . . . subscribe to at least two services that provide information on what's happening. One of them . . . tries to keep track of everything.

[The service] update[s] it daily [and] we plug into that. . . . The other
service . . . monitors committee meetings and other things going on, and
we get reports that help us analyze what's going on, as opposed to just
saying the nuts and bolts [and] the mechanics of it.

Third, many lobbyists obtain information from government sources.
For example, governmental bodies at all three levels of government often
conduct their business in public, and lobbyists can attend government
proceedings and monitor them. Legislatures and administrative agencies
frequently hold public hearings, and these hearings provide information
about what government is up to. In addition, governments publish reams
of material and make it available to the public. Lobbyist no. 6 noted that
the state of Tennessee (where he works as a contract lobbyist) regularly
publishes (on its Web site) the status of proposed legislation, as well as
the details of committee action. Similarly, Lobbyist no. 4 noted that after
they adopt regulations, federal agencies publish "guidance documents"
that attempt to explain the regulations to interested parties. Moreover,
before federal agencies adopt rules or regulations, the federal government
publishes the proposed actions in the *Federal Register*. States have similar
publications, and lobbyists peruse them regularly.

Finally, all of my sample public policy lobbyists told me that they obtain
information from people, most frequently from government officials and
their staff members, and lobbyists or personnel from other organizations.
There was consensus among my respondents that while these people are
generally not the most important sources of information, they can be very
important. Lobbyist no. 8, for example, told me that he often receives
information from government officials: "There's a reason I have five people on staff in Washington: because they have an extraordinary array of
contacts." Lobbyist no. 7, an in-house state lobbyist for a railroad, told me
that while he regularly "checks in" with government officials, his most
important contacts work for other organizations:

[Getting quality information] is where your networking really comes in
helpful. For example, the Chamber of Commerce is a good ally. The Coal
Association is a good ally. [And] the Business and Industry Council is a
group of association lobbyists – in other words, pro-business lobbyists. We
don't have a lounge up there [in the state legislature], so we congregate
at what we call "the well" in the center between the House and Senate
and we shoot the sh**. [That is], we exchange information and we try to
warn [each other about things that might affect us. We'll say], "Did you
see such and such a bill that might affect you?"

In closing, it is worth noting that several of my respondents told me that monitoring is easier today than it has ever been, largely due to the Internet. For example, according to Lobbyist no. 17: "[I]t is amazing... the information you can find on the Internet. It's just something that people are used to now – having immediate access." Several other respondents made comments almost identical to this one.

Lobbyists Manage Their Clients and Members

Public policy lobbyists spend much time on what political scientist Rogan Kersh calls "client interaction." In addition, public policy lobbyists who represent membership organizations spend considerable time communicating with members. In this section, I briefly discuss how lobbyists interact with their clients and/or their members.

Educating Clients or Superiors. Public policy lobbyists transmit information to their clients (in the case of contract lobbyists) or their superiors (in the case of in-house lobbyists). In most cases it is political information. What kind of political information? The facts about what is going on. As Lobbyist no. 21, who works as a contract lobbyist in Texas, told me: The public policy lobbyist's job is to "present a clear set of facts...to [people] at the highest level [of the organization he or she represents]." What this means, according to the data, is that public policy lobbyists pass on the information they have gleaned from monitoring. Over time, they learn what kinds of information to look for when they engage in monitoring. Lobbyist no. 6, for example, told me that he was once hired by a land title insurance company and spent months getting "up to speed" on that business. Specifically, he worked hard to learn what sorts of public policy issues affected his client. Once he learned about those issues, he knew what to look for. From here, anytime he detected a law or rule or regulation or court decision that affected the land title insurance business, he passed this information along to his client.

The information that lobbyists pass along to their clients or superiors often concerns the policies that are "coming down the pike" and the status of certain policies. Is a proposed policy almost certain to pass? Or does it look dead? With this information, clients or superiors decide what to do next.

Advising. Once public policy lobbyists locate information they deem worthy of passing on to either their clients (in the case of contract lobbyists) or their superiors (in the case of in-house lobbyists), they are often intimately involved in discussions about what to do next. Of course, because every organized interest is different, it is impossible to generalize about who ultimately makes decisions within an organization as to how to proceed in a specific lobbying campaign. But one thing is clear: Lobbyists are often involved in these decisions. Lobbyist no. 10, a Washington contract lobbyist, told me that although his clients generally decide where they stand on a specific policy proposal, they often ask him for advice on how best to achieve their policy goals. He said: "If I had to typify [the process, I would say that] if someone in the organization knows there's a problem [out there with a proposed policy], then they come to us and say, 'Hey listen, [what do we do?].'" Lobbyist no. 27, a California contract lobbyist, told me something similar:

> [I may have] a long-standing client. [And I go] through [all the information I can find] ascertaining all the different bills that may affect them. So I spotted . . . one and said to them, "Gee, this is what I think that we should spend a lot of time on. [This is what we should do on] it. Do you agree?"

A contract lobbyist hired by a business firm may report to a client that a bill is being considered in the state legislature that would cost the firm millions of dollars, and the lobbyist may well be asked what the firm can do to derail the bill. In sum, lobbyists often advise the organized interests they represent about how to proceed.

Lobbyists Report to Members. The data show that lobbyists who represent membership organized interests spend some of their time keeping their members up to date on what's going on. In other words, they share with their members the results of their monitoring activities. Lobbyist no. 19, a Washington in-house lobbyist for a coalition of small trade and professional associations, told me:

> Part of what I do is a weekly newsletter that I send out on Monday mornings. It's . . . for [the] membership. [The newsletter contains information on] what is [happening], what has happened, what's going to happen, and what we want to happen. For instance, today, [I sent out a newsletter with information on] what's going on right now with foreign tax repeal, which should happen in March. . . . We're letting them know the status of these manufacturing and small business tax cuts . . . letting them know that . . . they need to let their members of Congress know that they are going to support this, and it is imperative that we get the tax cut we need.

Lobbyist no. 1, a state lobbyist who works for an association of cities and towns, told me something similar:

> I found that the deal is, you keep them [i.e., members] informed along the way. You know, keeping them in the loop is the huge thing because the lobbying and the legislative process is a foreign thing. . . . It is such a foreign process that people don't understand all the work it takes to get a bill passed. And if you inform your membership and let them know all this, they're grateful that you're doing all the nasty work and getting in the gutters and the trenches and they don't have to.

The data show that lobbyists spend substantial time reporting information to members for two reasons. First, members expect it and like it. In other words, many members of organized interests expect that the organizations they belong to will keep them abreast of what's going on; they consider such information a nice benefit of belonging. Lobbyist no. 23, who represents a professional association of doctors, put it this way:

> [A]s with anything, in a voluntary association it gets down to value. And you know, I need to . . . tell our whole membership what we're doing on their behalf because quite frankly, next May they're going to get a membership dues bill and I want them to understand throughout the whole year that we've communicated what the society is doing to benefit [them] . . . so that they don't have any hesitation to say, "Well gee I wonder what [this group] did for me this last year?"

According to my respondents, members value the information they receive from the organizations they belong to because it allows them to act on their own if they wish (by, for example, writing letters or making telephone calls to elected officials), and because it allows them to feel that their views are being represented.

A second reason lobbyists spend time providing information to members is that it allows them to prepare those members for grassroots lobbying campaigns. As I mentioned in Chapter 2, grassroots lobbying efforts (to be discussed in depth in the next chapter) are increasingly common among organized interests of all kinds, and they are widely considered to be very effective. Keeping members abreast of what's going on enables lobbyists to "call on them" when they are needed. Lobbyist no. 17, for example, who lobbies for a Washington organized interest that works on behalf of senior citizens, told me that she regularly keeps her members informed via a periodic newsletter, as well as a web site. Keeping her members informed and interested, she noted, is a good way to prepare them for grassroots efforts. Every now and then, she told me, "if there's a hot issue on the Hill, I will craft a one page letter and get it sent out to ... our supporters. It often encourages them to contact their member of Congress on a specific issue." Several respondents indicated that a well-informed and "plugged in" membership is easier to mobilize than an ignorant and passive membership.

Justifying Their Existence. As the two previous subsections attest, lobbyists must spend considerable time reporting to others in the organizations they represent. For contract lobbyists, this means passing along information to their clients; for in-house lobbyists, this means passing along information to superiors and members. In my interviews, I learned that many public policy lobbyists in particular spend nontrivial amounts of time reporting to their bosses (in the case of in-house lobbyists) and/or clients.[20] I call this activity "justifying their existence." Lobbyists are forced to justify their existence primarily because of the expense. Organized interests spend billions of dollars on lobbyists each year, and it is not surprising that they want to make sure this money is well spent.

Lobbyist no. 27, a state contract lobbyist, told me that justifying his existence to his clients is not always easy:

> You know, I think that's a difficult thing. Unlike a sales force, you can't say, "Gee, this year Joe had sales of a million dollars." We're a cost center. We cost companies money as opposed to make them money. Even if you can say, "Gee I got involved in this bill, [and] if we hadn't done [it] ... this would have cost you X dollars," I don't think that people look at it that way on their bottom line.

Clients who hire lobbyists and superiors who supervise lobbyists like to keep tabs on them. As such, lobbyists spend some of their time keeping them up-to-date on what they are doing. Many lobbyists have periodic (e.g., weekly) meetings with their superiors or bosses to prove that they are busy. For example, Lobbyist no. 19, an in-house Washington lobbyist, told me:

> The conversations I have with my boss ... I let him know what I'm doing. I let him know where I'm going, and [I tell him about] the 10 members [of Congress] who I went to call on last week, [and I tell him that] seven of them signed on as cosponsors [of a bill I liked].

Some bosses are more demanding and "plugged in" than others. Lobbyist no. 29, who works for a university, told me:

> I talk to the chancellor three or four times a day, because he is interested. He is interested in a lot of ideas. . . . He's interested in public relations and government relations, and I keep him briefed throughout the day, and if anything happens that is more significant, I will do something more formally.

Three to four times a day is quite often. Lobbyist no. 19 has a more typical arrangement with his boss, "[A]t the end of the week . . . I update my boss . . . in my weekly [report]. I will note that I have worked this issue . . . not in great detail, but the overall picture of it. I tell them I am out lobbying on these issues and this [is what I did]." Most of my respondents told me that they are required in one way or another to prove to either their clients or superiors that they are keeping busy, usually on a weekly basis. The reason looking busy is so important, many pointed out, is that actually *evaluating* a lobbyist's performance is exceedingly difficult. Lobbyist no. 19 pointed out:

> I think a lot of what I do – it would be hard to claim any legislative victory on because what I'm doing is being done by a lot of other people as well. There really aren't a lot of clear-cut victories. And a lot of the stuff I am working on, we are not going to see action on this year. It's going to be next year [or] next summer because we're on a two-year cycle. Just because we are working on it now doesn't mean it's going to get acted on now. [Often] there is really no sign if I am doing a good job or not.

From time to time, of course, a lobbyist can point to a clear-cut, tangible success. Lobbyist no. 29 told me: "We have been lobbying this year very actively on some specific appropriations from Congress for some projects here, and we were successful. And literally, we get a check – earmarked funds." But more often lobbyists cannot point to definitive success stories. As a result, they must constantly justify their existence to their bosses. They do this primarily by convincing their clients or their superiors that they are busy – busy doing things like testifying before committees or agencies, meeting with government decision makers, responding to requests for information, and carefully watching for important pending proposals.

Summary

Monitoring is absolutely critical for most public policy lobbyists. So how much time do public policy lobbyists spend monitoring government? Unfortunately, it is impossible to say. Some of my respondents told me that they would not hazard a guess as to how much time they spend monitoring; others told me they spend as little as 10 or 20 percent of their time monitoring, and still others told me they spend "a majority" of their time monitoring. In any case, the amount of time that public policy lobbyists spend monitoring is nontrivial. In addition to monitoring, they also spend considerable time interacting with their clients (in the case of contract lobbyists), their superiors (in the case of in-house lobbyists), and their members (in the case of lobbyists who represent membership organizations).

WHAT PUBLIC POLICY LOBBYING LOOKS LIKE

In this chapter, I have given you a general idea of who public policy lobbyists are and what they do in addition to lobbying. In Part Two I describe what public policy lobbyists do when they lobby government. At the conclusion of the next chapter, I will address the question: What does public policy lobbying look like? Although I raise it here, I am deferring the answer until our discussion of public policy lobbying is complete and until insight is provided into how it differs from land use and procurement lobbying.

4 Public Policy Lobbying, Part Two

Now that I have provided you with some basic information about the public policymaking process and told you a bit about who public policy lobbyists are, what interests they represent, and what they do in addition to lobbying, I can move on to a general discussion of what public policy lobbyists do when they lobby government.

In the broadest sense, public policy lobbying entails attempting to affect laws, regulations, court decisions, nondecisions, and other types of public policy decisions. How precisely do these lobbyists attempt to affect public policy decisions? In this chapter, I answer the question by summarizing what my respondents told me about the process, beginning with a discussion of legislative lobbying. From there, I discuss executive branch lobbying, grassroots lobbying, and electoral lobbying. I conclude by asking: What does public policy lobbying look like?

LEGISLATIVE LOBBYING

Surveys of lobbyists consistently show that the legislature receives an enormous amount of attention from lobbyists. For example, surveys show that almost all lobbyists testify at legislative hearings.[1] Similarly, many studies show that lobbyists regularly meet personally with legislators and legislative staff.[2] My data support the general conclusion that the legislature is the primary target of public policy lobbying. The reason is obvious: The legislature has considerable power over public policy by dint of its power to pass laws and confirm executive appointments, among other things. Moreover, the legislature is very accessible. At the federal level, there are 535 members of Congress and thousands of legislative staff members. State and local legislatures are generally much smaller, but they too have numerous members and, in many cases, large staffs. Finally, many legislatures are broken into committees. This provides yet more points of access for public policy lobbyists.

Every public policy lobbyist in my sample spends some of his or her time lobbying the legislature. And while I did not ask my respondents to quantify the time they spent lobbying each branch of government, the data indicate that all but a few public policy lobbyists spend more time lobbying the legislative branch than they do the other branches of government.

Background Legislative Lobbying

The data indicate that when public policy lobbyists lobby legislators, they engage in two general types of lobbying: (1) background legislative lobbying and (2) proposal-specific legislative lobbying. I define *background legislative lobbying* as *broad-spectrum lobbying not aimed at influencing a specific piece of legislation, but rather designed to make legislators aware of who a lobbyist is, what organized interest(s) he or she represents, and what the lobbyist's general policy interests are.* Lobbyist no. 26 told me, for example: "I often buy tickets to political events – mostly fund-raisers [for legislators].... These things are like any social activity – my mere presence there is important. Being seen is important. It's an important end to itself." Lobbyist no. 7, a state lobbyist who works for a railroad, told me something very similar. "I tend to work with the [legislative] staff. We invite staff to functions.... [We] go buy donuts and [things like that]."

As these two examples show, background lobbying often takes place in informal settings. Lobbyist no. 3, an in-house Washington lobbyist who represents a cosmetology school, summarized both the "how" and the "why" of background lobbying:

> [Our group], they've been doing [this] for about three years. [T]hey do [this] over on Capitol Hill, sometimes in a reception room in one of the Senate or House office buildings, [it's] something called "Welcome to Our World." [We] set up massage tables – it's like a mini-salon. It's not even mini, it's pretty big! They have chairs, they have massage tables and everything. They invite senators and congressmen and their aides to come. They serve them food. They get together – volunteer cosmetologists and massage therapists and nail techs and so on. They orient them, give them a brief orientation on what the main issues are, and then these people [members of Congress and their aides] come and they get services – they get a haircut or they get a manicure or they get a massage.

When I asked Lobbyist no. 3 why her group engaged in this massive lobbying effort, she told me that it was not to affect any specific piece of legislation, but rather was designed to let legislators know who she was and what issues were of interest to her group. Most importantly, the event was designed to let members of Congress and their aides know that she and her group were readily available if they ever needed any information about issues of interest to the cosmetology industry. She told me:

> ["Welcome to Our World"] gives them [i.e., legislators and legislative staff] an introduction to a lot of people so that when we later go to actually lobby [on] an issue, they say, "I went in and had my nails done," or "I had my hair done," or whatever, "and it was a really great event." So that sort of helps "oil the wheel" a little bit.

Later, when summing up her background legislative lobbying efforts, Lobbyist no. 3 told me: "[One of] the main things we want is that people on the Hill – if they're dealing with an issue that has to do with cosmetology or with cosmetology schools – see us as a resource that they can tap for getting information."

Lobbyist no. 3's comments nicely illustrate the two things that happen during background lobbying sessions. First, lobbyists "show their faces" and make legislators and staffers aware that they are around and accessible. This is much more important than it sounds. The old adage "out of sight, out of mind" comes to mind here. Many of my respondents clearly believe that lobbyists who show their faces, make the rounds, and regularly encounter legislators or their staff are on legislators' and staffers' minds more than lobbyists who do not do these things. And this increases their chances of success. Second, when public policy lobbyists engage in background lobbying, they provide general information to legislators about the organized interests they represent and what kinds of issues they care about. For example, a lobbyist for a senior citizens group will gently remind legislators and staffers that she represents elderly people who are always concerned about the status of Medicare and Social Security. Similarly, a contract lobbyist for several small business firms and trade associations might remind legislators and staff members that he represents, let's say, a medical device manufacturer, a coalition of dry cleaning businesses, and a firm that makes baskets for export to China.

My respondents told me that this sort of background lobbying is potentially very rewarding. Lobbyist no. 7, the railroad lobbyist, explained that his donut buying and periodic informal socializing with legislators and staffers often leads to telephone calls from them: "[If] we invite staff to functions . . . and go buy donuts occasionally, and [there is a bill out there that is] affecting us, or more importantly, looks like it's pending . . . we get a call from [these] staff." Lobbyist no. 11, an in-house lobbyist for a Washington think tank, told me a very similar story. She said that in her previous job for a conservative advocacy group (she now works for a think tank), she had regular informal contacts with legislators and staff members, and regularly took officials out for meals, went on golf outings, and generally "schmoozed." She said that she did not particularly like it, but that it paid off. "I may get four to five phone calls a day from Congress," she told me. The telephone calls, she and other lobbyists told me, may stop if the background lobbying stops. Not only does background lobbying lead to requests for information and advice from legislators and their aides, but it also makes it easier for lobbyists to gain access to legislators and staffers for proposal-specific lobbying (which I describe next). Many of my respondents believe that legislators and their staff members are much more likely to take meetings with, and respond to telephone calls from, lobbyists with whom they are familiar than lobbyists they do not know. In sum, background lobbying paves the way for subsequent proposal-specific lobbying. It leads to requests for information and advice from legislators and staff members, and makes it easier for lobbyists to get opportunities to engage in proposal-specific lobbying.

Background lobbying sometimes seems downright silly. Lobbyist no. 10, a Washington contract lobbyist once retained by a university, told me the following story:

> When [a major southern university] won the national [football] championship two years ago, we brought them to Washington [and] got them a document out of the Senate that acknowledged that they were the best football team in America. It's huge public relations. It's about bragging rights and visibility. When the university then comes to lobby to get research funding . . . they [legislators] will go, "Oh yeah. We remember you were up here. What a success you are!"

While the data suggest that most background lobbying is designed to keep a lobbyist's profile high, they also suggest that some background lobbying is designed to "float" new policy ideas. As I mentioned in Chapter 3, before the government makes a public policy decision on a given issue, that issue must first reach the governmental agenda. One way (though certainly not the only way) issues reach the agenda is for lobbyists to convince government decision makers to put them there. And one way lobbyists do this is by convincing policymakers that there is a serious problem out there that deserves governmental attention. It is not unusual for public policy lobbyists to engage in "issue awareness" campaigns designed to convince legislators or their staffers that a specific issue deserves government attention. These types of background lobbying efforts can be broadly construed as attempts to set the governmental agenda. For example, Lobbyist no. 17, who works for a Washington citizen group that represents retirees, told me that she often tries to get legislators and their staffers to pay attention to specific issues related to Social Security and Medicare – even if these issues are not on the agenda. Indeed, her goal is to get these issues on the governmental agenda. To this end, she says that her organization "has commissioned numerous independent studies" that she then passed on to congressional offices. The studies highlighted problems with the current entitlement system and proposed solutions as well. The ultimate goal of reports like these is to convince legislators that a specific issue deserves to be on the agenda.

Reports designed to convince legislators and staff members that a particular issue deserves to be on the governmental agenda often present facts and figures that highlight societal problems (e.g., poverty among the elderly). The data indicate that some types of organized interests are more likely than others to engage in this sort of lobbying. Think tanks, for one, regularly publish research reports, books, and magazines designed to highlight problems. Lobbyist no. 11, who works for a think tank, says that after her organization publishes research reports, she sends them to what she calls her "Hill list" and her "Senate list" – that is, to members of Congress.

Proposal-Specific Legislative Lobbying

Sometimes public policy lobbyists engage in *proposal-specific legislative lobbying*, which I define as *lobbying designed to affect how legislators act on a specific piece of legislation*. The legislative process is not always straightforward. In fact, it is often quite arcane. Nonetheless, the process generally proceeds as follows. First, a legislator formally introduces a bill. Next, the bill is sent to a committee that discusses the bill, modifies it (if desired), and ultimately votes on it. From here, if the committee supports the bill, it is sent to the full chamber of the legislative body in question. Finally, members of the legislature vote on the bill. If a bill passes – assuming that the other house of the legislature (if there is one) passes it in identical form – it is sent to the chief executive.[3]

In general, then, the legislative process officially begins when an issue reaches the governmental agenda and a legislator proposes a bill concerning that issue. While background lobbying is generally not aimed at influencing a specific piece of legislation, proposal-specific lobbying is. When I asked my respondents how they went about trying to influence specific pieces of legislation, it became very obvious that one proposal-specific legislative lobbying technique is much more common than the others: *meeting personally with legislators and/or legislative staff.* What happens at personal meetings between lobbyists and legislators and/or their staffers? My respondents were quite consistent in their answers to this question: During these meetings, lobbyists present information that makes their side look good. In many cases, they also present information that makes the other side look bad. I asked my respondents to tell me about the information they provided to legislators and their staffers. Their responses varied, but the data highlight a few basic findings.

The Provision of Policy-Analytic Information. First, when they engage in proposal-specific legislative lobbying, lobbyists rely heavily on policy-analytic information. For example, when I asked Lobbyist no. 21, a contract lobbyist in Texas, about the type of information he provided to legislators and their staffers, he responded: "It's almost always...policy [information]." Many respondents gave similar answers. When I asked respondents for more detail about the type of policy-analytic information they provide, they told me that they generally emphasize information about how a particular policy will affect a legislator's constituents. Lobbyist no. 1, for example, told me the following:

> With policymakers, with legislators, I definitely [give them] tangible examples as opposed to making general statements to them. They really do want to hear [how a bill affects] their district, [or] the 12 cities that they have in their county, or the two counties that they represent. [They want to know] how [a bill] is affecting [their constituents].

Lobbyist no. 10, a Washington contract lobbyist, told me that invariably, the first thing legislators want to know when he contacts them is "are you a constituent?" "That," he told me, "bears a lot on success." He continued:

> Success is usually determined if you've got something in [their district]. If you've already got manufacturing facilities or employment in their state or district, then you have relevance...even if your headquarters are in New York and you've got some minor activities in their state.

After lobbyists have established that the organized interest they represent does indeed have a "district presence," they proceed to demonstrate how a proposed bill might affect the organization. Lobbyist no. 7, the state railroad lobbyist, gave me a concrete example of information he provided legislators when they considered a recent bill on tort reform, which the railroad company strongly favored because it was the target of repeated lawsuits:

> [I] prepare[d] a fact sheet with statistics and ... our reasoning [as to] why we need the law changed – just something very brief. On this ... bill we were showing that there were about 7,000 cases at the time filed [in this state] about the railroads, and that 90 percent of them weren't from [this state]. [We showed the chairman of the committee] dealing with the bill information that all these lawsuits were being filed in his district, and he realized it was clogging the courts up there and so he let the bill pass out of his committee.

Lobbyist no. 33, who is not a public policy lobbyist but lends some of his time every year to support a federal government job-training and education program run by the Department of Defense, personally showed me some policy-analytic information that he presented to legislative aides. During a recent policy battle, Lobbyist no. 33, who supports more funding for the program, showed legislative staff members detailed information on the number of people who yearly take advantage of the program, and information about what happens to the program's "graduates." In very clear charts and graphs and tables, this lobbyist showed the staff members that the program graduated a large proportion of its "students," and that a large proportion of these students went on to graduate from high school and then college. He also presented findings showing that the program had a startlingly high success rate compared to many programs of its kind.

The policy-analytic information that lobbyists provide to legislators and their aides focuses heavily on the effects of a proposed bill on a legislator's district. Lobbyists want to show legislators that a certain bill will create jobs, or decrease air pollution, or increase funding for local schools, or help a local business expand. I asked lobbyists where they get the policy-analytic information they present to legislators, and their answers suggest that two sources are particularly important. First, the organizations for which lobbyists work are important sources of policy-analytic information. Lobbyist no. 27, a California contract lobbyist who lobbies for a trade association of pet stores, told me that recently he alerted his client to a bill in California "that would prohibit the sale of any un-neutered or spayed dog from a pet store." He was not sure, he told me, how his client felt about this bill, and so he discussed it with the leaders of the group. He explained:

> I think that your clients know their business very, very well and how specific legislation affects them. So you talk to your client and you go,

"Okay, is this good or bad?" There's a lot of controversy over pet over-population and what you find is that it would really affect sales because a lot of people want to make that decision [to neuter or spay their pets] themselves.

The trade association in question, Lobbyist no. 27 told me, had done research on the topic, and passed the results of this research – which showed that such a law would hurt the pet business – on to him. From there, he passed this policy-analytic research to legislators. His message was clear: this bill will hurt pet stores.

Like the association of pet stores represented by Lobbyist no. 27, organized interests of all kinds devote resources to policy analysis – that is, research designed to discover the effects of specific pieces of legislation. Sometimes organized interests do this research themselves. Many trade and professional associations, citizen groups, and business firms, for example, do research internally. Sometimes, however, organized interests hire outside consultants such as academics, think tanks, and consulting firms.

Another source of policy-analytic information is the government itself. The data show that government reports of all kinds are common fodder for the public policy lobbyist. An environmental lobbyist, for example, might cite a Department of Housing and Urban Development (HUD) study on population density to back its claim that "smart growth" legislation is necessary at the state or local level. Similarly, a business firm that opposes stricter environmental regulations might cite an Environmental Protection Agency study showing that air quality in the United States has improved considerably since the early 1970s, and that further regulation is unnecessary.

The Provision of Career-Relevant Information. While lobbyists rely heavily on policy-analytic information when they engage in proposal-specific legislative lobbying, they also regularly deploy career-relevant information. Specifically, public policy lobbyists rely heavily upon information about how legislators' votes on a particular piece of legislation will affect their chances of reelection. Lobbyist no. 1, an in-house state lobbyist, told me that legislators are generally quite blunt about how electoral calculations enter into their decisions about voting on specific pieces of legislation: "They [i.e., legislators] will ask you: 'You're not going to get me in trouble if I vote for this, right?'" Lobbyist no. 1 went on to explain that what legislators want to know from lobbyists is how a particular course of action will affect their electoral fortunes.

The rawest and purest form of career-relevant information a lobbyist can provide to a legislator or legislative staff is polling data concerning how constituents feel about a bill. Some of my respondents told me that they provide this type of polling data to legislators or legislative staff to convince them that their constituents feel a certain way about an issue. Lobbyist no. 21, a Texas contract lobbyist, put it simply: "We will make use of polling.... [S]upporting polling data are important." Nonetheless, the majority of my respondents told me that they generally eschew polling data. The reason they do so, my research shows, is that using it is simply not necessary. In most cases, they said, conducting a sophisticated large-scale poll of a legislator's constituents is not worth the cost because information on how an organized interest's members, supporters, or (in the case of a business firm) employees and executives feel about a bill is enough to "make a lobbyist's case." Lobbyist no. 8, for example, who represents a professional association of architects, told me that when he lobbies on specific bills, legislators often ask him: "Are there any architects in my district that care about this?" Similarly, Lobbyist no. 20, an in-house big-city lobbyist who works for a police officers' union, told me that when he lobbies local legislators about a proposal, they are not as concerned with the feelings of the the public as a whole as they are with the feelings of the union's members: "[Legislators] will see a bill that affects police officers and . . . they'll [want to know] the opinions of the working [police officer] out on the street." Later he told me: "We poll our own members quite often on issues just to see where they are. And with those statistics, we'll always tell [local legislators], 'this is what police officers think.'" Lobbyist no. 19, an in-house Washington lobbyist, told me that before becoming a lobbyist he was a legislative staff member. As a lobbyist, he told me, he always emphasizes how much grassroots (i.e., citizen) support the organized interests he represents have, because this is what he and his boss really cared about when he worked in government:

> When I was a legislative staffer we had two people in the office. I han-
> dled half of what was going on in Congress, and I did not have time
> to study all the issues. [When I interacted with lobbyists], I wanted to
> know where they stood on the issue [and] what the issue was.... And
> most importantly, I wanted to hear about their grassroots support for the
> issue.

The data show that most of the time when public policy lobbyists present career-relevant information to a legislator or his or her staffers, they do not attempt to make statements concerning how a legislator's constituency as

a whole feels about an issue, but rather how a subset of the constituency –
constituents represented by the lobbyist – feels about an issue.

Why do public policy lobbyists tend to speak only for their members, supporters, or employees and executives when they present career-
relevant information to legislators? The answer to this question is twofold.
First, many public policy lobbyists believe that legislators already have a
good general idea of how their constituency as a whole feels about a given
bill. Lobbyist no. 1 told me: "We really don't always have to [tell them how
their constituents feel]. They're pretty savvy on their own because all politics are local and they're generally wired into their community." Lobbyist
no. 7, the railroad lobbyist, told me: "I guess it depends on the issue. But all
of them [i.e., the legislators] have e-mails now, and direct phone numbers.
And so their constituency knows how to get in touch with them. So they
know that kind of stuff." Legislators keep very close tabs on how many
letters, e-mail messages, faxes, and telephone calls they receive on specific
pieces of legislation, and they are careful to record the precise position of
each constituent who contacts them. While legislators know that these
communications are only rough indicators of overall constituent opinion,
they tend to assign great importance to them because citizens who take
the time to contact them are more likely to vote than are other citizens.
To lobbyists, speaking for citizens with whom they have no relationship
is neither necessary nor wise. Second, public policy lobbyists understand
that in many cases, the question of how a legislator's constituents feel
about a given bill is a moot one because constituents have no opinions
on many issues. Lobbyist no. 8, for example, lobbies on issues of interest
to architects but not of much interest to anybody else. Many respondents
appear to realize that they lobby on issues that are not particularly salient
to large swaths of the public.

In sum, my public policy respondents left little doubt that career-
relevant information is highly valued by legislators and legislative staff.
However, most respondents told me that they rely more heavily upon
policy-analytic information than upon career-relevant information. In a
way, this is not surprising. I say this because after analyzing my data, I
came to the conclusion that for public policy lobbyists, the line between
career-relevant information and policy-analytic information is unclear.
These lobbyists believe that a great deal of the policy-analytic information
they provide to legislators *is* career-relevant information. After all, information about how a particular piece of legislation will affect air pollution,
or economic growth, or crime, or tax rates *is* information about how a
particular piece of legislation will affect a legislator's electoral fortunes. Or
at least public policy lobbyists see it as such. By focusing on policy-analytic

information, they are indirectly telling legislators, "supporting my group's position is akin to supporting a bill that will do great things for your constituents, which will translate into electoral victory for you."

What about Political Information? In Chapter 2, I mentioned that the communications theory of lobbying (which I draw upon heavily in this book) holds that in addition to policy-analytic and career-relevant information, lobbyists also provide political information to government officials. Political information is defined as information about the status and prospect of a proposed or potential government decision. I specifically asked public policy lobbyists what kinds of information they provide to legislators and legislative staff when they lobby, and not a single respondent mentioned political information. Thus, the data suggest that public policy lobbyists rely less upon political information when they lobby legislators and legislative staff than they do on other kinds of information.

I cannot say for certain why this is the case. However, I can offer a guess. The most obvious and reasonable explanation is that legislators and their staff do not *need* political information as much as they need other types. It makes sense to conclude that legislators and legislative staff have more information about the status and prospect of a proposed or potential government decision than lobbyists do. In fact, my respondents' comments on monitoring suggest just this. Specifically, the data show that information about all aspects of proposed or potential government decisions is highly valued by lobbyists and that they seek this information from legislators, rather than the other way around. After all, it seems obvious that legislators and staffers – people who are directly involved in making public policy decisions – often would have better political information than lobbyists.

Summary
Lobbyists at all three levels of government lobby legislators heavily. The data strongly support the conclusion that legislatures garner more attention from public policy lobbyists than either the executive or judicial branches of government. The data show that public policy lobbyists engage in two basic types of legislative lobbying. First, there is *background legislative lobbying*, which, rather than affecting single pieces of legislation, is designed to make legislators and legislative staff aware of who lobbyists are, whom they represent, and what issues they are working on. Background lobbying often takes place in informal settings. Second, public policy lobbyists engage in *proposal-specific legislative lobbying*, which is designed to affect specific legislative proposals (e.g., a bill that has been introduced by a legislator). The data show that public policy lobbyists rely

heavily upon meeting personally with legislators and/or legislative staff when they engage in proposal-specific legislative lobbying. When public policy lobbyists meet with legislators and/or legislative staff, they present policy-analytic and career-relevant information. They believe that legislators respond best to information that is relevant to their constituents. Above all, legislators want to be certain that whatever they do is beneficial for the people who determine whether or not they keep their jobs (i.e., the voters).

EXECUTIVE BRANCH LOBBYING

While the legislature is the most common target of public policy lobbying efforts, the executive branch receives a great deal of lobbying attention as well. As I mentioned in Chapter 2, the executive branch (except in some local governments, where the chief executive is part of the legislature) consists of two parts: the chief executive's office and the bureaucracy. All of my respondents told me that they have some contact with the executive branch when they lobby. In this section, I examine what my respondents told me about how they attempt to affect public policy decisions by lobbying the executive branch.

Lobbying the Chief Executive

No matter where a lobbyist lobbies, it is quite a coup to have direct contact with the chief executive. Chief executives are not easily accessible to lobbyists, but most of them have staff people who are slightly more so. For example, the president has literally thousands of individuals who work for him in one way or another, and governors and mayors typically have sizable staffs as well (though size varies widely across jurisdictions). Nonetheless, aides and advisors to the chief executive are also quite inaccessible. Previous studies of lobbying indicate that though a large majority of lobbyists – approximately 90 percent – lobby the executive branch, very few lobbyists have any contact with chief executives or their top aides.[4] My data support the conclusion that public policy lobbyists do not spend substantial time or energy lobbying chief executives or their aides. I asked all my respondents about executive branch lobbying, and only three mentioned lobbying the chief executive (Lobbyists 8, 9, and 29).

What do public policy lobbyists do when they lobby the chief executives and/or their aides? To be honest, the data do not allow me to answer this question to any satisfactory degree. They do, however, suggest that when they lobby chief executives and/or their aides, it is a personal meeting where they present the same types of information they present to administrative agency personnel.

Lobbying the Bureaucracy

Although public policy lobbyists seldom lobby chief executives or their aides, they lobby the bureaucracy quite regularly. While I do not intend to make this a treatise on bureaucratic lobbying, a bit of background on how bureaucratic agencies make regulations (or rules) is necessary. At the federal and state levels, bureaucratic agencies write regulations through a process generically called "rule making." The process is quite complicated but can be summarized as follows. First, the legislative branch passes legislation that grants some discretion to an executive agency. For example, as I mentioned earlier, Congress may grant discretion to the EPA to clean up America's lakes and rivers. Second, the executive agency drafts a regulation to serve this end. For example, in our hypothetical case the EPA may draft a regulation that specifies the types of materials that can and cannot be dumped into rivers and lakes by manufacturing plants. Third, the agency publicizes the regulation. In our hypothetical case, this would mean publishing the proposed regulation in a federal government periodical called the *Federal Register*, which contains the text of proposed federal regulations. Finally, after a certain period of time, the agency decides whether or not to adopt the regulation.

Local governments also issue regulations or rules, but the scope of their regulatory powers and the process by which they issue regulations vary widely. Thus, it is very difficult to make any blanket statements about precisely how local bureaucratic agencies go about adopting rules or regulations. For now, suffice it to say that like state and national bureaucratic agencies, local agencies proffer regulations and rules, and as such are powerful policymaking bodies.[5]

So where do public policy lobbyists fit into the rulemaking process? My data indicate that public policy lobbyists lobby the bureaucracy in three main ways. First, lobbyists meet personally with bureaucrats. Second, they submit written comments on proposed rules and regulations. Third, bureaucrats testify at agency hearings.

The Techniques. All of my public policy respondents who lobby the bureaucracy reported that they frequently meet personally with bureaucrats. Most of the time these meetings take place in formal settings. At the state and federal levels, meetings often take place after the third step in the rule-making process – that is, after the agency has publicized the regulation or rule and invited comments from interested parties. Lobbyist no. 23, a Washington in-house lobbyist for a professional association of doctors, told me:

> [A] lot of times what happens [is that it is up to] the agency to develop regulations to implement a legislative act.... In some cases ... agencies will go ahead ... and put out proposed regulations in the *Federal Register*.... They're [i.e., the agency is] asking for contact. They want people to comment. You know, you have a 30- to 60-day comment period on a proposed regulation.... At that point, you really use your facts [and] it may take several meetings [with agency bureaucrats].

This was a common sentiment among public policy lobbyists: Agencies are often given broad discretion by legislatures to make policy, and it is vital for lobbyists to meet with bureaucrats to make their opinions known about pending regulations. In fact, bureaucratic agencies are generally required to publicize pending regulations and to allow comments from interested parties. Not surprisingly, these comments often come from lobbyists. This is one place where monitoring comes in handy: Lobbyists monitor pending rules and regulations and then meet with bureaucrats to comment upon them.

In addition to meeting personally with bureaucrats to comment on proposed regulations, public policy lobbyists also submit written comments. Generally, bureaucratic agencies are required to allow interested parties to submit written comments on proposed rules and regulations. These comments often take the form of brief written reports that present the lobbyist's view on the proposed regulation or rule. Lobbyist no. 3, who represents a group of cosmetology businesses, told me that when the Department of Education publishes proposed regulations in the *Federal Register,* she usually submits written comments to the agency: "[When there are regulations] – issues that affect us and the schools that we accredit – we submit our comments to the Department of Education."

Finally, public policy lobbyists lobby the bureaucracy by testifying at agency hearings. At the state and federal levels, it is not uncommon for agencies to have administrative hearings between the third and fourth stages of the rule-making process. In other words, after a regulation is publicized and before a final regulation is adopted, agencies hold public hearings at which lobbyists can testify. Testifying at agency hearings is a common bureaucratic lobbying technique. For example, Lobbyist no. 6, a state contract lobbyist who represents a major telecommunications company, told me: "We also will become involved on the administrative side. . . . Just as an example . . . we do a lot of environmental work . . . with the [state] Department of Environmental Conservation. Sometimes it becomes formalized – [we testify at] administrative hearings." Lobbyist no. 23, who earlier told me he relies heavily upon personal meetings with bureaucrats when he lobbies the bureaucracy, also told me that he testifies regularly at agency hearings: "[In addition to personal meetings], there are also commission hearings. I think they're equally intense but different."

It is important to note that these three bureaucratic lobbying techniques – meeting with bureaucrats, submitting written comments, and testifying before agency hearings – are not the only ways that public policy lobbyists lobby the bureaucracy. Indeed, as you can see from Table 2 in Chapter 2, there are several more ways. Nonetheless, these are the most common and widespread techniques used by public policy lobbyists to lobby the bureaucracy, according to the data.

The Information. What kind of information do public policy lobbyists present to bureaucrats when they lobby them? The data show that public policy lobbyists primarily employ policy-analytic information primarily when they lobby bureaucrats. They also occasionally employ career-relevant information.

My data show generally that when public policy lobbyists lobby bureaucrats, they emphasize policy-analytic information. Lobbyist no. 18, a Connecticut contract lobbyist, put it this way: "The bureaucrat who is not a political appointee . . . they're able to be insulated. So it [i.e., the information I provide] can be a little more esoteric and it can be more about policy." Various respondents weighed in on the effectiveness of policy-analytic information. Lobbyist no. 6, for example, told me: "On the executive branch side . . . the arguments we would use [are about] the fairness or unfairness of it [a proposed regulation or bureaucratic decision], and the economic benefit or detriment." Lobbyist no. 11, the Washington think tank lobbyist, told me that her group – a think tank opposed to many government regulations – regularly presents information on the detrimental economic consequences of certain regulations. She told me: "When the new Bush administration came in there was a bunch of Clinton regulations that were on the books that were going to take effect. . . . You know, they have to go through a certain process, and we basically shut them down." The organization, she told me, conducts its own sophisticated economic analyses of the cost of regulations to the American people, and they often contract with academics to do so. Lobbyist no. 23, who works for a professional association of doctors, told me that he presents the same type of policy-analytic information to bureaucrats that he presents to legislators. "You have to be fact based," he said. When he deals with a proposed regulation, he told me, he tells bureaucrats: "Here's the consequence of an action not taken or taken. We … view it [from the perspective of] quality patient care. [We say], 'If this is not done or this is done, [this is how it will] affect patients.'" The policy-analytic information Lobbyist no. 23 provides comes from in-house studies conducted by the organization's fellows, or from academics.

Overall, my respondents portrayed bureaucrats as open to well-conducted policy-analytic research. Policy-analytic research may not "save the day" for a lobbyist, but my respondents suggested that bureaucrats tend to give this type of information serious consideration when they are trying to determine what to do.

While policy-analytic information is generally emphasized when public policy lobbyists lobby bureaucrats, many public policy lobbyists also present career-relevant information to them. For example, Lobbyist no. 6, a state contract lobbyist, told me:

> [With a] legislator … among other things [they want to know] is: "How is this going to play in my district to the people who elected me and [who will] be voting for me again?" But some of those factors come into play on the executive side too. You know, no commissioner [i.e., head of an executive branch agency] likes to read about himself in the paper when it's a negative article.

Lobbyist no. 18 told me something different about bureaucrats – that while they are not elected, they too have constituents that they like to keep happy:

> You could say [bureaucrats] have constituents though too. I mean, if they [i.e., the bureaucrats] were proposing a regulation that is so stringent and it has the potential to put some small businesses out of business, those are constituents of the state agency and they need to be aware of these anecdotes. So that can be just as compelling to them.

These two comments nicely illustrate two facts about bureaucrats: (1) they do not want to attract bad publicity and (2) they want to please the people whom they perceive to be their constituents.

Before leaving this topic, I wish to note that my public policy lobbyist respondents consistently downplayed the importance of political information in lobbying bureaucrats. Again, this does not mean that public policy lobbyists never ply political information when they lobby bureaucrats. It does suggest that when public policy lobbyists lobby bureaucrats, political information is often less important than either policy-analytic information or career-relevant information. I cannot say for certain why this is the case. But as with legislators, it is possible that bureaucrats simply do not need much political information from lobbyists because they already get most of it from other sources.

Permits. Most general treatments of bureaucratic lobbying emphasize the role of lobbyists in affecting regulations and rules. My respondents, however, told me that their interactions with bureaucrats often do not concern the adoption of regulations at all but, rather, *permitting*. To put it simply, in this country, people and organizations of various kinds must get permits to engage in certain types of activities. For example, in my home state of Tennessee, "Anyone who performs a dye trace study in streams," "Any ginseng dealer who purchases ginseng collected in Tennessee with the intent to resale," and "Every used oil collection center" must obtain a special permit from the state's Department of Environment and Conservation.[6] These are just three of the multitude of activities that require a permit in Tennessee. Other states, local governments, and the federal government similarly require permits for various activities. The City of Los Angeles, for example, has a Web page that links Angelinos to a variety of permits, including tree removal permits, entrance canopy permits, street closure permits, and water discharge permits. I could go on, but I think you get the point: In most places, many activities require permits.

The data show that in addition to lobbying the bureaucracy in an attempt to influence regulations, public policy lobbyists also lobby bureaucrats for permits. Lobbyist no. 6, a Tennessee contract lobbyist, told me: "Just as an example, in our law firm we do a lot of environmental work. Environmental work involves among other things working with the Department of Environment and Conservation, getting permits [and] approvals of all sorts." Similarly, Lobbyist no. 18 told me: "We do a lot of that – [helping clients apply for permits]. [We represent] a lot of utility companies and manufacturing companies."

Lobbyist no. 25 is not a public policy lobbyist, but in the course of our conversation about executive branch lobbying, she told me that others in her firm do a lot of work on permits:

Let's say Pacific Gas and Electric . . . out in California [was] having problems with the permitting process in [some] states . . . or they want to expand. [This] is a full service, government relations lobbying firm . . . however you want to deem it. [We do] anything and everything dependent upon what the client wants.

The data show that when public policy lobbyists lobby for permits, they rely almost entirely on technical information – information showing that a particular activity (for example, emitting pollution into the water, collecting ginseng for resale) conforms to the law. Regarding permitting, according to Lobbyist no. 6, it is often the case that "there's nobody lobbying against you. . . . [Y]ou've . . . got to convince the bureaucrats, the technical people, that you're okay [i.e., that what you're doing is legal]." Lobbyist no. 18, the Connecticut contract lobbyist, told me that receiving permits is often a function of negotiations between an applicant and an executive agency. To paraphrase her comments, a client applies for a permit (by filing paperwork), and then the agency gets back to the client, specifying what is wrong (if anything) with the application. At this point, Lobbyist no. 18 said, she acts as a conduit between the two parties: She relays the "department's feedback" to her client, and then counsels the client on how best to modify the application to allay the department's concerns. Ultimately, her goal is to make sure that "the dialogue [between a client and a department] can continue" until the client eventually receives the permit.

Summary
Public policy lobbyists at all three levels of government lobby the executive branch heavily. The executive branch consists of both the chief executive's office and the executive bureaucracy. Though the chief executive is generally a powerful player in local, state, and national politics, he or she receives relatively little lobbying attention. The bureaucracy is a different story. Public policy lobbyists regularly lobby the bureaucracy by meeting personally with bureaucrats, submitting comments, and testifying at agency hearings. No matter what technique(s) they use, public policy lobbyists tend to emphasize policy-analytic information when they lobby. However, when they lobby bureaucrats for favorable permitting decisions, they rely primarily on technical information.

GRASSROOTS LOBBYING

As I pointed out in Chapter 2, grassroots lobbying is lobbying that is aimed at ordinary citizens rather than government decision makers. Although public policymakers do not always respond to citizen demands, studies show that government officials (especially elected officials) generally consider ordinary citizens' opinions when they make decisions.[7]

The Techniques

Although I did not specifically ask my public policy respondents about grassroots lobbying, nine respondents (Lobbyists 4, 8, 9, 10, 11, 17, 19, 23, and 29) spontaneously mentioned that they utilize grassroots lobbying techniques. Four (Lobbyists 4, 17, 19, and 23) of these 9 respondents explicitly mentioned the second technique under grassroots lobbying in Table 2 – engaging in e-mail, letter, telegram, or telephone campaigns. This technique is straightforward. It entails a lobbyist contacting an organized interest's members, supporters, or employees and executives, and urging them to contact policymakers about a specific issue. I will have more to say about this later.

Four other lobbyists (Lobbyists 9, 10, 11, and 29) mentioned using the media to "get out their message." Each of these four does something different. First, Lobbyist no. 9, an in-house state lobbyist for a large trade association, told me that his group regularly stages "media events" to garner free press coverage:

> We work with a large consulting firm and we do media events in various cities. This week we did one in [a big city] and then I flew down and did [another big city]. We had all the major networks, and what we do is we talk about the anti-business climate in California. [I] stand up there with [some members] and talk about how bad the business environment is. The message gets across.

Second, Lobbyist no. 10, a Washington contract lobbyist, told me that he lobbies the media by issuing press releases to various media outlets. For example, to try to convince Congress to reform the Internal Revenue Service (IRS), which in his opinion was interpreting a tax law in a way that hurt some of his clients in the energy business, Lobbyist no. 10 said that he issued numerous press releases: "We go to the media, and we express it through business media that the IRS is running afoul.... [We] try to bring pressure on them [i.e., the IRS] to admit that they're doing something wrong." Third, Lobbyist no. 11, who works for a Washington think tank, told me that her group issues reports that are then circulated in Washington, and writes "op-ed" pieces that appear in the pages of major newspapers. Finally, Lobbyist no. 29, who works for a big-city university, told me that he regularly attempts to get certain issues covered in campus and local media in an attempt to disseminate the university's point out view:

> We also report a lot of [information] in our campus media. One of the advantages of having the community relations and government relations combined is that if there is something big in government – state, local, or federal – we will report on it in campus media.[8]

The Information

Grassroots lobbying is designed to do one or both of the following: (1) to influence people's opinions and (2) to encourage people to contact policymakers and make their opinions known. Organized interest expert Jeffrey Berry has called this first kind of grassroots lobbying "lobbying for values."[9] The premise of the second type of grassroots lobbying, which I call "lobbying for contact," is that because government decision makers (especially elected officials such as legislators and chief executives) want to keep their jobs, they pay close attention to the opinions of ordinary citizens. Though my data are limited, they suggest that engaging in e-mail, letter, telegram, or telephone campaigns is lobbying done for contact, while most media lobbying is done to affect values. In addition, the data suggest that when lobbyists lobby for values, they are usually attempting to affect the governmental agenda; when they lobby for contact, they are lobbying to affect the alternative the government ultimately chooses when it is considering an item on the agenda.

Engaging in E-mail, Letter, Telegram, and Telephone Campaigns. When public policy lobbyists engage in e-mail, letter, telegram, or telephone campaigns, they contact ordinary citizens – usually group members – and encourage them to contact policymakers and express their opinions. For example, when lobbyists contact citizens and encourage them to contact policymakers, they often tell them that the passage of a certain bill or adoption of a specific regulation is imminent. A lobbyist might contact citizens and tell them, for example: "A really bad bill is before Congress and I need you to help me defeat it." This is designed essentially to frighten citizens into action. In a previous section of this chapter, I talked about how public policy lobbyists who represent membership organizations often keep their members abreast of what's happening in government so that they can utilize them as lobbying resources later. When a particularly bad or good bill is before Congress, a lobbyist will "call in his chips," as Lobbyist no. 19 did when he asked his members to call their representatives to support a pending congressional proposal to cut taxes on manufacturers.

It is reasonable to assume that lobbyists who lobby citizens for contact rely on policy-analytic information. My data, however, do not support this assumption. Indeed, none of the public policy lobbyists I talked to who lobby for contact mentioned using policy-analytic information. The data suggest that the reason lobbyists do not provide policy-analytic information to citizens in such cases is that they do not have to. As Lobbyist no. 4 told me, he does not really have to explain why a specific bill or regulation would help or hurt one of his clients, because "if they're in a business, they know their business, probably better than I do." In other words, his clients (Lobbyist no. 4 is a Washington contract lobbyist) usually know why a particular bill or regulation is good or bad for them and they don't have to be told. Lobbyist no. 17, who works for a Washington senior citizens group, told me that her members are quite well informed about politics in Washington, partially because she keeps them up to date via a periodic newsletter. If Lobbyist no. 17 decides to launch a grassroots lobbying campaign and urge her members to contact their members of Congress and the president, she need only alert them that a specific bill (e.g., a bill that would ban importation of cheaper prescription drugs from Canada) is before Congress, because many of them are already well informed about the impact of the bill. In short, when public policy lobbyists lobby citizens for contact, they generally emphasize political information rather than policy-analytic information.

This portrayal of citizens as informed and up-to-date on policy issues affecting them flies in the face of a great deal of research showing that the typical American is not very well informed and pays little attention to politics. It is important to remember, however, that when public policy lobbyists lobby for contact, they generally do not cast a wide net and lobby everybody. Instead, in the case of lobbyists who represent membership organizations, they contact members – people who are by definition politically active (by dint of their group membership). And lobbyists who represent nonmembership organized interests (e.g., business firms), contact the people who hire them (e.g., a CEO, or the president of a university) – people who are generally well informed.

Using the Media. When public policy lobbyists use the media to engage in grassroots lobbying, they provide information to a large swath of the public in an effort to affect people's attitudes and opinions. What kind of information do they provide? The answer appears to be that when using the media, public policy lobbyists provide policy-analytic information. This information is generally quite broad – it is not necessarily specific to one policy proposal or issue. For example, Lobbyist no. 9 told me about the type of media event he orchestrates on behalf of his trade association: "We have boxes with pink slips coming out of them, and each box has [a particular bill's] name on it, the author [of the bill], and what the bill did." The idea of the media event is to send the general message that the state legislature has passed a lot of bills that have led to layoffs. Lobbyist no. 9 told me that rather than dwelling on how each specific bill affected each specific industry in the state, he instead emphasized a general message "about how bad the business environment is."

Of course, there are exceptions to the tendency that the policy-analytic information provided to citizens is quite broad. Think tanks, for example, are well known for publishing studies and research reports that go into considerable detail about specific policies. Lobbyist no. 11, who works for a Washington think tank, told me that her organization often puts out research reports that are rife with detailed policy-analytic information. Nonetheless, when public policy lobbyists use the media, they are aiming at a fairly broad audience and must make a general, rather than detailed and specific, pitch.

What Information Is Being Conveyed to Public Policymakers?

As I noted at the beginning of this section grassroots lobbying is ultimately intended to affect public policy decisions. If lobbying for values is successful, it will probably affect public opinion in the long run, rather than in the short run. In other words, since lobbying for values is not designed primarily to convince citizens to contact policymakers, it often does not do so.

In contrast, the reason public policy lobbyists lobby for contact is to get citizens to put pressure on public policymakers to do something (e.g., vote for or against a specific bill). Grassroots lobbying, then, unlike other forms of lobbying, involves a two-part flow of information. First, the lobbyist conveys information to citizens. Second (if the grassroots lobbying is successful), the citizens convey information to policymakers. If a grassroots lobbying campaign is successful, the information a citizen provides to a policymaker is straightforward: "I want you to do X." An example will clarify what I mean. Imagine a hypothetical situation in which a lobbyist for an environmental group is very concerned about a bill before Congress that would allow coal-burning power plants to emit more mercury into the air. The lobbyist decides to launch a grassroots lobbying campaign.

Specifically, he or she sends e-mail messages to all of the group's members, tells them about the mercury bill pending in Congress, and urges them to contact their representatives and express their opposition to the bill. From here, if the lobbyist's entreaty is successful, the group members call their representatives and say, "I think this mercury bill is a disaster. I want you to vote against it." So what kind of information are citizens conveying to policymakers when they respond to grassroots lobbying appeals by public policy lobbyists? The answer is clear: It is career-relevant information, because it is information with the following message: "If you do what I want you to do, you can count on my support in the upcoming election."

Does this type of information actually influence what government officials do? A wealth of information suggests that the answer is yes. In short, study after study show that elected officials – at whom most grassroots lobbying campaigns ultimately are directed – are quite responsive to the demands of their constituents.[10] My respondents were unanimous in this belief. In virtually all of my interviews with public policy lobbyists, I heard a variation of the following statement: If it comes down to a choice between what their constituents want and what a lobbyist wants, elected officials will almost always do what their constituents want. The influence of constituent opinion on the behavior of elected officials – especially legislators – cannot be overestimated. In the previous section subtitled "Legislative Lobbying," I presented several quotes that attest to the importance my respondents attach to constituent opinion in determining how elected officials behave. Because elected officials depend upon their constituents to keep their jobs, they pay close attention to constituents' opinions. And one way constituents convey these opinions is through letters, e-mail messages, and telephone calls at the behest of lobbyists.

Summary

Public policy lobbyists at all three levels of government engage in grassroots lobbying, defined as lobbying aimed at ordinary citizens rather than policymakers. Lobbyists lobby citizens because they know that citizens often have a profound impact on public policy. Although there are several grassroots lobbying techniques available to lobbyists, my respondents rely primarily on e-mail, letter, telegram, or telephone campaigns, and use of the media. Lobbyists who urge citizens to contact policymakers generally do so to affect specific policy alternatives that policymakers choose. Lobbyists who use media strategies often do so to affect the issues that reach the governmental agenda. My data indicate that lobbyists believe grassroots lobbying to be very effective, primarily because it provides elected officials with information about how their constituents feel about an issue. And constituent opinion, according to my respondents, is an extremely important determinant of the ways in which elected officials behave.

ELECTORAL LOBBYING

Few lobbying techniques receive as much media attention as monetary contributions. As Table 2 shows, there are many ways that organized interests and lobbyists engage in electoral lobbying. My data show that when public policy lobbyists engage in electoral lobbying, they do so primarily by making individual or PAC contributions to candidates. Indeed, not one of my respondents mentioned any other form of electoral lobbying.

Why Give Money?

In all, only six of my respondents told me that they regularly contribute money to candidates or parties (Lobbyists 7, 8, 9, 27, 29, and 32).[11] There is an ongoing debate in the political science literature about what campaign money buys. Though not a complete list, here are a few general findings produced by this literature. First, there is no consensus on whether or not campaign money buys votes.[12] On the one hand, several studies show that legislators who receive monetary contributions from PACs tend to vote the way their PAC donors want them to.[13] On the other hand, several studies show no link between monetary contributions and legislators' votes on legislation.[14] Second, extant research indicates that monetary contributions can buy contributors *access – the ability to see and to speak with government decision makers*.[15] In other words, money can "open doors." Third, monetary contributions can buy effort. Studies show that while a monetary contribution to legislators may not change their minds about a specific piece of legislation, it may cause them to push harder for a specific proposal or to "put in a good word" for a donor.[16] Ultimately, the research indicates that money may not determine how legislators vote on a piece of legislation, but it may affect their behavior on the margins and determine to whom they grant access.

Of course, my limited data do not allow me to determine definitively what campaign money buys. The comments of my respondents do, however, allow me to weigh in on the topic. Specifically, the data point to two general conclusions about lobbying with campaign money. First, lobbyists contribute money to public officials – mostly legislators, but chief executives as well – because they believe it buys them access.[17] For example, Lobbyist no. 8, who works for a state professional association, told me: "What we'll try to do is . . . help foster relationships [with] legislators. . . . So if we're going to contribute to a legislator . . . I mean, it's all about having an opportunity to have your opinion heard." Lobbyist no. 9, a state trade association lobbyist, told me something similar: "Our members gain access [to legislators and the governor] that way." In all, my respondents who contribute money were unanimous that money helps them gain access to the policymakers they support. Lobbyist no. 8, a state professional association lobbyist, told me that many legislators are quite open about how money affects access:

> I heard it explained by a Texas legislator one day. . . . He was saying [to a group of us lobbyists], "Let me tell you, most of us, we're not experts in all issues. You know, a lot of the bills that come up and that you guys come and talk to us on, we know nothing of it. Let's say there are two people talking to you about something you don't know anything about. One [is] a person you've never seen before [and] the other person helped 'bring you to the dance' [i.e., contributed money to your campaign]. Who are you going to listen to? You come back to your office and there are 30 phone messages. You go through, you recognize five of them because they helped bring you to the dance. Which five are you going to return your calls to? And the other [25], you're going to give [those calls] to staff."

Does this mean that money never buys votes? Of course not. In fact, Lobbyist no. 8 told me that he knows of legislators who *do* respond to money when deciding how to vote. But ultimately, as several respondents said, money is not in and of itself a particularly effective lobbying weapon because legislators who receive money from lobbyists still primarily vote according to, as Lobbyist no. 18 put it, "political ideology and political [party] loyalty."

My second general finding is this: My respondents believe that contributing money is not a principal weapon in a lobbyist's arsenal. To be sure, as my data and previous studies suggest, contributing money is one of the many tactics that public policy lobbyists use. Nonetheless, it is striking how little my respondents talked about money. Even those who told me that they contribute money told me that doing so was more of a sideshow than the main event. Money can buy access, they reported, but the real work of lobbying is done elsewhere.

A Better Way to Buy Access

Before I leave the topic of money I have one additional point: There is a way to buy access to policymakers that does not involve giving them money, and that way is to hire a contract lobbyist. In all, nine of my public policy lobbyists are contract lobbyists (Lobbyists 4, 6, 10, 18, 21, 26, 27, 28, and 32). Moreover, several in-house lobbyists told me that their organization had hired a contract lobbyist at some point (Lobbyists 3, 7, 8, 9, 17, and 23). I asked both groups of respondents the following question: Why do organizations hire contract lobbyists in addition to or in lieu of in-house lobbyists? Their answers were remarkably consistent: Organized interests hire contract lobbyists because of their connections. My respondents said that contract lobbyists are most valuable because they provide the organized interests that hire them with instant (as opposed to earned) access to public policymakers. Lobbyist no. 17, a Washington citizen group lobbyist, was very blunt about it: "There is a consultant who works with us [sometimes]. He is a former member of Congress." When I asked why her group retains a contract lobbyist even though she works as a lobbyist full time, her answer was simple: access. Contract lobbyists themselves agree that they bring instant access to the groups that hire them. For example, Lobbyist no. 27, a California contract lobbyist, told me: "I think that [what] I have is . . . tentacles into a lot of different areas for lots of different clients. I'm able to maybe seek out legislators that they wouldn't normally have access to." Lobbyist no. 4, a Washington contract lobbyist, told a similar story. One of the clients he represents has several in-house lobbyists that have extensive relationships with key members of Congress. But they hire him nonetheless. He told me:

> We have the relationships on the key committees that they don't have. Their relationships are strongest with the area delegation members [i.e., members from the area where the client's office is], so what makes them unusual is that they provide the primary point of contact . . . with area delegation members. They hired us because we have people who have relationships with members of Congress from all three jurisdictions [where they operate]: DC, Maryland, and Virginia, as well as the senators [from all three states].

Other contract lobbyists also argued that access appears to be the primary reason they are hired by most organizations.

In the course of my discussions with respondents as to why organized interests hire contract lobbyists, several told me that in-house lobbyists with extensive contacts are also hired. In fact, Lobbyist no. 21, whose firm lobbies the executive branch extensively, told me that his firm hires only people with high-level government experience: "We hire people who have long-standing relationships . . . that have these relationships long-term . . . people who have worked for the agencies in the past." This comment points up an important fact about hiring lobbyists with experience, rather than contributing money to get access: Because bureaucrats do not run for office, they are ineligible to receive monetary contributions from lobbyists and organized interests, and so contributing money to gain access to them is not an option. Contributing money is not a particularly versatile lobbying technique – the number of policymakers who are eligible to receive monetary contributions is limited (i.e., only candidates for elective office can receive campaign money). In contrast, hiring a person with built-in access is an extremely versatile lobbying tactic. Once an organized interest determines its needs, it can scan the universe of contract lobbyists and find one who has access to the policymakers it wants to influence. Of course, hiring a contract lobbyist or a new in-house lobbyist is expensive. For many organized interests, either option is simply not possible.

Summary

Lobbyists and organized interests can give money to policymakers in a variety of ways. My data indicate that most money lobbying is done primarily through direct contributions made to candidates. The respondents who contribute money told me that they do so primarily to gain access to decision makers. Money, they noted, helps a lobbyist build a relationship with a policymaker, and can help a lobbyist get a foot in the door. While many scholars and observers of lobbying and lobbyists are preoccupied with money, my data suggest that electoral lobbying is a relatively minor form of lobbying.

WHAT DOES PUBLIC POLICY LOBBYING LOOK LIKE?

Chapter 3 and the preceding sections of this chapter have given you a broad overview of who public policy lobbyists are and what they do. In this section, drawing upon the data presented there, I ask the question deferred from the end of Chapter 3: *What does public policy lobbying look like?* The answer requires a series of other questions – questions that can be adapted to explore land use and procurement lobbying in the chapters that follow.

Where Does Public Policy Lobbying Take Place?

Public policy lobbying takes place at all three levels of government, where public policy decisions are made. Although all three levels of government are involved, the data suggest that public policy lobbying is more common at the federal and state levels than at the local level, where more time is spent on questions of land use. Our federal system of government has evolved such that state governments and the federal government tend to make the most important public policy decisions, leaving fewer public policy decisions to local governments, which make most of the nation's land use decisions.

Who Lobbies?

The data indicate that the range of organized interests engaged in public policy lobbying is far greater than the range of organized interests engaged in either land use or procurement lobbying. In fact, my data indicate that professional associations, labor unions, governmental entities, think tanks, charities, and coalitions engage in public policy lobbying almost exclusively, while trade associations, universities and colleges, hospitals, and churches focus the bulk of their attention on public policy matters, rather than on land use or procurement matters. In contrast, business firms are at least as prolific and active in land use and procurement lobbying as they are in public policy lobbying (and probably more so).

Why are so many more types of organized interests active in public policy lobbying than in either land use or procurement lobbying? The fact is that we simply do not know. It is tempting to conclude that a wider range of organized interests attempts to affect public policy decisions because they are more important. After all, public policy decisions relate to some of the most contentious and salient issues of our time, including abortion, affirmative action, the environment, and the war on terror. Surely, the argument goes, these issues are more important than the type of trash receptacle a county government buys or where Wal-Mart is allowed to build its newest superstore. But are they? Just because more Americans are fired up about abortion, affirmative action, the environment, and the war on terror does not mean that these issues are necessarily more important in any objective sense. In fact, it is arguably the case that land use decisions – which manifest themselves in changes in our neighborhoods, schools, and roads – and procurement decisions – which affect how much money we pay in taxes and how the government spends that money – are more important to a wider range of people and organized interests than are public policy decisions. Thus, a facile "public policy decisions are more important than either procurement or land use decisions" explanation for the relatively wide range of organized interests involved in public policy lobbying does not pass muster.

Although my data cannot definitively explain why the range of organized interests that engages in public policy lobbying is so broad, they do point to a possible (though admittedly partial) explanation. Specifically, the data show (and you will see for yourself in the following two chapters) that the procurement and land use decision-making processes are highly technical and complex. Moreover, they often involve, for lack of a better word, rather mundane matters. People simply do not generally get excited about zoning or government contracts. In contrast, issues such as abortion and affirmative action, just to name two, tend to be emotional and salient. Part of the reason is that they are relatively easy to understand. Because many public policy issues are relatively easy to understand and emotionally charged, the people who form and maintain organized interests (the literature calls them "organized interest entrepreneurs") that lobby on such issues have a relatively easy time attracting and maintaining members and supporters. For now, suffice it to say that the data indicate that because some public policy issues are easier to understand than either procurement or land use issues, organized interests concerned with public policy issues tend to be more successful at attracting and retaining members and supporters than organized interests concerned with either procurement or land use matters.

No matter what the reason, it is clear that a relatively wide range of organized interests is active in public policy lobbying. Among those represented by my public policy respondents are business firms, charities, citizen groups, government entities, labor unions, professional associations, trade associations, think tanks, and universities and colleges – almost the entire range of organized interests.

What Nonlobbying Activities Do Public Policy Lobbyists Engage In?

You will recall from Chapter 3 that public policy lobbyists spend considerable time on two types of nonlobbying activities: (1) monitoring government and (2) managing clients (for contract lobbyists) or members and supporters (for in-house lobbyists). Of these two activities, the first is the most important. Based on discussions with my respondents, I estimate that the typical public policy lobbyist spends between 20 and 40 percent of his or her time on policy monitoring and compliance monitoring.

Monitoring. For public policy lobbyists, monitoring is absolutely essential for successful lobbying. Several respondents told me that politics is a fast business – things develop quickly and unpredictably. They must keep up with what is happening, what policies are being considered, and what proposed policies affect the organized interest(s) they represent. In short, only after public policy lobbyists learn what is happening in government can they decide what to do when they lobby.

How much time public policy lobbyists spend monitoring government partially depends upon the type of organized interests they represent. The data show that lobbyists who represent business firms monitor government because it is part of their job to advise and counsel their clients on how to stay out of trouble by complying with current laws, rules, and regulations. Compliance monitoring is especially important for lobbyists who represent business firms in heavily regulated industries such as energy, health care, and insurance. Lobbyists for such membership groups as citizen groups, labor unions, professional associations, and trade associations monitor extensively to gather information that they then pass on to their members. Members of environmental citizen groups, for example, like to keep themselves up-to-date on environmental issues and pending environmental laws and regulations. Similarly, business firms that belong to trade associations value information that they receive on pending rules, regulations, and laws in their industry.

Although many people assume that the primary goal of most organized interests is to influence government decisions, this is not the case. Rather, the primary goal of every organized interest is to *survive*. Survival takes money, and membership organized interests get a great deal of the money they need to survive from their members. And one way for a membership organized interest to attract and keep members is to offer them information they value in exchange for membership fees. The typical membership organized interest publishes magazines and/or newsletters and sends periodic e-mail or regular mail alerts.

Finally, many membership organized interests engage in monitoring and pass information on to their members because they use them periodically in grassroots lobbying campaigns. By providing members with information about what is going on in government, a membership organized interest can keep its members at the ready in case they are needed for a grassroots lobbying campaign.

Interacting with Clients. In addition to monitoring, many public policy lobbyists also spend time managing their clients (in the case of contract lobbyists) or members (in the case of in-house lobbyists), and justifying their existence to the people who either hire them (in the case of contract lobbyists) or supervise them (in the case of in-house lobbyists). Based on discussions with my respondents, I estimate that the typical public policy lobbyist spends approximately 10 to 15 percent of his or her time on client management. Contract lobbyists tell the organized interests that hire them what policies are in the pipeline and offer them advice about what to do. In-house lobbyists tell their bosses (i.e., the people they report to) what government decisions are pending. Finally, public policy lobbyists are periodically asked to justify their existence by accounting for their activities.

Whom Do Public Policy Lobbyists Target?

The data show that public policy lobbyists lobby the legislative branch (i.e., legislators and their aides) more than the executive branch, the judicial branch, or the public. The data also show the second most common target to be the executive bureaucracy and the third to be the public. Public policy lobbyists lobby chief executives (e.g., mayors, governors, the president), chief executive aides, and the judiciary the least.

The Legislature. Why does the legislature attract so much lobbying attention from public policy lobbyists? The data suggest two answers. First, legislators and their aides are more accessible than government officials in other branches of government. Because they must obtain money to fund their periodic election campaigns, legislators regularly interact informally with lobbyists at bars and restaurants and fund-raising events. They tap lobbyists for donations, and this breeds familiarity. Second, the legislature regularly provides formal forums (legislative committee hearings) at which lobbyists provide input about pending and proposed decisions. In sum, legislators and their aides are unusually accessible to public policy lobbyists.

Executive Agencies. Bureaucrats (especially midlevel) attract substantial attention from public policy lobbyists because they too are accessible. Like the legislature, the executive bureaucracy provides formal opportunities for public policy lobbyists to add their input on pending agency decisions. Executive agencies typically allow lobbyists to offer comments about pending or proposed regulations, often at hearings akin to legislative hearings. My data suggest that bureaucrats are not as busy as many other government officials. Legislators and their aides, especially at the national and state levels, tend constantly to legislative work, casework (i.e., constituent service), and campaign-related activities. Several of my respondents lobby middle-level bureaucrats, therefore, because they are more likely *to pick up the telephone*. They are less harried and less busy than many other government officials, and they enjoy being targeted by lobbyists who shower them with attention.

The Public. While public policy lobbyists focus the bulk of their attention upon legislators and bureaucrats, on occasion they also target the public at large, which can sometimes influence public policy decisions. While numerous recent studies (many of which I cite in Chapter 2) attest to the fact that grassroots lobbying is more common than ever before, my data nonetheless illustrate that it is still far less common than legislative or executive branch lobbying. So when do public policy lobbyists resort to grassroots lobbying? The most common response was a variation of "I'm not really sure," which suggests one thing: Many organized interests are not the rational, logical, calculating actors that we often assume them to be. After all, if the people who actually *run* grassroots lobbying campaigns cannot articulate precisely why they choose to run them when they do, what chance do we have to understand the phenomenon?

All is not lost, however, in our quest to understand the whys and whens of grassroots lobbying. One result that emerges from the data is that the type of organized interest lobbyists represent has little impact on whether or not (and how often) they engage in grassroots lobbying. Several previous studies suggested that lobbyists for membership organizations – especially citizen groups and labor unions – often engage in grassroots lobbying, while lobbyists for nonmembership organized interests (especially business firms) tend to eschew the practice. My data suggest that this simply is not true, for several reasons. First, some nonmembership organized interests – think tanks, for example – rely almost exclusively upon grassroots lobbying techniques. Second, lobbyists for business firms regularly utilize grassroots lobbying techniques. Business firms, my data show, regularly run advertisements ("advertorials") in media, and many also use other grassroots lobbying techniques including e-mail, letter, telegram, or telephone campaigns. Although business firms do not have members per se that they can mobilize in grassroots lobbying campaigns, they *do* have employees for that purpose. Finally, "lobbying for values" requires no membership or employee base whatsoever to be successful. While it seems intuitive to conclude that an organized interest with a substantial membership or employee base would be more likely to "lobby for contact" than without such a base, there is no reason to believe that it would be more likely to lobby for values. All that is required to do this is money.

To summarize, although my data do not allow me definitively to answer the question of why lobbyists turn to grassroots lobbying techniques when they do, one thing is clear: It is not the case that lobbyists who work for organized interests without members tend to eschew grassroots lobbying techniques.

The Rare Targets. The data indicate that some government officials – specifically judges, and chief executives and their aides – do not attract much lobbying attention. It is certainly not the case that public policy lobbyists never lobby them. As a wealth of research attests, they do. However, in the large scheme of things, the judiciary, and the office of the chief executive attract relatively little lobbying attention.

Which Techniques Do Public Policy Lobbyists Use Most?

When public policy lobbyists lobby government decision makers and/or the public, they use a wide range of lobbying techniques. There is no doubt, however, that they rely upon two techniques more than any other: meeting personally with legislators and/or their aides, and meeting personally with executive agency personnel. In addition to meeting personally with decision makers, public policy lobbyists also regularly use grassroots lobbying techniques, such as engaging in e-mail, letter, telegram, or telephone campaigns, talking to the media, staging media events, and running advertisements in media outlets.

Rarely Used Techniques. Public policy lobbyists seldom use many of the techniques listed in Table 2. For example, they rarely use any direct democratic techniques, or electoral techniques other than contributing money to candidates. Moreover, even within the three major categories of techniques that public policy lobbyists use – legislative, grassroots, and executive branch techniques – several are used sparingly. Among them are doing favors/providing gifts for legislators, engaging in adjudication, mounting demonstrations or protests, interacting with special liaison offices within the chief executive's office, and personally meeting with the chief executive or chief executive's aides. This does not mean that these techniques are unimportant or insignificant. But it does mean that many lobbying techniques are not prime weapons in the public policy lobbyist's arsenal. Since I did not (as many large-scale surveys do) present my respondents with a list of techniques and ask them which ones they utilize, I cannot make any definitive statements about the techniques that my sample lob-byists use and do not use. I can, however, state without doubt that of the extensive array of techniques available to them, most public policy lob-byists rely upon a relatively limited repertoire – a repertoire dominated by techniques that entail personal, face-to-face interaction with public officials.

Which Techniques Are Most Effective?

I must again caution that my data do not allow me to answer this question definitively. However, they are suggestive, and point to three general conclusions.

Meeting Personally with Government Officials and Their Aides. First, my respondents clearly believe that meeting personally with legislators and/or their aides and meeting personally with executive agency personnel are extremely effective lobbying techniques. Why is meeting personally such an effective tactic? First, meeting with policymakers lodges the lobbyist's image in the policymaker's mind. In other words, as filmmaker and former comedian Woody Allen once said: "Eighty percent of success is showing up."[18] Earlier I mentioned "background lobbying" that makes legislators and/or their aides aware of lobbyists and the organized interest(s) they represent. Background lobbying is akin to "showing up." Public policy lobbyists can engage in it by sending press releases, or policy papers, or monographs, or e-mail messages to legislators and/or their aides; *or* by showing up and personally meeting with legislators and/or their aides. My respondents agreed that the latter tactic is much more effective. The data suggest that showing up and meeting with policymakers face-to-face increases the chances that they will call upon lobbyists and ask for their views on policy. Such a meeting is effective because it makes a deep-seated impression. When policymakers want information from lobbyists, they tend to call upon those they have met and whom they know.

Second, meeting personally with government officials and/or their aides is effective because it affords lobbyists the opportunity *to listen* as well as to talk. In fact, lobbyists have a much easier time winning when they are trying to *kill* a pending policy proposal than they do when they are trying to get a new policy proposal adopted. As such, lobbyists' success often rests upon their ability to identify policy proposals that are in the pipeline. Only after a lobbyist finds out about a potentially damaging policy proposal can he or she work to kill it. Once a proposal is adopted, getting the government to rescind it or change it is much more difficult, and so it is best to kill it beforehand. Meeting personally with policymakers allows lobbyists to keep abreast of new proposals that they may wish to defeat.

Finally, meeting personally with policymakers is effective because government officials like it. There are, of course, policymakers who do not particularly enjoy personal contact and schmoozing and hobnobbing with citizens and lobbyists. But in talking with my respondents, I was struck by how often they implied that policymakers meet with lobbyists partially because *it is fun*. Politics is still a *people* business. Many of the people involved in politics enjoy the give-and-take of personal interaction.

Joining Coalitions. According to the data, my respondents also clearly believe that joining coalitions with other lobbyists and/or organized interests is an effective lobbying technique. (I have not yet mentioned this technique because it does not fit nicely into the categories of legislative lobbying, executive branch lobbying, and grassroots lobbying.) Again, although I did not ask my respondents about specific lobbying techniques, nine of my public policy respondents mentioned that they regularly engage in coalition activity with other organized interests, and all nine agreed that this it is extremely effective.

Why is joining coalitions so effective? Respondents cited two reasons in particular. First, to paraphrase one respondent, joining into a coalition with other organized interests increases an organized interest's resource base (more later about the advantages of having lots of resources). Second, joining into a coalition with other organized interests shows policymakers that a lobbyist's position is popular. As I have mentioned, policymakers (especially legislators) do not like to do things that are unpopular with their constituents. Therefore, a lobbyist who can say "Mine is not the only organization that wants this; there are 28 others as well" helps assure policymakers that a particular position has wide support.

Grassroots Lobbying. The data indicate that grassroots lobbying – lobbying for contact in particular – can be very effective. To repeat once again, policymakers do not like to do things that flout public opinion. The flipside is that policymakers *enjoy* making decisions that conform to public opinion, especially if the public feels strongly about an issue. One way for a lobbyist to convince them of public support is to mount a grassroots lobbying campaign that results in large numbers of citizens contacting policymakers. It is interesting to note, however, that a relatively small number of my respondents told me that they lobby for contact. This does not mean that my other public policy respondents never lobby for contact, but it does mean that the technique is not as prevalent as, for example, meeting with policymakers personally.

Why if respondents believe that lobbying for contact is so effective do so few do it regularly? The answer appears to be threefold. First, there may be a lingering feeling among many public policy lobbyists that there is a limit to how much citizens will participate in politics. Several studies indicate that the typical American citizen does not care much about, or participate much in, politics.[19] As such, many lobbyists believe that they should not "go to the well too often" by repeatedly asking their constituents to contact policymakers. Second, in many (perhaps most) cases, public policy lobbyists do not think that lobbying for contact is necessary. I was surprised at the number of respondents who said that policymakers have a fairly good idea of how citizens (and especially their constituents) feel about issues. They constantly monitor their mail, their telephone calls, and even the media to take the pulse of the public. In many cases, because policymakers have already heard from citizens who support a lobbyist's point of view, this technique is simply not necessary. Finally, lobbying for contact can be expensive. Few organized interests have pockets deep enough to mount numerous grassroots lobbying campaigns.

The Importance of Versatility. In closing this section, I want to mention one thing that both meeting personally with government officials and entering into coalitions with other organized interests have in common: *Both are versatile lobbying tactics* that can be used in many situations and deployed in a wide variety of ways. If a lobbyist masters the art of meeting personally with government officials and/or their aides, this technique can be used to lobby legislators, legislative aides, bureaucrats, the chief executive, and chief executive aides on a number of issues and in a variety of contexts. Being good at meeting personally with policymakers allows a lobbyist to have a chance to succeed, no matter what else is done. Coalition building is similar. No matter the issue, the level of government, or the branch of government, a lobbyist who can bring other people on board has a chance to be successful.

Coalition building and meeting personally with policymakers are the most versatile lobbying techniques in the lobbyist's arsenal. To understand why, consider a few lobbying techniques that are *not* versatile. For example, imagine you are a lobbyist who is exceptionally good at mobilizing voters to support candidates, or at issuing voter guides. These are nice skills to have, but they are really only valuable during an election year and are of no use if you are trying to affect what bureaucrats do. Similarly, assume that you are very good at engaging in litigation. Again, this is a nice skill to have, but it cannot help you much if you are dealing with bureaucrats or legislators. Virtually all lobbyists wish to master the skill of meeting personally with policymakers because it can serve them well no matter what they want and no matter what else they do. Similarly, mastering the skill of building coalitions with other groups is valuable no matter where lobbyists work and what issues they work on.

In sum, public policy lobbyists use a wide variety of lobbying techniques, two of which stand out above all others: meeting personally with legislators and/or their aides, and meeting personally with executive agency personnel. These are the most commonly used techniques in the lobbyist's arsenal, and they are widely perceived to be the most effective.

Which Types of Information Do Public Policy Lobbyists Provide?

In Chapter 2, I described the three types of information that lobbyists provide when they lobby: political, career-relevant, and policy-analytic information. What types of information do public policy lobbyists generally ply? The answer to this question is fivefold.

Background Information. First, the data show that public policy lobbyists often ply background information. This is basic information that lobbyists provide to legislators about the organized interest(s) they represent, and where and how they can be reached. Background lobbying is designed to lodge a lobbyist's basic information in policymakers' heads. And the data suggest that it works. Many respondents told me that as a result of their background lobbying efforts, public policymakers regularly contact them and ask them for advice and counsel. Apparently, for policymakers seeking information, the answer to the question "who you gonna call?" is "lobbyists you know."

Technical Information. Second, the data show that public policy lobbyists provide technical information (which, like background information, does not fit neatly into the three categories of information I mentioned in Chapter 2). In many instances, public policy lobbyists lobby not for policies per se but for permits of various kinds. When lobbying for permits, they present detailed technical information and advise bureaucrats on how a particular activity conforms to the law.

Policy-Analytic Information. Third, the data indicate that public policy lobbyists rely heavily upon policy-analytic information. When my respondents provide such information to legislators or legislative aides, they focus on the consequences of a policy for a legislator's constituents, rather than the public at large. They also emphasize policy-analytic information when they lobby bureaucrats. Finally, my data show that when public policy lobbyists lobby the public by using the media, they use a broad form of policy-analytic information.

Career-Relevant Information. Fourth, public policy lobbyists rely heavily upon career-relevant information, particularly when they lobby legislators and/or their aides. Specifically, when my respondents engage in proposal-specific legislative lobbying, they rely primarily upon information about how a legislator's vote on a certain piece of legislation will affect his or her chances of reelection. While some of these lobbyists poll the general public to support their efforts, typically public policy lobbyists pass along information about how the members, supporters, or employees of the organized interest they represent feel about a particular policy.

Public policy lobbyists rely less upon career-relevant information when they lobby bureaucrats, but they utilize it nonetheless. Although bureaucrats do not answer to voters, they do have constituents. Many bureaucratic agencies are designed to serve specific constituents: The Department of Veteran's Affairs (a federal agency) serves veterans, the Department of Agriculture (another federal agency) serves farmers, and state fish and game departments serve hunters and people who fish. While bureaucrats do not answer solely to the primary constituents of their agencies, my respondents told me that most do indeed take the opinions of these constituents into account when they make decisions. And lobbyists are good sources of information on how these constituents feel about proposed rules and regulations. In addition, like most of us, bureaucrats do not want to make mistakes. Accordingly, they attend to the information that lobbyists provide them and try to avoid actions that they think are unpopular, controversial, or detrimental to their careers.

Political Information. Fifth, although public policy lobbyists provide political information when they lobby government officials, it is of less importance than other types of information. Apparently policymakers tend to have access to this kind of information themselves and do not often need lobbyists to provide it to them. When public policy lobbyists lobby the public, however, they do often rely upon political information. Specifically, when they lobby for contact, they often attempt to fire up members, supporters, employees, or the mass public by informing them that a particular policy change (usually detrimental, but sometimes beneficial) is imminent. This information is designed to goad citizens into acting.

In sum, public policy lobbyists provide background, technical, policy-analytic, career-relevant, and political information when they lobby. However, the data suggest that they rely less upon political information than they do on other types of information.

What Determines Whether or Not Public Policy Lobbyists Win?

What factors determine a win? I must caution that this question is difficult to answer. A plethora of factors and actors enter into each public policy decision, and isolating one or a few as determinative is risky. Moreover, because I spoke to the lobbyists who try to affect public policy decisions, rather than the government officials who actually make public policy decisions, I have no definitive conclusions about why some public policy lobbyists win and others lose. Nonetheless, the data provide us with clues about the factors that affect a public policy lobbyist's chances of winning. Drawing upon my data, I identify six "keys to success" for a public policy lobbyist.

Key 1: Don't Ask for Too Much. The first key to success for a public policy lobbyist is *not asking for too much*. Time and time again during my interviews, respondents told me that asking for too much is a virtual kiss of death in the lobbying business. What is "too much"? Something that represents a radical departure from existing public policy. A hypothetical example helps illustrate the value of not asking for too much. Several citizen groups in this country believe that the easy availability of guns contributes to a high crime rate. A lobbyist for one of these organized interests can ask the federal government to (1) ban all guns, (2) ban some guns, or (3) restrict who can own and buy guns. My data (and common sense) suggest that the lobbyist will be more likely to win by pressing for the third option. Banning even some guns in this country is a fairly radical departure from public policies concerning gun ownership. Asking the government to ban some or all guns is asking the government radically to alter its course. And my respondents told me repeatedly that government officials do not like radical alterations of existing public policy.

   Ironically, because lobbyists are most successful when they minimize their demands, they seldom ask for big changes in public policy, which means in turn that the impetus for big changes typically comes from government officials, rather than lobbyists. In other words, when the government radically alters course – for example, if the president decides to send troops to war, or Congress enacts massive tax cuts or increases, or a state government enacts monumental education reforms – it is government officials, rather than lobbyists, who are responsible for the shift. The data show that even when lobbyists truly want to press for radical changes in policy, they tend not to because they know that government officials are averse to radical change.

Key 2: Have Lots of Resources. Second, the data show that *resources* are a key to a public policy lobbyist's success. In short, they indicate that, all things being equal, lobbyists with lots of money at their disposal have a higher chance of succeeding than lobbyists with little money to spend. Money is important for several reasons, but three in particular stand out. First, money allows lobbyists and the organized interest(s) they represent to buy access to policymakers. Public policy lobbyists buy access by contributing money to elected officials' campaigns. Public policy lobbyists and the organized interests they represent also buy access by hiring other lobbyists – especially contract lobbyists who are valued primarily for their connections with public officials. "Buying" a contract lobbyist who has extensive connections is a quick and easy (though expensive) way for an organized interest to gain instant access to policymakers. None of this, of course, means that buying access ensures that public policy lobbyists always get everything they want, but it's a good start. And access affords lobbyists the opportunity to learn about what policymakers are up to, in other words, to listen as well as to talk, and to keep them abreast of impending government actions that affect their interests.

The second reason that resources increase lobbyists' chances of success is that resources allow them to *do more*. As the data show, governments in the United States are amazingly permeable. Local governments, state governments, and the federal government all have numerous points of access. Public policy decisions emanate from the legislature, from the office of the chief executive, from the bureaucracy, and from the judiciary. Moreover, within each of these branches there are hundreds if not thousands of individual policymakers. The more money an organized interest has, the more lobbyists it can hire and the more public officials it can lobby. In a hypothetical example, let's assume that a state environmental protection department is considering a new regulation to loosen emissions standards for power plants. On one side of the issue is an environmental citizen group with a budget of $1 million and one full-time lobbyist. On the other side is a business firm with a budget of $8 million and 10 full-time lobbyists. Let's also assume that each side in this conflict has good, solid policy-analytic information to support its viewpoint. Ultimately, the decision on whether or not to adopt this regulation is to be made by a group of 10 bureaucrats. The citizen group manages to meet with 3 of these bureaucrats. The business firm, however, because it has more lobbyists, manages to meet with all 10. Moreover, while the citizen group lobbyist is spread thin and must limit his or her time meeting with each of the 3 bureaucrats, the business firm has one lobbyist devoted to each bureaucrat. When the time comes for the bureaucrats to make a decision about the regulation, they are far more familiar with the arguments and evidence *for* the regulation than they are with the arguments and evidence *against* the regulation. This does not mean that the bureaucrats will automatically side with the business firm. But it does mean that the business firm has a decided edge – it has the money and personnel necessary to make the best possible case. The citizen group, in contrast, cannot make as good a case as it wishes. It does not have the people power or the resources to do so. Does this mean that in any conflict that pits two organized interests against each other the one with the most money wins? Of course not. But ask yourself this question: If you were battling an organized interest and its lobbyists, would you rather have more or less money than your opponent?

The third and final reason that resources can contribute to a lobbyist's success is that plentiful resources allow lobbyists and the organized interests they represent to lobby for values. As mentioned, some grassroots lobbying is designed to affect people's opinions and attitudes. Studies suggest that over the long term these lobbying campaigns can be quite successful at molding citizen opinion.[20] Many lobbyists, including several in my sample, clearly believe this to be the case. Lobbying for values, however, is expensive.

Key 3: Do Not Flout Public Opinion. Third, the data show that another key to a public policy lobbyist's success is *not asking for something that is counter to public opinion*. My respondents were unanimous in the opinion that policymakers never want to make decisions that contradict the wishes of ordinary citizens. Legislators are especially reluctant to make such decisions because they face election on a regular basis. According to my respondents, one subset of the public is especially important to legislators – their constituents. The respondents were insistent and consistent about the power of constituency opinion. When legislators are faced with a choice between doing something that their constituents want them to do and doing something that a lobbyist wants them to do, the legislator will side with the constituents every time. Legislators, however, are not the only ones who pay attention to public opinion. Bureaucrats are also loath to make a decision that runs counter to public sentiment.

That policymakers do not like to make decisions contradicting public opinion has two important implications. First, it means that public policy lobbyists go to great lengths to show policymakers that what they want is good for ordinary citizens. When these lobbyists present policy-analytic information to policymakers, it almost always includes facts and figures about how the lobbyist's favored course of action will positively benefit ordinary citizens in general and a policymaker's constituents in particular. Second, it means that some public policy lobbyists have an enormous advantage over other public policy lobbyists. Specifically, the most successful public policy lobbyists are those who (1) lobby on issues that media outlets and citizens tend to ignore, and/or (2) lobby on issues that are highly technical and complex, and/or (3) lobby on issues that are not highly partisan or ideological. Why is this the case? The answer is simple: Issues that the media and the public tend to ignore, and issues that are technical and complex, and issues that are nonpartisan and nonideological, are issues on which the overwhelming majority of citizens have no opinion.

To illustrate this point, let us consider two issues. The first is abortion. This is an issue that both the media and the public at large pay a great deal of attention to. In addition, it is not particularly complex, but it is highly partisan and ideological (as conservatives and Republicans tend to come down on one side, while liberals and Democrats tend to come down on the other side). The second issue is agricultural subsidies. The media and the public spend little time on this. Moreover, agriculture policy in this country is technical and complex, and there is no easily identifiable Republican, conservative, Democrat, or liberal "side" of the issue. Whereas most citizens have well-formed, deeply held opinions about abortion, most do *not* have well-formed, deeply held opinions about agricultural subsidies. What this means is that a lobbyist working on the issue of agricultural subsidies has a built-in advantage over a lobbyist working on the issue of abortion: There is no worry about advocating something that large numbers of people oppose. The fact is that no matter what the agricultural lobbyist asks for, it is highly unlikely that he or she is going face substantial (or even minimal) opposition from the public. Why? Because the public is not paying attention. Does this mean that the lobbyist can count on the *support* of the public? No. But it does mean that no matter what is being asked for, the agricultural lobbyist is not likely to encounter substantial public opposition. This makes the job easier, as the lobbyist can essentially say to a policymaker, "If you do as I say, your constituents will not be upset." Policymakers like making decisions that do not upset their constituents. As for the abortion lobbyist, no matter what he or she asks for, there is liable to be strong public opposition. This makes it more difficult to convince policymakers about a favored course of action. In sum, lobbyists who work on issues that do not attract much attention from the public have a built-in advantage over lobbyists who work on issues that make news.

Key 4: Play Defense Rather Than Offense. To many of my respondents, another key to lobbying success is playing defense rather than offense. They were unanimous in the belief that it is much easier for a lobbyist to convince a policymaker *not* to do something than *to* do something. Ironically, then, lobbyists who are under constant attack have much higher success rates than lobbyists who are constantly on the offensive. This does not mean that lobbyists like to be on the defensive. After all, if lobbyists are constantly under attack (like, for example, tobacco company lobbyists were during the 1990s), they will probably eventually lose. But the data unequivocally show that public policy lobbyists are much more successful when they ask the government *not* to do something than when they ask the government *to* do something.

Because it is the conventional wisdom among public policy lobbyists that it is easier to win when you play defense, they devote much time to monitoring. Monitoring is the way that public policy lobbyists become aware of impending policies that may hurt the organized interests they represent.

Key 5: Have Good, Credible Policy-Analytic Information to Present to Policymakers. Though lobbyists have a reputation for getting what they want by strong-arming, bribing, and harassing policymakers, the data suggest that presenting convincing policy-analytic information is much more effective than doing anything else. Policymakers want reasons to do or not to do things. Lobbyists provide them with the reasons they need. Policymakers who support a bill that limits car emissions, for example, want solid, credible evidence that the limits will clean the air and make people healthier. Without this evidence, they may not take a chance on limiting emissions, even if they want to. Policymakers do not always do what the policy-analytic information they receive tells them to do, but all things being equal, especially on technical, complex, obscure, and nonpartisan issues, having credible policy-analytic information can help lobbyists make their case.

Key 6: Have a Member or Supporter Base That Can Be Mobilized for Grass-roots Lobbying. Because policymakers care so much about public opinion, my respondents say that lobbying for contact can be enormously valuable in helping public policy lobbyists get what they want from government. In short, lobbyists who generate mail, telephone calls, or e-mails messages to policymakers in support of their position are much more likely to win than lobbyists who do not. My data indicate that some lobbyists have an easier time lobbying for contact than others. Specifically, lobbyists who work for organized interests with a large member or supporter base are better at lobbying for contact than lobbyists who do not. Large trade associations, citizen groups, and labor unions, for example, have a relatively easy time mobilizing their members for political action. Similarly, large business firms, though they do not have members per se, *do* have employees and executives who can be mobilized by lobbyists. In contrast, small businesses, small membership citizen, professional, and trade organizations, as well as nonmembership organized interests including think tanks, universities and colleges, and hospitals, have a tougher time successfully lobbying for contact.

In sum, the data suggest that there are six "keys to success" for a public policy lobbyist: (1) Don't ask for too much; (2) have lots of resources; (3) do not flout public opinion; (4) play defense rather than offense; (5) have good, credible policy-analytic information to present to policymakers; and (6) have a member or supporter base that can be mobilized for grassroots lobbying. There are undoubtedly other factors that determine whether or not a public policy lobbyist wins. These, however, are the factors that were highlighted most often and most prominently by my respondents.

CONCLUSION

Each year, the federal government, the 50 state governments, and tens of thousands of local governments in the United States make public policy decisions on an amazing array of issues. Many of these decisions are accompanied by lobbying. In this chapter and the previous chapter, I have attempted to describe and explain where public policy lobbyists fit into the policymaking process. It is impossible in such a short space to reach definitive conclusions about where lobbyists fit into this process, but the data suggest a number of general conclusions.

First, public policy lobbyists represent a wide range of organized interests. Indeed, virtually all types of organized interests engage in public policy lobbying. Second, public policy lobbyists spend substantial amounts of time on nonlobbying activities, among which the most important is monitoring government. It is impossible to know for certain what percentage of their time public policy lobbyists spend monitoring, but my respondents told me that it is well into double digits. Third, public policy lobbyists operate at all three levels of government and lobby all three branches of government. Nonetheless, they are less active in local politics than in either state or federal politics, primarily because local governments spend more time on land use matters. In addition, though lobbyists lobby the judiciary, my data indicate that they spend far more time on the legislature and the executive. Fourth, no matter where they lobby or what they want, public policy lobbyists rely heavily upon two lobbying techniques: meeting personally with legislators and/or their aides, and meeting personally with executive agency staff. No matter who lobbyists are, where they work, or what they want, meeting personally with policymakers is a good way to "make a case."

Fifth, my data show that public policy lobbyists rely primarily upon background information and policy-analytic information when they lobby policymakers. While many lobbyists also present career-relevant information to policymakers, policy-analytic information and background information are clearly the typical lobbyist's stocks in trade. Policy-analytic information that shows that a particular course of action will *help* (or not hurt) policymakers do things is a very valuable asset for the lobbyist. Sixth, some lobbying techniques, including judicial, direct democratic, and many electoral lobbying techniques, are relatively rare. While surveys indicate that the typical public policy lobbyist uses a wide variety of techniques, the data here show that a few techniques are used persistently while others are used only rarely. Seventh, though grassroots lobbying can be effective, it is not very common. My respondents told me that this is the case because it is expensive and because the public has a limit on how much grassroots lobbying it will respond to. Thus, while many lobbyists do indeed engage in grassroots lobbying, they do not do so very often. Eighth, the data show that while contributing money to candidates is a reasonably common lobbying technique, lobbyists believe that money seldom determines what a policymaker actually does. Public policy lobbyists believe that money buys access to policymakers rather than votes.

Finally, public policy lobbyists sometimes win and sometimes lose. Lobbyists can do a number of things to improve their chances of success. They can, for example, not ask for too much, not flout public opinion, and deploy good, credible policy-analytic information. In addition, some

lobbyists are simply advantaged over others. Specifically, lobbyists who are playing defense are more likely to be successful than lobbyists playing offense, lobbyists with a large base of supporters that can be mobilized are more likely to be successful than lobbyists without a large base, and lobbyists with lots of resources at their disposal are more likely to be successful than lobbyists without these resources.

5 Land Use Lobbying

Mukunda Lal Ghosh was born in Gorakhpur, India, in 1893. At the age of 17, the spiritually restive Indian became a devoted student of the renowned spiritual leader Swami Sri Yukteswar Giri. A few years later, he took his vows as a monk of the Swami Order and received the name Paramahansa Yogananda ("bliss of spiritual discipline").

Yogananda made an impression on India's religious community almost immediately. In 1917, he started a school for boys where he taught yoga and spiritual principles, in addition to the standard curriculum. His successful school drew praise from many religious quarters, and in 1920 he was asked to travel to Boston as a delegate to a world convention of religious leaders. Also in 1920, Yogananda founded the Self-Realization Fellowship (SRF), an organization designed to spread his teachings. Yogananda clearly enjoyed his trip to America. From late 1920 to 1924, he crisscrossed the United States speaking and teaching. In 1925, the peripatetic Yogananda settled in Los Angeles. There, he bought the dilapidated Mount Washington Hotel, which rested on a pastoral hillside a few minutes from downtown Los Angeles, and established the worldwide headquarters for SRF. In the years that followed, Yogananda continued spreading the word, and he was even invited to the White House in 1927, where he got a warm reception from President Calvin Coolidge. From his home on Mount Washington, Yogananda continued to teach, travel, meditate, and write until his "exit from the body" (death) in 1952.[1]

Today, SRF headquarters remains a quiet oasis in the middle of a massive metropolis. SRF's bustling Mount Washington compound serves as the administrative base for the organization, acts as a clearinghouse for information on Yogananda's teachings, houses a shrine to Yogananda, contains a chapel for prayer and meditation, and is home to dozens of monks and nuns of the Self-Realization Order. By all accounts, SRF coexisted relatively peacefully with its neighbors – well-off Angelinos who live in the expensive homes on and around Mount Washington – for most of its existence.[2] The peace was shattered in late 1997 when word spread that SRF planned to relocate Yogananda from his eternal resting place in a Glendale, California, cemetery to a new shrine at its Mount Washington retreat. SRF did not simply plan to put Yogananda in the ground. It had bigger plans. Specifically, it planned to build a 20,000-square-foot museum and a large round dome under which Yogananda would lie for eternity in a marble sarcophagus. These plans did not sit well with some of the neighbors. By the time the SRF released details of its proposed reentombment in 2000, many area residents were up in arms. Foremost among their concerns was that reentombment would bring untold thousands of visitors to SRF headquarters, which would lead to traffic congestion, noise, pollution, and crowding.[3]

This case may seem out of place in a book about lobbying, but it is not. In fact, it illustrates the following important point about land use in the United States: *Landowners cannot do whatever they wish with their land.* If you own a piece of land – be it residential, commercial, industrial, or agricultural – the government circumscribes what you can and cannot do with it. The case of SRF and the proposed plan to reentomb its long-dead guru illustrates this point very well. To put it briefly, the land on which SRF proposed building its new mausoleum was not "zoned" for such a project. As such, SRF could not simply build the mausoleum and its attendant structures. Rather, it had to receive special government permission to proceed with its ambitious project. In its quest to win government permission to erect its funereal edifice, SRF did what many landowners do when they need government permission to proceed with land use projects (especially large ones): It hired a lobbyist (actually, it hired several). The lobbyists were hired to convince city officials and public opponents that the proposed development would not be harmful to neighboring residents and would conform with local zoning and building rules. All told, media reports suggest that SRF spent hundreds of thousands of dollars trying to shepherd the project through city government. The money was wasted. In 2003, in the face of opposition from residents, a neighborhood organization formed expressly to block the project, and a rival religious sect that also claims Yogananda as its spiritual lodestar (and wished to have continued access to Yogananda's tomb), SRF withdrew its proposal to build a new home for Yogananda's body.

This case is not unique. Landowners throughout the country regularly hire lobbyists to help them get permission to develop land. In this chapter,

I examine land use lobbying – the lobbying that accompanies government decisions rendered in response to specific requests for permission to utilize land in a certain way. I begin with an overview of how land use decisions in America are made. (I should warn you that this overview is somewhat arcane, but you will need to become familiar with the complex regulations and rules that govern land use in the United States). From there, I examine who land use lobbyists are, whom they represent, and what they do. I conclude with a summary of the land use lobbying process.

GOVERNMENT REGULATION OF LAND USE: PLANNING AND ZONING

Urban affairs specialist Paul Peterson has noted that "[u]rban politics is above all the politics of land use."[4] The same can be said of local politics in general. There are tens of thousands of local governments in the United States, and many of them regulate how landowners can develop their land. As you read of the ways that local governments in the United States regulate land use through the process of zoning, please keep in mind that zoning varies substantially from place to place. Thus, this overview provides only the most basic outline of the zoning process.

Zoning Basics

Zoning is a complex process that involves a variety of political actors. It begins with a grant of power from the state government to a local government – for example, a county, city, town, or village. This grant of power comes in the form of state enabling legislation, a special charter, or a "home-rule" provision in a state's constitution that allows a local government "to engage in planning and undertake zoning."[5] From here, a local governing body (e.g., city council, county commission) adopts a zoning ordinance that comprises a map and accompanying text.[6] The map divides the community into a number of zones or districts. For example, a generic zoning ordinance might distinguish between agricultural, commercial, industrial, and residential land use. Many zoning ordinances distinguish between a larger number of districts. The text of the zoning ordinance explains what is and is not allowed in each district. An ordinance might, for example, dictate the "size and placement of buildings in each type of zone."[7]

The Ordinance. Historically, many zoning ordinances were hierarchical and pyramidal in structure, with agricultural and open space at the top of the pyramid, residential uses and commercial uses in the middle, and heavy industrial uses at the bottom. In such a scheme, restrictions on land use are very stringent at the top of the pyramid and become less stringent as you move to the base of the pyramid. Moreover, in a hierarchical scheme like this, a landowner is generally free to develop "'higher,' less intensive uses – such as residences – in the 'lower' zones" that allow "more intensive uses – such as commercial uses."[8] Today, many communities adopt ordinances that are exclusive rather than pyramidal, in that they do not allow this sort of movement from higher uses to lower uses.[9]

The Comprehensive Plan. Many communities have a "comprehensive plan" (or "master plan") in addition to a zoning ordinance. A comprehensive plan is

> a long-range roadmap for the future of a community which examines and makes recommendations on a variety of planning activities such as land use, transportation, utilities . . . community facilities, housing, the environment, recreation, economic development, etc. It provides information about conditions, and trends and issues in a community and identifies actions needed to address such issues.[10]

A comprehensive plan is a set of policies intended to guide land use decisions, including changes to the zoning ordinance.[11] This plan is like a zoning ordinance in the sense that it designates how specific tracts of land within a geographic area may be developed. However, the typical comprehensive plan allows for a range of uses for a specific piece of property, whereas a zoning ordinance is much more detailed and designates one specific usage. In most communities, the comprehensive plan has the force of law, and government officials cannot make land use decisions that contradict it.

The Three Main Types of Land Use Decisions

The typical zoning ordinance specifies three things. First, it specifies what uses are permitted as a matter of right (i.e., no special action is required for approval) in each zone. For example, an ordinance might specify that a single-family home is permitted as a matter of right in a residential zone, and a store or office building is permitted as a matter of right in a commercial zone. Second, the typical zoning ordinance spells out what uses are permitted conditionally or upon review by the local government. For example, a zoning ordinance may not allow the building of a church in a residential zone as a matter of right, but it may allow it if the landowner is able to get a "special use" or "conditional use" permit from the local government. The inclusion of special or conditional uses in zoning ordinances "allows a city or county to consider special uses which may be essential or desirable to a particular community, but which are not allowed as a matter of right within a zoning district."[12] Third, the typical zoning ordinance specifies the standards that specific structures and developments must meet. For example, most zoning ordinances contain height limitations (i.e., limitations on the maximum height of a building), density limitations (i.e., limits on the number of building units allowed per acre), and setback requirements (that dictate the minimum-required distance between a structure and some specified line, such as another structure, an adjacent lot, or a right-of-way).

If a landowner wishes to do something with a piece of land that is allowed as a matter of right, he or she usually need only apply for a permit, fill out some forms, and proceed. However, if a landowner wishes to do something on a piece of land that is not allowed as a matter of right, then special permission must be sought from the local government. Government decisions to grant such permission come in three main forms: rezoning decisions, conditional use decisions, and variance decisions.[13]

Rezoning Decisions. In some cases, a landowner wants to develop land in a way that is explicitly disallowed by the zoning ordinance. This is the case, for example, when a landowner wants to build homes in an agricultural zone or a factory in a residential zone. A landowner that wishes to develop land in a way that is explicitly disallowed by the zoning ordinance must get the land "rezoned" by the local government – let's say, from residential to commericial in order to build a large grocery store on a piece of land in a residential district.

Zoning experts Charles Hoch and Linda Dalton call a rezoning decision "the most important and most common zoning action of any local government."[14] In most communities, because a rezoning action is essentially a change in the law, it must be approved by the local legislature. The process by which rezoning applications are considered is a long one. In most places, an application for rezoning goes initially to the local planning commission, which typically consists of five, seven, or nine commissioners appointed by the local legislative body. The first thing the planning commission does is refer the application to planning commission staffers, who review it and make a recommendation (for or against approval) to the planning commission. Next, the planning commission holds a public hearing on the rezoning application. The applicant invariably participates in the public hearing, and interested citizens are invited to participate as well. Generally, planning commissions are bound by law to notify the public in advance of these hearings. On the basis of the staff recommendation and the public hearing, the planning commission then makes a recommendation (that is, gives the proposal a thumbs-up or a thumbs-down) to the local legislative body. From here, the application is referred to the local legislative body. At this point, the local legislative body holds one or more public hearings on the application. Again, generally the law mandates that citizens be informed of these hearings. After the hearings and deliberation, the local legislative body takes final action on the application.

Scholars of rezoning note that the process is quite anarchic. As zoning expert Eric Damian Kelly notes, "the granting or denial of rezonings is generally performed without reference to significant standards."[15] In other words, many (if not most) communities have no clear-cut, unambiguous standards for rezoning. This means that the legislators, planning commissioners, and planning staff involved in rezoning decisions generally have substantial discretion to do as they please in rezoning cases. As such, it is not surprising that land use decisions attract lobbyists. In the absence of concrete standards on which to judge rezoning applications, land use decision makers are open to all sorts of appeals from lobbyists and citizens.

Conditional Use Decisions. As noted, most zoning ordinances contain a list of what local governments call "conditional uses," "special uses," or "uses on review" that are allowed in a zoning district if special permission is granted by the local government. (For the purposes of this discussion, I will call all such uses conditional uses.) Many local governments, for example, allow churches, day-care centers, and parking lots in residential or commercial zones, but only with explicit government review and permission. In addition, in many localities certain land uses, including cemeteries, car washes, hazardous waste storage or processing facilities, and landfills are considered conditional uses no matter where they are located, and must be approved by the local government. Expanding an existing conditional use project (for example, adding on to a church located in a residential zone) is also considered a conditional use in many communities.

For something conditionally permitted by the zoning ordinance, the landowner must obtain a conditional use permit (henceforth, CUP) from the local government. The typical zoning ordinance contains a list of criteria for the granting of these permits. The criteria are generally vague and so open to interpretation. For example, many zoning ordinances state that conditional use permits will be granted for projects that "are not injurious to the public welfare," are "in harmony with the purpose of the zoning ordinance," "are generally compatible with surrounding land uses," and "do not have adverse impacts on the project area."[16]

The process a landowner must follow to obtain a CUP varies somewhat from place to place. Generally, the process works as follows. First, the landowner submits a CUP application to the planning commission (or in some places, a board of zoning appeals or a zoning hearing officer). Next, as in the rezoning process, the planning commission holds a public hearing at which the landowner explains the proposed project and attests to its worthiness, and opponents and supporters are invited to testify for or against the project. Most zoning ordinances specify that CUP applicants must notify nearby landowners before the public hearing. After the hearing, the planning commission votes on the CUP application. In some communities, the planning commission's decision is final. In other communities, the planning commission's decision acts as a recommendation to the local legislative body. In these communities, the local legislative body holds an additional public hearing and then makes the final decision regarding the CUP application.

Zoning Variance Decisions. The typical zoning ordinance, as noted, spells out the standards that structures and developments must meet. In some cases, landowners wish to be exempt from these standards or wish to deviate from them in some way. For example, a retail developer may want to build a store that is slightly taller than zoning rules allow, or a homeowner may want to build an "add-on" that makes the home bigger than the zoning ordinance allows. In cases like these, most communities allow property owners to apply for zoning variances, which are minor deviations from the zoning ordinance. The difference between a zoning variance and a conditional use permit is that a variance generally deals with technical aspects of a building project, rather than the use of the land per se. Pierce County, WA, defines a variance as an "adjustment to the development standards of the zoning regulation, that does not apply to use or required density."[17] Typically, the county government goes on to note, variances are "used to request reductions in setbacks, increase in height, and other deviations from bulk standards [e.g., size or dimensional restrictions]."[18] (A setback is the "distance from a curb, property line or other reference point, within which building is prohibited . . . ")[19] In more accessible terms, this means that a variance is a relatively trivial deviation from the zoning ordinance.

A landowner wishing to get permission to deviate slightly from zoning regulations must obtain a zoning variance from the local government. In most communities, a board of zoning appeals (BZAs) or a board of zoning adjustment has the power to grant zoning variances. BZAs are typically composed of five or seven people appointed by the governing body. Most communities require a public hearing by the BZA before a zoning variance is granted. Different communities use different standards to evaluate variance requests, but this set of criteria from Westport, CT, is somewhat representative. To obtain a zoning variance in Westport: (1) the project must be "in harmony with the general purpose and intent of the zoning regulations"; (2) "due consideration" must be "given for conserving the public health, safety, convenience, welfare, and property values"; (3) there must be "physical conditions that are unique to" the project; and (4) "the enforcement of the regulations would result in exceptional difficulty or unusual hardship. The hardship must be defined as a condition affecting the specific property, not a monetary hardship."[20]

A Word about Comprehensive Plan Amendments. To recap, a landowner wishing to do something with a piece of land that is not allowed as a matter of right must receive special government permission. In most cases, this permission comes in the form of a rezoning decision, a conditional use decision, or a zoning variance decision. However, in some cases, especially those in which a landowner wishes to develop land in a way that is radically different from what the zoning ordinance allows, that landowner must receive special government permission in the form of a comprehensive plan amendment. Comprehensive plan amendments are not required in the vast majority of cases on which land use lobbyists work. In other words, a rezoning or conditional use or zoning variance decision usually suffices. Therefore, in this chapter I do not examine either the process by which comprehensive plans are amended or the role of land use lobbyists in amending comprehensive plans.[21]

Summary

Local governments in the United States regulate what landowners can do with their land. A community's basic regulations are set forth in a zoning ordinance that divides land into categories based on how the land can be used. In some cases, what a landowner wishes to do with a piece of land is allowed as a matter of right under the ordinance. In many cases, however, it is not. Depending upon precisely what a landowner wants to do, permission from the government must be sought in the form of an affirmative rezoning decision, CUP decision, or zoning variance. The process by which a landowner gets government permission to do something is complex, protracted, and sometimes contentious. No one knows for certain how often landowners who seek to rezone their land, obtain a zoning variance, or obtain a conditional use permit actually hire lobbyists to help them. Anecdotal evidence suggests, however, that in large projects such as the SRF venture I describe at the beginning of this chapter, lobbyists are common players.

LAND USE LOBBYISTS: BACKGROUND INFORMATION

The data reveal three notable general findings concerning who land use lobbyists are and what organized interests they represent.

Most Land Use Lobbyists Represent Business Firms

According to the data, most land use lobbyists lobby on behalf of business firms. Not surprisingly, the kinds of businesses that use land use lobbyists the most are those that own, develop, and manage land – for example, real estate investment firms, real estate development firms, property management firms, construction companies, homebuilders, and comprehensive real estate services firms. Other types of businesses that commonly retain land use lobbyists include cellular telephone companies, power companies, railroads, and other types of firms that own and/or manage land.

My respondents agreed that virtually any time business firms want to develop undeveloped land (that is, build something on it) or expand an existing facility or development (e.g., a factory, oil refinery, golf course, retail store, apartment complex, office building, cellular telephone tower, or mall), they must get government permission. Even if a plot of land is zoned for a particular use and the owner or developer of that land wants to use it for that particular purpose, it is virtually unheard of for the landowner to be able to proceed without explicit government permission. Lobbyist no. 28, a land use lobbyist in Los Angeles, summed up the situation nicely when he told me: "There are not a lot of projects anymore other than single family homes, or small duplexes, or small shopping centers . . . that go straight to building permit."

While business firms appear to be the most common clients of land use lobbyists, they are certainly not the only clients. For example, Lobbyist no. 30, a land use lobbyist in San Francisco, once represented a charitable organization that sought to build housing for low-income people, and Lobbyist no. 2, a lobbyist in San Diego, once represented a church that wished to expand its facilities. Moreover, Lobbyist no. 29, who works in a large southeastern city, represents a university exclusively. He explained why he is so active in land use lobbying:

> Pretty much everything that we do . . . involving land, construction, [and] everything else, involves some land use permit or permission. [For example], we need zoning permits for the construction and building . . . of new building[s]. Every one of [our new] buildings has parking impact [and] has environmental impact, [and] we have special zoning [rules] for the campus; [so] we have to tend to these things.

In short, virtually any organization or individual that owns or manages land might at some point need approval from the government to do something with that land, and thus might require the services of a land use lobbyist. Among the types of nonbusiness clients that have hired my respondents are universities and colleges, churches, charities, and government entities.

Despite the fact that most land use lobbyists represent business firms when they lobby, the data indicate that citizen groups are also frequent players in land use politics. The data indicate that two types of citizen groups are particularly active: "NIMBY" groups and neighborhood associations. People who study land use politics use the acronym NIMBY ("not in my backyard") to describe local citizen groups that mobilize to thwart businesses' efforts to develop land. Extant research indicates that NIMBY groups can be quite effective.[22] Neighborhood associations – organized groups of residents who live in the same neighborhood, condominium complex, or cooperative – also are regular participants in land use politics, and they too often are successful in forcing developers either to modify or to cancel development projects.[23] This, of course, begs the following question: If NIMBY groups and neighborhood associations are frequent players in land use politics, how come none of my respondents report ever representing such groups? The answer, several respondents noted, appears to be that when NIMBY groups lobby, they tend to rely upon volunteers and community activists rather than professional land use lobbyists. It is not unheard of, of course, for NIMBY groups to hire land use lobbyists. For example, several large nationally active environmental groups have local chapters that utilize paid professional land use lobbyists. But several of my respondents acknowledged that only occasionally do the NIMBY groups or neighborhood associations they tangle with hire professional land use lobbyists. This does not, however, mean that citizen groups are inactive in land use politics.

Finally, it is worth noting that some land use lobbyists work on behalf of individuals rather than organized interests. Several respondents told me that some areas have such restrictive zoning rules that individual landowners who want to make even small changes to their property require the services of a land use lobbyist. Lobbyist no. 2, who works in San Diego, told me: "We will probably get three or four cases a year representing homeowners who just need a permit to remodel their home in a coastal zone." Coastal zones, this lobbyist told me, often have very restrictive zoning rules. Even relatively such simple jobs as home expansion or remodeling are controversial in places with highly restrictive zoning rules.

Many Land Use Lobbyists Are Contract Lobbyists

If you recall, in Chapter 2 I distinguished between in-house lobbyists (who work for and are employed by the organized interests for which they lobby) and contract lobbyists (who work for whoever wishes to pay them). My data suggest that most land use lobbyists are contract lobbyists who are employed by consulting, law, lobbying, or public relations firms, and are hired by outside clients to lobby on land use issues. In fact, of the eight land use lobbyists I interviewed, seven are contract lobbyists. The other is an in-house lobbyist employed by a university. Of course, I cannot say on the basis of my small sample whether or not this 7:1 ratio of contract to in-house lobbyist is reflective of overall tendencies. But this ratio coupled with the comments of respondents, suggests that land use advocacy is a highly specialized field practiced primarily by contract lobbyists.

Why are so many land use lobbyists contract lobbyists? The answer, it appears, is that land use rules and regulations vary from jurisdiction to jurisdiction (that is, from place to place). As such, a business firm that operates in several jurisdictions may need a *different* land use lobbyist for each and every one. Let us consider, for example, the hypothetical case of a large development firm that is working on projects in five different jurisdictions in two different states. It is possible (and indeed likely) that each of these five jurisdictions has a different land use approval process. What the firm needs is a lobbyist who is familiar with the land use rules and regulations in all five jurisdictions. This is probably too much to ask of an in-house lobbyist (or even several in-house lobbyists). Moreover, even if an in-house lobbyist (or a group of in-house lobbyists) gets up to speed on the rules and regulations in all five of these jurisdictions, there is no guarantee that the firm will ever do business in any of the five again. Thus, hiring a contract lobbyist in each jurisdiction makes sense. I asked

Lobbyist no. 14, who is a contract lobbyist in Florida, why so many land use lobbyists are contract lobbyists, and this is her answer:

> I'm speaking from a Florida context. In Florida everything is very localized in that each local government has its own comprehensive plan and its own set of land development regulations, which are different from every other local government's comprehensive plan and land development regulations. Each local government also has its own staff and operates in a political context that derives from the personalities and philosophies of the individual elected officials. As a result, I work almost exclusively in those Central Florida counties and cities where I know the codes, the people, and the politics.

In other words, while firms' in-house lobbyists may be able to offer the company some general advice on land use matters, they most likely are not well versed in the politics and policy of each individual jurisdiction in which the firms operate.

In sum, the data suggest that the highly localized nature of land use politics explains the relative surfeit of contract lobbyists in the ranks of land use lobbyists. Indeed, according to Lobbyist no. 22, it is the conventional wisdom among firms that hire land use lobbyists that the best way to win is to hire local lobbyists who know the "ins and outs" of the jurisdiction in question. In the end, however, I must caution that my data are not extensive enough to explain this phenomenon completely. This is a matter that I continue to study.

Not All Land Use Decisions Are Accompanied by Lobbying

Although local governments spend a great deal of time on land use decisions, not all are accompanied by lobbying. In other words, many landowners go through the process of obtaining government permission to do something with their land without using the services of a land use lobbyist. So who needs a land use lobbyist?

My data, as well as previous research on land use decisions, suggest that the developers of large projects – for example, industrial facilities, "big box" retail stores, massive shopping centers, and housing subdivisions – are the most likely to require the use of a land use lobbyist. Large projects are likely to require substantial lobbying because (1) they receive more government scrutiny than smaller projects, (2) they are more technical and complex than smaller projects, and (3) they are often more controversial and draw more community opposition than do smaller projects. Speaking to the first issue, in most places the law mandates that large projects be reviewed and approved by many government decision makers. A homeowner who wants to build a garage will probably just have to fill out some paperwork and get a building permit from a single city department, whereas a housing developer who wants to bulldoze several acres of land and build dozens of single-family homes must deal with multiple city departments and get permission from the city's elected governing board (e.g., city council). As for the second issue, big projects tend to be complex projects. A new garage added to a home is not nearly as complex as a new mall that entails the building of several structures, the planting of hundreds of trees, the laying of tons of water pipes, and the paving of new parking lots. The more complex a project is, the more technical the expertise that is necessary, and lobbyists have technical expertise. Finally, larger projects are often controversial. The more controversial a project is, the more lobbyists are needed to present the facts and issues to the planning commission staff, the planning commission, and the legislative body, as well as to interface with the project's opponents to "educate" them and to facilitate compromise solutions.

Summary

My data suggest that business firms – especially those that specialize in developing land – are the most prolific users of land use lobbyists. This is not surprising. Land use decisions are about land development, so it makes sense that businesses that develop land lobby most on land use issues. It is important to note that while my data point up the prevalence of lobbyists who work for business firms, the literature on land use politics and the comments of many of my respondents show that other types of organizations – especially citizen groups – are also active in trying to affect land use decisions. Research shows that neighborhood associations and NIMBY groups often mobilize to thwart the plans of developers and other types of business firms.

WHAT LAND USE LOBBYISTS DO OTHER THAN LOBBYING

In addition to lobbying, lobbyists fit into the zoning process by doing three things in particular. First, land use lobbyists advise, inform, and counsel clients about land use matters. Second, they consult with local bureaucrats about the land use decision-making process. Third, they do paperwork. Here's a summary of what my respondents told me about these three aspects of their work.

Land Use Lobbyists Advise, Inform, and Counsel Landowners and/or Potential Landowners

Many respondents told me that they engage in land use advising and coun-seling in addition to land use lobbying. Land use advising and counseling entails one or both of the following: (1) telling a landowner or potential landowner what projects are and are not allowed under the law, and (2) explaining to a landowner or potential landowner what steps will be nec-essary to develop a piece of land in a certain way. Lobbyist no. 28 provided an example of the first type of activity:

> My feeling is that before you buy a piece of land you want to under-stand the current condition as it relates to that land, and what its poten-tial opportunities and limitations are. I think it's absolutely essential. That's what we do. If someone is looking to buy a piece of land and they have an idea of what they want to do, they ask us, "Can we do it?" We look at it and say, "Yes you can, no problem. [However], you have to go through a minor process," or "You're going to have to get some serious deviations from the code, and these are the things that are necessary."

The same lobbyist provided an example of the second type of activity: "Most of [my clients] have an idea of what they'd like to do [with a piece of land]. But they don't have an idea what they *can* do." This is where the lobbyist comes in – telling the client what sorts of things are allowed or disallowed on a specific piece of land.

Lobbyist no. 28, a contract lobbyist in Los Angeles, explained that the zoning process is exceedingly complex and technical, and that clients often come to him just to get an idea of what might be necessary to complete a specific project:

> The zoning code and/or specific plans that relate to the properties them-selves which articulate what you can do and cannot do and what you need to do to get your project done ... are extraordinarily complicated. I'll tell you, [we] spend hours trying to figure out what the issues are and what we have to file and what discretionary permission is necessary [to do what we want to do].

Lobbyist no. 14 told me that many of her clients know that some gov-ernment action is required for them to be able to use their land as they desire, but they do not comprehend how much power the gov-ernment holds over the use of their property. Educating clients about this reality is an important and often difficult aspect of the land use lobbyists' role as advisors to their clients. Lobbyist no. 14 gave the following example:

> I have represented clients that I affectionately refer to as the "landed gentry." By that I mean people whose family has owned the land for generations and who have been good stewards of that land. They have been farming the land for years and caring for it; they love the land. They have expected that one day their land would be in the path of growth and then it would be their turn to develop the land for its "highest and best use." They now have decided the time is right to rezone the land for development. They often believe they are entitled to have their land rezoned just as their neighbors a little closer into town have been doing for years. Because of their history and their long-term ownership of the land, these clients have a very keen sense of property rights – particularly the right to use land for their desired purpose. One of my jobs is to bring a dose of reality to these clients. In the political arena, changing the use of land is not a matter of right, it is a matter of discretion vested in the local government. Before beginning the rezoning process, the client needs to know that the change in land use may not be easy to obtain. In order to temper unrealistic expectations, the client also needs to know in advance that he or she is not entitled to the "highest and best use" of the land, but only to a reasonable use. The neighbors and the local government may believe that farming continues to be a reasonable use for the land. My job is then to persuade the opponents and the local government that the use being requested by the client is both reasonable and appropriate given the changes that have occurred in the area since the land was first given its existing agricultural designation.

In other words, some landowners know little or nothing about what they can and cannot do with their land, and a land use lobbyist is there to enlighten them.

Sometimes land use lobbyists go beyond simply informing their clients by offering them advice about how to proceed. Lobbyist no. 14 told me, for example, that she often spends a lot of time at the beginning of a project trying to adjust her client's expectations:

> One of the toughest things that I do in my practice is controlling my clients' expectations. Once they have spent money on preparing a land use plan, they fall in love with it no matter how aggressive or unrealistic the plan may be. I often remind the client that obtaining land use approvals is a matter of compromise and that their plan will very likely need to change during the review and hearing processes. I can think of only one or two instances where the plan initially presented was the one approved.

Lobbyist no. 28, who works in Los Angeles, told me that he sometimes must be the bearer of bad news:

> Sometimes people will come to me with an idea for a project. And some-
> times I say, "Look, I know this community well enough to tell you that
> what you want to do [on that piece of land] you'll never get support for.
> So if you want to spend your time and money, I'm happy to do it, but
> I'm telling you right now you're going to be wasting it."

Several respondents said that some clients refuse to take their advice and forge ahead with ill-advised projects that have no chance of getting approved. These clients waste a lot of time and money due to their stubbornness.

The fact that clients often hire land use lobbyists not to lobby but to advise them raises the following question: Why do landowners and potential landowners hire lobbyists to give them advice, rather than lawyers or other professionals who do not engage in political activity? The answer, the data suggest, is that clients hire lobbyists because they know that land use decisions are political decisions rather than simply technical or legal decisions. Yes, most of them said, advising clients of the rules and regulations of zoning is a big part of the job. But getting permission from a local government almost always requires political as well as technical expertise. Lobbyist no. 28 told me: "The political process is one part of the equation. The code can say one thing, and [the city government] can say, 'we're just not doing it that way.'" In other words, while knowing the law and the code is very helpful for developers and potential developers, knowing how government officials interpret and administer the law is also crucial. Lobbyists – people who deal with government officials on a regular basis – are ideally suited to provide this kind of information.

Land Use Lobbyists Consult with Local Government Bureaucrats

Land use lobbyists try to influence land use decisions by lobbying planning commissioners, planning commission staffers, and local legislators – that is, the government officials who ultimately make rezoning, conditional use, and zoning variance decisions. Nonetheless, all of my respondents told me that these are not the only local government decision makers with whom they deal on a regular basis. Specifically, my data show that land use lobbyists spend considerable time consulting with – though not necessarily lobbying – bureaucrats in local government agencies. According to Lobbyist no. 28, for example: "On [any] development project, we have to deal with the Bureau of Engineering who will oversee the street standards, [and the Department of] Public Works, [which deals with] street lights [and] street trees." Lobbyist no. 29, who works for a large urban university, told me something similar:

> There is no aspect of local government that doesn't affect this university – police, fire, water and sewer, electricity, public works. We have, for example, streets that are city streets running through our campus. Some of them we own, but others are city streets. But maintenance, traffic control...that's all under the jurisdiction of the Department of Public Works.

Land use lobbyists consult with bureaucrats in local government agencies primarily because they are good sources of information. Lobbyist no. 28 told me that the agencies

> provide us with the information we need to make sure the project meets city standards. Let me give you an example [involving a] 480,000-square-foot development project [I recently worked on]. We were well under way, we had submitted our application, we had had a predevelopment meeting where the city sat down with them and we talked about the project. We described it, gave them the plans, and they tell us in turn what they're going to be looking for. The Bureau of Engineering came in, and we had 1,000 linear feet of street frontage along a major street, and they said, "We're not going to require any widenings but we want a seven foot dedication along the entire frontage."

This information was essential in enabling this land use project to conform to the law.

Lobbyist no. 2 said that in some cases, his consultations with city bureaucrats provide him with information he later uses to lobby land use decision makers. Once he was hired to represent a biotechnology firm that wanted to build a facility in a residential neighborhood. He consulted extensively with bureaucrats in the city's Health Department who eventually concluded that the facility did not provide a health risk to area residents. Lobbyist no. 2 subsequently cited this "clean bill of health" from the Health Department when he lobbied planning commissioners, planning staffers, and local legislators.

Land Use Lobbyists Do Paperwork

Not surprisingly, no matter what type of decision land use lobbyists are trying to affect, they must fill out copious amounts of forms. Conditional use and rezoning applications, for example, typically run 10–15 pages and require numerous supporting documents. Moreover, once an application for rezoning, conditional use, or a zoning variance has been approved, the applicant must obtain a building permit, and in many cases other approvals including fire, electrical, plumbing, and concrete permits. In addition, most jurisdictions require large development projects to undergo some type of environmental review. What all of this adds up to is hundreds of hours of paperwork. And land use lobbyists often help clients with this paperwork. According to Lobbyist no. 2:

> The first thing they [the client] did is they hired me to do their lobbying. In two months we were able to help [a client that wanted to build a golf driving range on an undeveloped piece of land] . . . secure a conditional use permit. . . . The second thing we did for this client was construction permitting. [After the CUP was granted], they still need[ed] to get through fish and wildlife agencies, resource agencies, [and the] Army Corps of Engineers to build their building.

Although land use lobbyists consider completing paperwork a part of their job, they typically delegate this unpleasant task to others. Lobbyist no. 31, a contract lobbyist in Los Angeles, told me:

> Well, usually I work with or hire experts – land use expeditors. I mean, I don't fill out the forms. That's not what I want to do in life and usually we bring in people – land use planners – to fill out the forms; or we hire the transportation consultants. . . . Those types of individuals . . . interface more directly with [agency officials] than I do. I usually do bigger picture stuff.

Several other respondents said that they regularly hire consultants, land use planners, and land use expeditors to help them fulfill their nonlobbying responsibilities during lobbying campaigns.

Summary

A substantial part of many land use lobbyists' job is advising clients about what they can and cannot do with their land. Some landowners and potential landowners are more sophisticated than others, my respondents agreed, and some know a lot about the rules that govern zoning, while others know little or nothing. Perhaps surprisingly, both kinds of clients – the sophisticated and the unsophisticated – hire land use lobbyists to advise them about the feasibility of certain projects and to get them up-to-date on relevant zoning rules, regulations, and procedures. Zoning decisions, especially in high-density jurisdictions, are contentious, technical, and political. In other words, they are fertile grounds for lobbyist influence and activity. In addition to advising their clients, land use lobbyists also spend time consulting with local agency officials on many aspects of the land use decision-making process. The primary purpose of these consultations is to ensure that a project conforms to the law.

LOBBYING TO AFFECT LAND USE DECISIONS

In the most general sense, land use lobbying entails attempting to affect a rezoning, conditional use, or zoning variance decision made by a local government. But how exactly do land use lobbyists attempt to influence these decisions? In this section, I answer this question by discussing what my respondents told me about the land use lobbying process. The data suggest that the process by which land use decisions are made proceeds, for the most part, in identifiable, more or less discrete, successive steps from start to finish, organized chronologically in this section.

Lobbying the Planning Staff

As mentioned, applications for rezoning and conditional use normally begin at the local planning (or zoning) commission, which makes a recommendation to the local legislative body about specific rezoning and conditional use proposals. In most jurisdictions, a professional planning staff considers each land use proposal (i.e., application for rezoning or a conditional use permit) and then makes a recommendation (i.e., to either approve or reject a proposal) to the planning commission. In other words, in most jurisdictions planning staffers get first crack at land use proposals.

My respondents were unanimous in the opinion that professional staff planners (generally known as "planning staff") are crucial players in land use politics. The first order of business in many lobbying campaigns is trying to convince the planning staff to give a proposal the thumbs-up. Lobbyist no. 14 summed it up nicely:

> [The] planning [or] zoning commission is . . . an appointed board. . . . The [planning] staff makes a recommendation to the planning commission, [which] then ultimately makes a recommendation to the elected body, either the county commission or the city council. And so my goal on any project that I start out with is to get a staff recommendation for approval. I work extremely hard at the front end trying to understand what staff's concerns are. Do they have problems? Can I meet whatever hurdles they throw at me before I get to the public? I want to know what their general reaction is to my project.

Lobbyist no. 31 concurred, noting that getting the support of "the professional staff – the unbiased professional staff . . . makes our life a lot easier." Getting staff approval is not always easy. It may require countless meetings.

Lobbyist no. 30, who works in San Francisco, told me: "For example, if we were building a high rise, by the time we were done, maybe two years down the line, we might have interacted with staff members several hundred times."

Several respondents said that planning staff are unique in the land use decision-making process – they are experts. Local legislators, and even planning commissioners themselves, respondents explained, are often amateurs and dilettantes who are unfamiliar with zoning rules and regulations. Lobbyist no. 30 was blunt about this:

> The decision makers are generally citizen volunteers with no or little knowledge about the subject [of land use]. Planning commissioners, city council members, mayors, and supervisors – they are not bureaucrats who are in a position by virtue of their expertise.

Planning staff – at least in theory – *are* in their positions by virtue of their expertise. Because planning staff are professional planners rather than politicians, they tend to consider the technical aspects of proposed projects more than do planning commissioners and local legislators. Therefore, land use lobbyists tend to emphasize technical information when they lobby planning staff. Lobbyist no. 28 told me: "In most cases, my feeling is it's very important to have a very strong technical argument when you are dealing with planning staff . . . it's important to have a good technical justification." In other words, virtually every large project has to meet manifold technical requirements, and planning staff are there partially to make certain that they do. Lobbyists are there to convince planning staff that their projects are in compliance with zoning rules and regulations.

However, generally speaking, getting the planning staff on board with a certain proposal is not as simple as convincing them that the proposal abides by the letter of the law. Several respondents noted that most large projects ask for deviations from the letter of the law – deviations that are allowed under the law, but generally only if they can be justified. Lobbyist no. 30 told me the following about such deviations:

> Well, exemptions and waivers [from the zoning code] are part of the current law. [For example, let's say] you . . . want to build a hotel [on a piece of land] and you want to get a variance so you can make it so you have less open space, and you [also] want a waiver on fees because you are going to be doing a joint venture with a non-profit for all the job creation. Well, all these things are allowed by law. The code is designed to allow those kinds of activities under certain circumstances – you know, things like variances, rezonings, exceptions, exemptions, [and] waivers.

While all of these exemptions, waivers, and variances are allowed by law, they nonetheless must be justified to be approved. The first step is convincing planning staff that there are good reasons for waivers and exemptions. Often, the criteria on which variances and exemptions are granted are somewhat vague. Again, this is where lobbyists come in. Lobbyist no. 30 went on to describe how she convinces planning staff and other land use decision makers to approve deviations from the letter of the law:

> [I] describe the project and ... say, "What are the criteria for approval?" Yes, we are going to be demolishing this old historic building. And whether or not it's legal to demolish an old building depends on whether it's designated a landmark. So these are your legal standards. So now let me describe how we meet those standards. This is an old building, and people like it, but it's not ever been designated an historic landmark. Therefore the demolition is completely appropriate.

In short, "getting to yes" with the planning staff generally involves more than simply convincing them that paperwork has been filled out correctly, that all relevant permits have been applied for, and that a project conforms with all rules and regulations. In most cases, it also involves convincing them that deviations, exemptions, and waivers are justified. In addition, getting staff approval often requires negotiations with staff. Several of my respondents said that they do not inform planning staff about their plans as much as they *negotiate* with planning staff about their plans. Lobbyist no. 30 told me: "We may be negotiating with staff ... about what the staff recommendation will be. [The] staff may want to impose very onerous conditions on a project that are more than we want. And we may counteroffer. [That's] the price we pay for the staff's recommendation of approval."

Lobbying for Planning Commission Support

As mentioned in the previous section, in most jurisdictions, the planning commission exists to advise the local legislative body on specific land use proposals. After the planning staff makes a recommendation to the planning commission, lobbyists turn their attention to the commission itself. Getting the planning commission's support generally entails one or both of the following: (1) mobilizing public support and/or demobilizing public opposition in advance of the planning commission hearing and (2) lobbying the planning commissioners themselves. Let's consider each of these two activities in turn.

Grassroots Lobbying: Mobilizing Public Support and/or Demobilizing Public Opposition. It is impossible to overstate the importance of public opinion in land use politics. All of my respondents agreed that, things being equal, receiving approval for a land use proposal is very problematic if substantial public opposition to the project exists. Lobbyist no. 31 said that in most of his cases, "You want as much [public] support as you can [get], and if you can't do that then you want to minimize opposition." Getting the public on your side is doubly important, my respondents agreed, because a public hearing takes place *before* the planning commission renders its decision *and* before the local legislative body makes its final decision. In sum, because in most jurisdictions the law mandates public hearings for all but relatively minor land use decisions, lobbyists use grassroots techniques (i.e., they lobby the public) extensively.

The best-case scenario for a land use lobbyist is to have active and vocal support for a project. This, however, is uncommon. According to Lobbyist no. 22, who works in Florida where land use is a big issue:

> The people who come to a land use hearing are not the people who are in favor of it, they're the people who are against it. So sometimes we actively go out and organize support to come to the hearing. But in the vast majority of projects the only one supporting the project is the developer and his consultant [lobbyist]....If you took a market sample and you had 82 percent of the people supporting the project, [only] 25 people [will show] up; or three people – a lady with a walker and a mother with a child....I'm not kidding.

In most cases, the data suggest, grassroots lobbying is designed *not* to convince supporters to show up at the planning commission's public hearing and show their support for the project, but rather to convince opponents and potential opponents *not* to show up and voice their opposition to a project.

So just how does a lobbyist demobilize public opposition to a project? Several of my respondents said that they start the demobilization process by beginning a dialogue with members of the affected community. For example, Lobbyist no. 2, who works in San Diego, told me:

> I always start our focus with the community and the neighbors. Having worked in government, I well understand that if you can make communities and neighborhood groups happy with a project it makes your job a heck of a lot easier.

Later in our interview, Lobbyist no. 2 reiterated the importance of public outreach:

> [In] almost all of our cases – 75% of the time – we start by dealing with immediate neighbors, environmental groups, [and] people out in the community who have a reason to care.... That's the very first thing I tell my clients, "Thanks. You hired us, you have something in mind. The very first thing we are going to do is talk to community groups and inform them." We say [to the neighbors], "Here's who we are, and this is what we are trying to accomplish." Let them hear it from us first.

The same lobbyist said (and several respondents concurred) that neighbors, environmentalists, and members of the community are often organized into neighborhood associations or NIMBY groups. Beginning a dialogue with these groups early on in the process is often seen as crucial to victory. Lobbyist no. 14 said that neighborhood groups can easily transform into an "angry mob." A big part of her job, she said, is trying to deal effectively with this mob, to either gain support for a project or lessen the emotional level of its opposition to a project:

> The largest local government in which I practice has institutionalized the practice of holding community meetings and sending notices to [neighborhood] associations and individuals within two miles of the site where new development is proposed. The elected representative for that area is the official "host" for the meeting. This approach easily creates an emotional, angry mob who want to show their collective opposition to the project. After all, they are the voters who put the meeting's host in office.

Demobilizing opposition, my data indicate, is particularly important today because in so many places the default position is "no growth." All of my respondents in one form or another made this point. Lobbyist no. 28 said, for example: "Oftentimes a community or a community of interest within a community [has a] philosophical interest to oppose everything." Lobbyist no. 22 concurred, stating: "[In] Florida, like [in] a lot of states, [people] are fairly anti-growth." I asked Lobbyist no. 22, who also does work outside of Florida, if he believed that the default position in most jurisdictions was no growth. He responded: "No question...other than [in] Henderson, Nevada."[24]

So what do land use lobbyists do to demobilize community opposition? My data suggest there are three primary answers to this question. First, land use lobbyists provide opponents and potential opponents with information that paints the project in a good light. Lobbyist no. 31 told me:

> We like to get involved in a project sooner than later, especially if it's going to be a controversial one, so that we can go out and "seed" the community with appropriate and proper information and try to mobilize our information prior to what I call the bad guys mobilizing theirs.

What type of information? Lobbyists often provide basic project information designed to appeal to opponents' and potential opponents' sense of fairness and reasonableness. Lobbyist no. 22 said, for example: "A lot of times, it's logic. Something is an appropriate use in an appropriate location, and even though people may oppose it, there's an argument to be made that this is fair and equitable." Not surprisingly, the "this project makes good sense" approach to demobilizing the public is seldom successful. This is why land use lobbyists also provide basic policy-analytic information to demobilize public opposition to a project. Lobbyist no. 31, for example, described a recent case in which his client wanted to expand "an existing oil facility in the middle of a very upscale residential community." His job, he said, was to convince the public that the expansion was to be accompanied by a modernization that would make the project "environmentally superior to the existing conditions." To prove this to community members, he showed them "the environmental impact report [and] environmental studies." Lobbyist no. 2 spoke about a controversial project in which he represented "a biotech company" that wanted to build a "300,000-square-foot office and research center in a residential neighborhood." Neighborhood and environmental groups, he said, were very worried about "pollution, chemicals, [and] toxics." His approach, he said, was calmly to present information to opposing groups that suggested their fears were overblown. The project, he told opponents, was simply not dangerous:

> [The biotech firm] had four schools and a day-care center within 1,500 feet of the [proposed] project – probably the highest concentration of schools near a biotech in the community. We said, "we need to get the client to conduct a health risk assessment report." I said to the biotech, "of course it will look like we told the consultants to give us the report we wanted." [So I suggested that] the school district conduct a health risk assessment. We were going to have to do one anyway. But the better messenger to defend and represent the interests of the schoolchildren was the school district itself.

Lobbyist no. 2 said that at first his client balked at allowing the school district to do the risk assessment. Eventually, however, he convinced the firm that his was the best way to go. Eventually, the school district hired a "consultant who does these things, who understands the levels of risk, who quantifies it everyday." The school district's final report suggested that the risk from the biotech firm was quite small. To this lobbyist's surprise, "not a single opponent" showed up at the planning commission hearing and the project was eventually approved.

Neighborhood associations and NIMBY groups often worry about traffic, noise, and pollution. Thus, according to Lobbyist no. 31, one type of policy-analytic information that land use lobbyists provide is information on "traffic counts, traffic mitigation plans ... and traffic improvements." While it is not always the case that opponents are convinced by policy-analytic information provided by land use lobbyists, it often helps the lobbyists overcome opposition. Several of my respondents said that to obtain technical information, they hire independent environmental consultants, traffic consultants, engineers, health and safety consultants, and other experts. Lobbyist no. 14 told me:

> For every controversial project I work on, a team of five or more technical consultants is required. For example, the project will always include a traffic engineer. It will also always include an environmental firm. Very often the team includes a geotechnical engineer to provide soils data, an urban land planner, a landscape architect, a civil engineer with expertise in storm water management and utilities, and a surveyor.

The second finding that emerges from my conversations about how to demobilize community opposition is that land use lobbyists believe that the best way to deal with opponents and potential opponents is to do so in small groups rather than large ones. In fact, I was surprised at how adamant my respondents were about this point. Lobbyist no. 14 explained: "You can't negotiate with the angry mob. You've got to get to a point where either you have a small delegation or somebody that is stepping up to at least control the mob." Lobbyist no. 2 concurred, stating:

> One of the other things I have learned is [that you must spend] . . . the time with people one on one, or in small groups, especially on controversial, emotional issues. If you get 100 people in a room about emotional issues, you lose control; emotions take over. The meeting becomes less than productive, negative, and a waste of time. [In one recent land use battle] we said, "OK, we know who those opponents are, or those who are most likely to be worried about it. Let's meet them one on one, talk to

them one on one, educate them one on one." [We did this] so that by the time we get to a group meeting of sorts the emotion has been cast aside.

Lobbyist no. 31 referred to meetings with large groups of opponents or potential opponents (e.g., open meetings with the entire membership of a neighborhood association or NIMBY group) as "group gropes." He told me: "I don't like 'group gropes' because what you do is you get fifty people in the room [and] you've got three loudmouths that intimidate the other forty-seven." Large group meetings are problematic for several reasons: They give activists, group leaders, and other vocal opponents a forum in which to shine. Without such a forum – in a smaller, more intimate setting – "loudmouth" opponents have less of an incentive to "show off" for others. Large groups also encourage bad behavior. In an angry-mob setting, several respondents noted, opponents and potential opponents are more likely to scream, yell, "boo," hiss, and generally engage in bad behavior. Finally, large groups are easier to disrupt than smaller ones. Convincing people not to oppose a controversial project, my respondents agreed, is easier to do one-on-one or in small groups than it is in large groups.

The third and final finding is that land use lobbyists believe that one of the best ways to demobilize opposition once and for all is to offer opponents and potential opponents concessions. Lobbyist no. 14 told me: "Obtaining land use approvals is basically a negotiation. In meetings with opposing groups you point out the merits of the proposed project and negotiate what concessions will be necessary to gain their support or at least neutralize their opposition." The same lobbyist said that during her campaign on behalf of a developer that wanted to build a resort hotel, she negotiated with neighbors and eventually convinced them to drop their opposition to the project by offering them a very valuable concession:

> This [was] a multiyear project . . . on about 730 acres – a big resort piece of land. We were negotiating with the neighbors over a three-year period. The client ended up having to sell to the School Board at a very, very discounted price, a high school site because the neighbors and the School Board wanted a high school in that area. In addition, the client landscaped the median of an entry road into an adjoining subdivision to help gain the support of a retirement-age neighborhood with no school-aged children.

I asked Lobbyist no. 14 if this sort of "wheeling and dealing" is common in negotiations with neighbors, and she said it was:

> It's basically just a negotiation on a lot of different topics. The opponents have wish lists, and sometimes the client is able to make contributions or

concessions that will either directly enhance their neighborhood, provide additional buffers,[25] or provide other amenities that are important to them in an effort to eliminate the opposition.

Lobbyist no. 22 said that on one recent project, after months of meetings with neighbors, he and his client decided to make the neighbors happy by agreeing to change their plans and pay for a road from the development to a local school. "This road," he told me, "[had] no impact on this [project, and] this project had no impact on the need for this road. This road is solely to serve a school to make people happy in this subdivision." One member of the planning staff told Lobbyist no. 22 that building this road simply to placate neighbors was ridiculous and maybe even illegal. The staffer supported the road nonetheless, and eventually the project was approved.

Lobbying the Planning Commissioners. As the previous subsection attests, the public attracts considerable attention from land use lobbyists. Ultimately, however, the goal is to convince planning commissioners to support a project. My data show that the kind of information land use lobbyists provide planning commissioners is similar to that which they provide to planning staffers.

First, land use lobbyists work on the technical aspects of a project. Lobbyist no. 28 told me that it is very important to have a strong technical argument when lobbying planning commissioners. Lobbyist no. 30, a San Francisco lobbyist who had earlier lamented the lack of expertise among land use decision makers in her city, said that when she deals with planning commissioners and members of the legislative body she focuses on the legal "facts of the case":

> You have to then describe what are the legal and public policy criteria for approval of [a project]. Because again, these are citizen volunteer politicians, and there is no reason to believe that they have all of that information or have it in an organized fashion in front of them. So you describe the project, you describe the legal and policy criteria for approval, and then you demonstrate how your project complies with those standards.

In short, like planning staff, planning commissioners value technical information about how well a proposed project agrees with the law.

Technical information, however, is seldom enough to convince planning commissioners to support a project. The data suggest that they are more concerned with nontechnical aspects of a project than are planning staff, as described by Lobbyist no. 28:

> I also find that the planning commissioners tend to be more prag-
> matic . . . they look at the bigger picture beyond the technical justifications
> of a project and use more intuition. [For example] there may be some'
> technical issues here that you cannot make that perfect finding for – a
> variance, for instance. But the variance makes sense and it's not going to
> have negative repercussions in an unmitigated manner. They'll look at it
> in a much more pragmatic basis than some of the technicians do.

Lobbyist no. 28 said that by "pragmatic," he meant more willing than planning staff to consider nontechnical aspects of a project, such as its impact on
economic development, job provision, and the good of the community. He
went on to say that the nontechnical side of lobbying speaks to "the beauty
of the project or its benefits." When I asked Lobbyist no. 31 what kind of
benefits he emphasized when speaking to planning commissioners and
local legislators, he said: "job creation, economic value . . . uniqueness."
Lobbyist no. 30 said that one of the things she explains to planning commissioners (as well as local legislators) is the tremendous value that some
projects have to the community as a whole, even if some opposition to
them exists:

> There are a lot of projects where the issue is not to serve [neighbors']
> interests. If you build a homeless shelter, no matter how well that shel-
> ter is managed, it is going to have some adverse impact on the people
> that surround it. And they have reason to be unhappy. So if this was the
> planning commission to serve just me and you, we'd be fine. But the
> planning commission has to do best for the entire city, not just for
> the proximate neighborhood.

While her job is to convince planning commissioners and local legislators
that a project is worth supporting on its legal and technical merits, it may
also have value to the community at large.

Finally, the data suggest that when land use lobbyists lobby planning
commissioners, they emphasize evidence that they have consulted the
public and worked hard to deal with their concerns. While land use lobbyists use grassroots lobbying techniques extensively to demobilize opposition, these efforts serve another purpose as well – they allow lobbyists to
demonstrate their "reasonableness" to planning commissioners and local
legislators. Several of my respondents said that planning commissioners (as
well as local legislators) like to know that lobbyists have done everything

possible to win public support for a project before they vote to support it. In other words, effort counts a great deal, as Lobbyist no. 2 can attest:

> As the project gets to the planning commission or the city council, decision makers want to know that the applicant has gone out of their way to be reasonable and accommodating to the people who might have differing opinions. So we subsequently get some success out of dealing with the neighbors, and we also tell that as a part of our story. You do get "brownie points" for being the good guy. [I tell planning commissioners and local legislators], "I did go out of my way, I did talk to the folks, we accommodated them reasonably, and here's how we did it." It almost turns the tables on reasonableness. [We can say], "We tried, we tried our best. If there are still opponents, they are being unreasonable." ... And the longer we have over the life of a project to do this [and] the more reasonable accommodations we make, the better decision makers feel about the project.

Lobbyist no. 28 said that he often contacts neighbors and potential opponents not so much to try to get their support but rather as a courtesy – a courtesy that may work to "soften" opposition to a project *and* allow him to tell planning commissioners and local legislators that he did the best he could to accommodate opponents:

> In many cases we are contacting people we know are going to be opposed to a project. But we do it as a courtesy to let them know. . . . And a lot of times they will disclose their displeasure, and if there's a way of working through that then we can figure out a way to work through it. And if we cannot work through it at least we know where they're coming from.

In sum, in several respects, lobbying the planning commission is like lobbying the planning staff. Specifically, such lobbying entails providing technical information to commissioners about the legality of a proposed land use project. In some ways, however, lobbying the commission is different. My data suggest that lobbyists begin by emphasizing their efforts to get the public on board when they lobby commissioners, and only after voters' concerns (successfully or not) have been addressed do they provide policy-analytic information.

Lobbying for Legislative Support

After the planning commission makes a recommendation to the local legislature about a land use proposal, the local legislature has a public hearing. Then it votes on the project. As I mentioned in the opening section of this chapter, virtually all large and/or controversial land use proposals must be

approved by the local legislative body. Not surprisingly then, land use lobbyists work to win legislative support, which usually entails one or both
of the following: (1) mobilizing public support and/or demobilizing public
opposition and (2) lobbying local legislators directly.

*More Grassroots Lobbying: Mobilizing Public Support and/or Demobiliz-
ing Public Opposition.* Again, it is impossible to overstate the importance
of public opinion in land use politics. My respondents agreed that receiving a "yes" vote in the local legislature is easier when a project has either
no opposition or active support than when there is vocal opposition. How
important is public support (or lack of public opposition)? Lobbyist no. 31
told me: "[For] the elected officials...out here, its [all] about where are
their constituents, [to which she added later:] It's very rare that an elected
official will go against a project that has public support." Similarly, it is
rare for a local legislator to support a project that has substantial public
opposition. Lobbyist no. 22 said that the worst-case scenario is to have a
lot of people at the legislative hearing: "Frankly, you know, [if] you get
50 neighbors at a [public hearing] . . . they can kick your ass."

The data show that the demobilization of opponents (and/or mobilization of supporters) that occurs before the planning commission hearing
continues unabated between the commission's vote and the legislative
hearing. Again, respondents told stories about negotiating with opponents
and potential opponents in small groups, providing them with information
that paints the project in a favorable light, and granting them concessions
when necessary. My respondents agreed that the demobilization (or mobilization) process is not appreciably different during this phase of the land
use decision-making process than it is at earlier stages. According to Lobbyist no. 31, the key is constant contact with opponents and potential opponents: "[It's very important to have] [d]irect contacts in the communities,
knowledge of the individuals in these various homeowners associations
or neighborhood councils. . . . We *live* in these neighborhood groups." In
short, in many cases, the demobilization of opposition and/or the mobilization of support that begins early on in a project's history continues to
the end. The goal, of course, is to make sure that no vocal opposition to
a project exists and that few or no opponents show up at the legislative
hearing.

Lobbying Local Legislators

The last step in land use lobbying is the direct lobbying of the local legislators who have the final say on land use decisions. In lobbying legislators, my respondents' campaigns emphasized four types of information:

(1) technical information about how the project conforms with the law, (2) career-relevant information about how neighbors feel about the project, (3) policy-analytic information about the beneficial aspects of the project for the community as a whole, and (4) information about the effort the client expended to get the public's support for the project. In essence, this is a combination of all the types of information they provide to other land use decision makers.

Starting with technical information, the respondents believe that local legislators must always be told about the technical aspects of the project – that is, how the project conforms to the law. Lobbyist no. 30, who repeatedly reminded me that local legislators are not land use experts, said that a big part of her job is constantly to remind local legislators that they do not have unlimited discretion in what to approve or disapprove. The ultimate decision, she said, should be based on whether or not the project in question conforms to the law:

> They don't always have as much discretion as they perceive. This gets into a real problem....If you don't outline what the legal and policy procedures are for approval, a decision maker might be under the misperception that a project should be only approved if it's popular.... So my job is to [try] to focus attention on the correct approval standards [and] to help decision makers focus on the fact that this is not just about making the people who live next door to the site happy, or the people who live in your district, or today's voters.

Lobbyist no. 28 said that he realizes that local legislators must consider the political aspects of a project. However, he added: "The politicians...I like to provide the technical [information] so they have a technical basis on which they can hang their hat."

The key difference between how lobbyists lobby legislators and how they lobby other land use decision makers is that with legislators, lobbyists emphasize career-relevant information. After all, my respondents repeatedly told me, local legislators are elected officials who worry about their constituents first and foremost. Not surprisingly then, land use lobbyists try very hard to convince them that neighbors are either on board or do not object to a project. The key, of course, is convincing legislators that supporting a project is not going to hurt them electorally. Lobbyist no. 30 said that she sometimes uses polling data to convince legislators to support a project:

> Let's say there's a controversial expansion of a hotel and the activists in the decision maker's [i.e., legislator's] district oppose it. You could just do a survey to show that the activists were the squeaky wheels and that yes,

it's true that thirteen percent of the voters in your district don't like it, but sixty-one percent do want the expansion, and the rest don't care one way or the other.

One other respondent (Lobbyist no. 22) sometimes uses polling data to help him make his case. Unfortunately for land use lobbyists, there is not much a lobbyist can do other than a survey to prove unequivocally to a legislator that his or her constituents are behind (or do not oppose) a project. My respondents agreed that the best way to demonstrate that the project does not have substantial opposition is to make sure that no one shows up at the legislative hearing, which is the primary venue for opponents to make their opposition known. Making certain that legislative hearings are not filled with opponents is much more important than providing survey information to legislators.

Neighbors, however, are not the only people who care about land use projects. Several of my respondents said that they remind legislators to consider the community as a whole when they make land use decisions. Thus, when they lobby local legislators, land use lobbyists often use policy-analytic information that touts a project's benefits to the community at large. Lobbyist no. 14 said that she often reminds local legislators in her city of Orlando, Florida, that while the impact of a project on a certain area may seem negative, it may nonetheless be good for the wider community:

> I think most local legislators are there because they want to do the right thing. They have different perceptions of what the right thing is, and they get a lot of misinformation. And the other thing I would say, at least in the land use arena, is that it is awfully scary to the residents who are about to see their area change. They fear a change in their lifestyle; they fear that a new development is going to adversely affect their biggest investment; they fear that the change is going to adversely affect their entire way of life. During the public hearing, I've seen residents cry and become extremely emotional because the vacant lot their children have played on for years – as trespassers – is now proposed for development. My job is to give the legislative body a different perspective, a factual perspective and a realistic view that the proposed development will benefit the community as a whole and will not be detrimental to the local neighborhood.

Of course, convincing legislators that a project is good despite some public opposition is not easy. But it is possible. One way to get legislators' support is to convince them that a project has supporters outside its immediate neighborhood or community. For example, Lobbyist no. 30, who works in the liberal jurisdiction of San Francisco, often invokes the name of supporters – in many cases supporters who are not immediate neighbors – when she lobbies. For example, she said, if she has "lots of people opposing . . . a high-density housing project" she tells legislators that "the Sierra Club is now endorsing high-density housing projects." Similarly, Lobbyists no. 30 and no. 28 sometimes seek the support of the local Chamber of Commerce as evidence that a project is beneficial for the community at large. Referring to the "good of the community" does not always work, but my respondents agreed that it is almost always part of the campaign to convince legislators to support a project.

Finally, when they lobby legislators, lobbyists emphasize how reasonable they and their clients are, and how they have bent over backwards to do right by opponents. Lobbyist no. 22, for example, told me that his presentations to local legislators emphasize his reasonableness and that of his client. By the time a project reaches the legislature, he has been working on it for many months and possibly even years. "Any land use deal must be something that is fair to everybody," he told me. And he tries to convince legislators that a project is fair by showing them that during earlier negotiations on a project, his client agreed to "give something back to the government" in the way of concessions. According to Lobbyist no. 2, as mentioned earlier, legislators, like planning commissioners, "want to know that the applicant has gone out of their way to be reasonable and accommodating to the people who might have differing opinions."

Legislators understand, my respondents agreed, that there is almost always going to be some opposition to a project. Thus, lobbyists know that often they cannot be completely successful in their demobilization efforts. So in addition to trying to show legislators how reasonable they are, lobbyists also attempt to convince legislators that opponents are *un*reasonable. They do this by demonstrating how hard they tried to overcome neighbors' objections.

In sum, lobbying local legislators combines all aspects of lobbying planning staffers, planning commissioners, and the public. Lobbyists provide technical and career-relevant information to local legislators, as well as policy-analytic information designed to show that a project is good for the community, and other kinds of information designed to demonstrate how reasonable a client is. The key difference between lobbying legislators and lobbying planning staff and planning commissioners, my data suggest, is that when land use lobbyists lobby legislators, they emphasize career-relevant information. In other words, they try to assure legislators that supporting a project will not have negative electoral consequences. This emphasis on career-relevant information is not surprising, as local legislators, unlike planning staffers and commissioners, are elected to their positions. Local legislators, like elected officials everywhere, want to keep their jobs. Moreover, some of them have aspirations for higher office.

The Public Hearings

To reiterate, for many land use projects, public hearings are required before both the planning commission decision and the local legislative body decision. As to the public hearings themselves, my data suggest that they are relatively inconsequential. I am not saying that they do not matter. They do. In fact, public hearings are important sources of information for both planning commissioners and local legislators. For it is there that commissioners and legislators receive career-relevant information about the level of community support and/or opposition to a proposed land use project. I say that hearings themselves are relatively inconsequential because the data suggest that the crucial lobbying work occurs *before* public hearings are held. Yes, public hearings provide information to decision makers, but my respondents suggested that almost all the heavy lifting in land use lobbying takes place outside the hearing rooms. Several respondents said, for example, that by the time a public hearing rolls around, they have met dozens if not hundreds of times with land use decision makers and members of the public. For opponents of land use projects, however, public hearings may well be more important, as they are the primary forums for making their case.

What Do Neighborhood Associations and NIMBY Groups Do?

My data have relatively little to say about the lobbying activities of NIMBY groups and neighborhood associations inasmuch as all of my respondents are professional land use lobbyists who generally lobby on behalf of business firms. Since this book is about lobbyists, rather than organized interests per se, it is fair to say that this chapter paints a more or less accurate picture of what the typical land use lobbyist does, because most do not lobby on behalf of neighborhood associations or NIMBY groups. Nonetheless, I would be remiss if I did not point out that because I did not interview representatives of these groups, this chapter does not tell the *whole* story of land use lobbying.

Despite the obvious limitations of my data, they do provide a crucial insight into the activities of neighborhood associations and NIMBY groups. Specifically, the data suggest that they frequently engage in grassroots lobbying. Several respondents told me that when these groups lobby, nearly all of them rely heavily upon such grassroots techniques as contacting public officials (especially legislators) directly by telephone, e-mail, or letter and participating in public hearings. Moreover, some respondents indicated that it is not unheard of for the groups to engage in "direct action" – that is, protests, demonstrations, or rallies. On the whole, it appears that while land use lobbyists, most of whom represent business firms, rely primarily upon "inside" techniques, such as meeting personally with legislators, planning staffers, and planning commissioners, neighborhood associations and NIMBY groups rely heavily upon "outside" grassroots lobbying techniques. Unfortunately, while my data have little else to say about their lobbying activities, I do not want to give you the impression that these groups are inactive or unimportant in land use politics.

Summary
Land use lobbyists target the public, planning staff, planning commissioners, and local legislators when they lobby. It is difficult to say precisely which of these groups of decision makers lobbyists target the most. It is clear, however, that the public is important at virtually every step of the land use decision-making process. Thus, it may be that the public gets more attention than other entities in land use lobbying, at least when land use battles are pitched. The information that lobbyists provide to land use decision makers runs the gamut. Lobbyists utilize technical, career-relevant, and policy-analytic information when they lobby.

WHAT DOES LAND USE LOBBYING LOOK LIKE?

Drawing upon the data I presented in the preceding sections, I address the following question: *What does land use lobbying look like?* As with the question at the end of Chapter 4 about public policy lobbying, the answer requires a series of other questions.

Where Does Land Use Lobbying Take Place?
Land use lobbying takes place primarily at the local level of government. This is the case because local governments are the primary entities in our political system that make important land use decisions. Although land use is not the only topic with which local governments deal, it is arguably the most important. Land use lobbying occasionally takes place at the state level as well, like in Florida where a state agency review is mandated. There, every comprehensive plan amendment affecting a tract of land greater than 10 acres in size must be reviewed by the state Department of Community Affairs, which has the right to halt an amendment

recommended by the local government if it believes it to be inconsistent with state law or the existing comprehensive plan. Still, my respondents indicated that most land use lobbying takes place at the local level of government.

Who Lobbies?

My data suggest that most of the lobbying that accompanies land use decisions is done by lobbyists representing business firms. All but one of my sample land use lobbyists spend the bulk of their time representing such businesses as real estate investment, development, and management firms. The data suggest that few full-time, professional lobbyists represent the interests of the citizen groups (i.e., local community, environmental, neighborhood, or NIMBY groups) that are active in land use politics. This does not mean that these groups are unimportant players. Clearly, citizen groups – especially NIMBY groups and neighborhood associations – *are* important players in land use politics, and indeed, have substantial power to modify and even block projects they oppose. Nonetheless, both the predominance of business lobbyists in my sample and the comments of my respondents show that in land use politics, business lobbyists outnumber nonbusiness lobbyists by a wide margin. In sum, people who lobby on land use issues for a living generally represent business firms – especially development firms.

What accounts for the dominance of lobbyists representing business firms in land use politics? The answer, it seems, is obvious: *the law*. The data show that businesses that develop land hire lobbyists because they have to. In virtually every community in the United States, businesses that wish to develop land must get permission from the local government to do so. Of course, some of the projects that they undertake are allowed as a matter of right, and so do not require lobbying. However, my respondents were unanimous in the opinion that most development projects require some sort of special government action. It is virtually unheard of, my respondents reported, for a large project *not* to require some rezoning decision, conditional use decision, or zoning variance decision. Lobbyist no. 30 summed this up nicely:

> The only kinds of projects that are entitled as of legal right, that are principally permitted, are such minor projects. Any major projects of social significance are politically designed to go before a political body. You might be able to put a rear deck on the back of your house [but that's about it].

The process by which landowners get government permission to develop their land is a political process, not an administrative one. The zoning ordinances in most communities mandate that large and significant projects go before a political body and undergo a thorough vetting in public. This is why landowners hire lobbyists, rather than land use planners or technocrats. Politics, my respondents told me, enter into almost every land use decision. This is especially true in densely populated localities, such as Chicago, Los Angeles, Miami, San Diego, and New York City, and virtually everywhere in rapidly growing sunbelt states like Florida.

The other types of organized interests mentioned in Chapter 2 – trade associations, professional associations, labor unions, governmental entities, think tanks, charities, universities and colleges, coalitions, hospitals, and churches – are only sporadically involved in land use lobbying, if they are involved at all.[26]

What Nonlobbying Activities Do Land Use Lobbyists Engage In?

Land use lobbyists, like public policy lobbyists, spend substantial time "lobbying their clients," as one of my respondents put it. What this means is that land use lobbyists (1) advise and counsel clients on what they are allowed to do with a piece of land they own or are thinking about buying and (2) make recommendations to clients about how to proceed with development projects. The complexity of most zoning ordinances (and in some cases accompanying comprehensive plans) makes hiring a land use lobbyist a virtual necessity for firms that manage and develop land. However, if understanding the ins and outs of zoning regulations were all there was to such advising and consulting, these tasks would probably fall to land use experts who are not lobbyists. It does not. Understanding the *politics* of land use is crucial. Land use lobbyists tell their clients what sorts of projects government decision makers are likely and unlikely to support, and they also make recommendations to their clients about how to proceed (e.g., what concessions and modifications to make).

In addition to advising and counseling clients, land use lobbyists consult with local government bureaucrats who work in agencies that deal with traffic, engineering, public safety, the environment, and public works. They also consult with bureaucrats from various agencies that handle complex development projects.

Whom Do Land Use Lobbyists Target?

The data show that within government, land use lobbyists target planning staffers, planning commissioners, and local legislators. In most communities, local legislators are arguably the most important decision makers in land use politics because they have the last word on projects that require either a rezoning decision or a conditional use decision. Moreover, the most substantial projects – huge housing developments, large industrial facilities, and massive shopping centers – are generally the most controversial. Yet despite the importance and preeminence of the local legislature, the data suggest that legislators attract about the same amount of attention (if not less) from lobbyists as planning staffers and planning commissioners. Though I cannot say for certain why this is the case, I think that land use lobbyists themselves believe that a land use proposal (i.e., an application for rezoning or a CUP) will never be seriously considered by the legislative body unless it is first approved by the planning staff and then the planning commission. Another way to put this is that land use lobbyists "front load" their work so they have an easier time getting what they want from local legislators. There is evidence elsewhere that this is a good strategy, as research suggests that land use proposals that have the support of planning commissioners and their staff are more likely to be approved than those that do not.[27]

Land use lobbyists also target the public – especially people who live near the site of a proposed project. In fact, what is perhaps most striking about such lobbying is the extent to which it involves the public. All of my respondents said that they targeted the public extensively, especially when they work on controversial, high-profile, or large projects. Whether it is true or not, these lobbyists believe that public support and/or lack of public opposition is vital to the success of land use proposals. A determined opposition, my respondents told me, can almost always derail a land use proposal.

Which Techniques Do Land Use Lobbyists Use Most?

When land use lobbyists lobby government decision makers (planning staffers, planning commissioners, and local legislators), they rely heavily on two techniques: meeting personally with legislators, and meeting personally with executive agency personnel. The data suggest, in fact, that meeting personally with government officials is by far the most common lobbying tactic used by land use lobbyists.

My data suggest that these lobbyists also rely heavily upon grassroots lobbying techniques, two in particular. First, lobbyists meet personally with citizens in small groups, which they prefer to large groups. The data suggest that whenever possible, lobbyists lobby citizens in small groups as it is conventional wisdom that large meetings are not effective at demobilizing opposition or mobilizing support. Second, land use lobbyists engage in grassroots lobbying by providing citizens with information through the mail, over the telephone, or door-to-door. I did not say much about this in the preceding section because meeting personally with citizens in planned meetings is much more common. But meeting briefly with citizens at their homes to deliver factual information about a development project, sending citizens information through the mail, and telephoning citizens to inform them of planned meetings or give them a heads-up about a hearing or a meeting are not uncommon grassroots lobbying techniques. It is interesting that these kinds of person-to-person techniques are seldom mentioned in studies of grassroots lobbying (and indeed do not appear in Table 2). This is probably the case because most of these studies focus upon public policy lobbying rather than land use lobbying. While public policy lobbyists who use grassroots techniques may rely on other grassroots techniques, land use lobbyists prefer more personal techniques designed to sway individual citizens to support (or not to oppose) their projects.

Finally, my data suggest that land use lobbyists regularly testify at legislative hearings and also at executive agency (i.e., planning commission) hearings. There are fewer opportunities to testify at public hearings than there are to meet personally with government officials or members of the public, and so land use lobbyists do more of the latter than the former. But the data show that they testify publicly whenever they get the chance.

Which Techniques Are Most Effective?

It is hard to say for certain which of the primary techniques is most effective. The data suggest, however, that neither testifying at legislative hearings nor testifying at agency hearings is particularly effective for professional land use lobbyists (though they may be effective for NIMBY groups and neighborhood associations). While public hearings are more than simple formalities and are, in many cases, required by law, my respondents told me that land use battles are not often won or lost in public hearings; they are won or lost in the previous months and years during personal meetings.

Meeting Personally with Government Officials and Their Aides. My respondents clearly believe that meeting personally with government officials is an important and effective lobbying tactic. Local government officials are not very sophisticated when it comes to land use issues and typically have little or no staff to help them. (Thus, they need to be educated.) Personal meetings with decision makers are important (and preferable to, say, written reports) because they allow lobbyists to simplify complex matters that government officials may not understand. Of course, meeting personally with decision makers has another advantage – it allows lobbyists to capitalize on their "connections." As one respondent told me, meeting personally with local legislators is effective because local legislators trust him. Another said the same thing, adding that years of lobbying and fostering personal relationships with legislators had paid off because legislators are eager to hear her client's side of the story. In short, meeting personally with government officials is the most efficient way to pass on relevant information.

Meeting Personally with Citizens. Meeting personally with citizens in small groups is also a very effective lobbying technique. My respondents cited three reasons. First, meetings allow a lobbyist to put a human face on a development project. Lobbyists' clients are often seen as "big business" interests with no concern for local communities or ordinary citizens. Lobbyists can counter this image by meeting personally with citizens and letting them know that there are actual people behind development projects, not just business firms. Second, as mentioned, meeting personally with citizens gives lobbyists ammunition they use when they lobby government officials. Specifically, lobbying citizens personally allows lobbyists honestly to tell government officials (especially legislators, who wish to curry favors with voters) that they did their best to understand and accommodate their opposition. Third, meeting personally with citizens shows legislators that a client is reasonable, responsible, and responsive. Several respondents told me that many citizens are satisfied by a simple consultation. In other words, lobbyists can demobilize (and in rare cases mobilize) some members of the public simply by meeting with them, listening to them, and letting them know they are a part of the land use decision-making process. When Lobbyist no. 14 lobbies citizens, she is not educating them about the merits of a development project, but rather "making them feel that they can be part of the process." For Lobbyist no. 31, meeting with citizens who are opposed to a land development project and telling them that they are important and that their concerns are being considered is often enough to take the rough edges off of their opposition. On the whole, my respondents clearly believe that for some citizens, being informed and consulted is important quite apart from the merits of the specific project under consideration.

Which Types of Information Do Land Use Lobbyists Provide?
Chapter 2 described the three types of information that lobbyists provide to government officials and the public when they lobby: political,

career-relevant, and policy-analytic information. Land use lobbyists generally ply two of the three – and two other kinds as well.

Policy-Analytic Information. First, the data show that land use lobbyists provide policy-analytic information to both government officials and the public. If you recall, I defined policy-analytic information (in Chapter 2) as information about the likely economic, social, or environmental consequences of a particular course of action).[28] In the context of land use lobbying, policy-analytic information is usually information about how a proposed land use project will affect the economy, employment, the environment, noise, pollution, population density, property values, and traffic. Many lobbyists hire outside consultants to estimate the impacts of their proposed projects. Policy-analytic information is especially important when lobbyists lobby the public. My respondents told me that the public thirsts for information showing that a proposed development project will not adversely affect their way of life. Lobbyists also provide policy-analytic information to local legislators and planning commissioners, who want reassurance that a development project will either benefit the community or not adversely affect it.

Career-Relevant Information. Second, the data show that land use lobbyists rely heavily on career-relevant information when they lobby. However, my respondents said that they use this kind of information only when they lobby local legislators, who have the final say on almost all controversial land use projects. The data indicate that local legislators crave information that helps them figure out what course of action is best for their political futures. Local legislators, like elected officials everywhere, worry about reelection, and look to lobbyists to provide them with information on public opinion about the land use proposals that come before them.

Political Information: Not That Important. None of my respondents mentioned political information, which I defined in Chapter 2 as information about the status and prospect of a proposed or potential government decision. Because I asked my respondents what kind of information they provided to government officials and the public, rather than specifically about political information, I cannot say for certain that lobbyists do not provide it. None of them mentioned political information, however. Thus, at the very least, we can conclude that political information is generally less important to land use lobbyists than either policy-analytic information or career-relevant information.

Technical Information. Two types of information that land use lobbyists provide to government officials (though not to the general public) do not fit into any of the three information categories mentioned in Chapter 2. First, there is what I call *technical information*, which I define as *detailed information about various (and sometimes minute) aspects of a specific land use project.* All of my respondents agreed that technical information is exceedingly important in land use lobbying. To paraphrase Lobbyist no. 30, zoning codes in most jurisdictions are technical, complex, and lengthy, and specify what kinds of things are allowed in what places. The typical zoning ordinance, for example, contains many requirements concerning building height, density, and acreage. Whether or not a proposed land use project meets height, density, or acreage requirements is not a political question; it is a technical question. And lobbyists provide government officials with the technical information they need to determine whether a land use project conforms to the law. As Lobbyist no. 30 makes clear, lobbyists are essential in the land use decision-making process because they serve as de facto staff members for government officials (especially legislators) who do not have extensive staff of their own.

Activity Information. In addition to technical information, land use lobbyists provide government decisions makers with what I call *activity information* – that is, *information about what they have done to accommodate a project's opponents.* As pointed out earlier by my respondents, local government decision makers are more likely to support a project if they believe that its proponents have worked reasonably hard to accommodate its opponents and have listened carefully and thoughtfully to their concerns. Because this is the case, land use lobbyists often let government decision makers know how hard they have worked to accommodate opponents.

What Determines Whether or Not Land Use Lobbyists Win?
The question of "winning" – like the question of lobbyist and organized-interest influence in general – is difficult to answer. Nonetheless, the data provide us with some clues as to the variables that affect a land use lobbyist's chances of winning. I should first note, however, that land use politics is seldom a "zero-sum" game. My respondents told me that very few land use proposals sail through the approval process without being modified. In fact, most projects go through several modifications before a final vote is taken, as lobbyists negotiate with government officials and the public alike, offering concessions in exchange for support. Moreover, land use lobbyists engage in extensive discussions and consultations with

local government officials in various agencies long before they officially submit their proposals. This gives them opportunities to modify proposals in ways that may make them more likely to be approved. In sum, the land use decision-making process is often long and protracted, and during this process lobbyists and their clients modify their proposals and offer concessions to government officials.

All of this notwithstanding, many land use proposals *do* get rejected – some by the planning commission, some by the local legislature, and some by both. So what are the crucial factors that affect a lobbyist's chances of winning? The data suggest three factors in particular.

The Disposition of the Public. First, there is *the disposition of the public*, especially neighbors. According to my respondents' unanimous opinion, a project that lacks public opposition has a much greater chance of being approved than a project that attracts it. For the land use lobbyist, having vocal and active public support is the best-case scenario. But mobilizing supporters is often more difficult than *de*mobilizing opponents. In either case, land use lobbyists believe that the disposition of the public is often the key to victory, and this is why they spend so much time courting opponents and potential opponents. If lobbyists cannot either demobilize opposition completely or mobilize support, they can improve their chances of winning by demonstrating a willingness to be reasonable and to compromise with opponents and potential opponents.

The Disposition of the Planning Staff. The second factor in winning is *the disposition of the planning staff*. A negative recommendation is decidedly not the way to start the process. The data indicate that few proposals can overcome the objections of the professional planning staff, and that is why my respondents were unanimous that winning the recommendation of the planning staff is paramount and is time well spent.

Good Technical Information. The third and final determinant of success is *the ability to formulate and deploy an airtight technical argument*. Though the disposition of the public is a crucial variable in land use decisions, proposals must conform to the law, and the law is complex and technical. Successful lobbyists must know all the details about the projects and clients they represent, and they must be intimately familiar with extant zoning rules and regulations in every local jurisdiction of their work. The ability to formulate and deploy an airtight technical argument is especially important because planning staffers are professionals who understand zoning rules and regulations better than either the public or other government officials, and they are also the government officials who have first crack at land use proposals.

CONCLUSION

This chapter about land use lobbying began with a general overview of the process by which land use decisions are made in the United States. Three things in particular stand out about the process. First, it is protracted and involves several distinct steps. Second, it involves multiple decision makers, including planning staffers, planning commissioners, local legislators, and the public. Third, land use decisions come in three basic forms: rezoning decisions, conditional use decisions, and variance decisions. Not all land use decisions are accompanied by lobbying, but many rezoning decisions and conditional use decisions are.

Next, I examined who land use lobbyists are and whom they represent. The data suggest that most are contract lobbyists who represent businesses – particularly real estate investment firms, real estate development firms, property management firms, construction companies, homebuilders, and comprehensive real estate services firms. While my data cannot speak definitively to the question of whether or not citizen groups are represented to any extent by land use lobbyists, the data suggest that they are not. NIMBY groups and neighborhood associations are indeed active in land use politics, but they are not often represented by professional land use lobbyists. It is not surprising that business organized interests dominate the world of land use lobbying, as businesses are the entities in America that develop land.

The bulk of this chapter described what land use lobbyists do. While land use lobbyists spend some of their time on nonlobbying activities, clients value them for their lobbying expertise. Land use lobbyists lobby planning staffers, planning commissioners, local legislators, and the public. Perhaps the most surprising finding in this regard is that they spend so much time and energy lobbying the public. As I pointed out in Chapter 2, the literature on lobbying suggests that the level of grassroots lobbying has increased substantially in recent years. However, this literature focuses almost solely on public policy lobbying. Apparently, as my data show, grassroots lobbying is quite prevalent in land use politics. When land use lobbyists lobby, they invariably provide information that makes their side look good, although the type of information they provide tends to differ across lobbying targets. Land use lobbyists emphasize technical information and policy-analytic information when they lobby planning staffers, policy-analytic information when they lobby planning commissioners and the public, and policy-analytic information, career-relevant information, and activity information when they lobby local legislators.

Summary

In summary, this chapter has highlighted the following general conclusions about land use lobbying: (1) Land use lobbying is primarily a local government phenomenon. (2) Most land use lobbyists represent business firms. (3) Land use lobbyists advise and counsel their clients in addition to lobbying. (4) Land use lobbyists target all of the players in land use politics, including planning staffers, planning commissioners, local legislators, and the public. (5) Land use lobbyists rely to a large extent on grassroots lobbying techniques and personal meetings with local government decision makers. (6) Meeting personally with government decision makers and members of the affected public is a very effective lobbying technique. (7) Land use lobbyists emphasize technical and policy-analytic information when they lobby planning staffers; policy-analytic information when they lobby the public and planning commissioners; and career-relevant, policy-analytic, and activity information when they lobby local legislators. (8) Finally, land use lobbyists have a much better chance of winning when they have the public on their side, when they have the support of the planning staff, and when they can make good, solid technical arguments.

6 Procurement Lobbying

Politicians, the media, and citizens alike argue incessantly about government spending. How much money should the government spend? What should the government spend it on? Where should the government *get* the money it spends? Questions like these pervade American politics.

Given the consistently high salience of government spending as a public policy issue, it is surprising that few people pay much attention to government *purchasing*. To be sure, government purchasing sometimes shows up on the public agenda. For example, during the 1980s it was widely reported that the Pentagon spent $436 on a hammer and $7,600 on a coffee pot.[1] Similarly, in the 1990s a spate of newspaper stories reported that Defense Department personnel used federal government credit cards to pay for prostitutes, lap dances at "gentleman's" clubs, and other unauthorized goods and services.[2] And since President George W. Bush sent troops to Iraq, the media have scrutinized the way the federal government has awarded reconstruction contracts. But these stories are exceptions to a general tendency. For the most part, the public, the media, and political leaders overlook government purchasing.

Perhaps this is a mistake. Government purchasing is big business. The federal government spends over $230 billion per year on procurement. More than 85,000 subnational governments in the United States (50 states and tens of thousands of local governments) spend an additional $1.1 trillion to $1.35 trillion.[3] These amounts are not likely to shrink in the near future. Federal government procurement spending has remained steady for over a decade, and state and local government procurement spending has grown dramatically since 1990.[4]

I must admit that until recently, I did not give much thought to the process by which the government purchases goods and services. Occasional horror stories aside, I more or less assumed that governments buy things the way you and I buy things – they shop around and buy the best products they can for the lowest prices. This was a bad assumption. The process by which state, local, and federal government entities decide what to purchase and then purchase it – a process called *procurement* – is protracted and complicated. Moreover, to add to the confusion, procurement rules, regulations, and processes differ across levels of government and individual bureaucratic agencies. Despite these differences, there is one constant in the procurement process: *lobbying*. In this chapter, I examine procurement lobbying – the lobbying that accompanies decisions concerning the specific goods and/or services that the government will purchase. I begin with a general description of the procurement process. (Again, I must warn you that this introductory section is somewhat arcane). From here, I examine who procurement lobbyists are, whom they represent, and what they do. I conclude with a brief summary of the procurement lobbying process.

GOVERNMENT BUYING

To understand procurement lobbying we must first understand the procurement process – the process by which government entities in the United States purchase goods and services. As you read, please keep in mind that this is not a definitive treatment, but rather a broad overview.

The Decision to Purchase Something: The Budget Process

Government entities in the United States buy a huge variety of goods and services, including everything from paper clips and printer cartridges to car parts and aircraft carriers. Generally, the procurement process begins with a government decision to purchase something. At all three levels of government, it is the legislature that appropriates money to purchase goods and services, usually with the consent of the chief executive. Legislatures decide what to spend money on by engaging in another process known as *budgeting,* which is an important part of the procurement process.

The processes by which state and local governments make spending decisions vary somewhat from the federal budget process. However, in their general outlines they are similar to the federal process.[5] Thus, a brief outline of the way in which the federal government makes spending decisions can help you understand how many governments in the United States make such decisions.

To make this discussion easier, I will assume that Congress is working on a budget for fiscal year 2008. The process begins in the summer of 2006, during which each executive agency within the federal government will send a budget request to the president that explains how much money it wants and what it wants the money for. Between the summer of 2006 and January 2007, the president and his staff will consider the agencies' requests and decide what to do about them. The president has three basic options for each agency request: (1) to leave it as it is, (2) to increase the amount of money requested, or (3) to decrease the amount of money requested. After the president considers all of the agencies' requests, he will compile them into one huge document referred to as the "president's proposed budget." He will then submit this budget to Congress in February 2007.

After the president submits his budget, Congress will consider it. Specifically, Congress will spend March to September 2007 looking at the president's budget and tinkering with it. In September 2007, Congress will stop its work and vote on 14 separate spending bills that together comprise what we call the federal budget – that is, the federal government's financial plan, which states how much money the government will spend and what it will spend money on. The last step in the budget process occurs when the legislative branch sends these spending bills to the president. The president usually signs the spending bills (because he has made it clear to Congress what he will and will not support). At this point, the federal government has made its final decisions on spending.

This brief discussion of the budgeting process points up three important facts about budgeting and how governments make spending decisions. First, *virtually all procurement spending must be approved by the legislature*. Ultimately, at all three levels of government the legislature has the power of the purse. Second, *while the government procurement process technically begins with a decision by the legislature to spend money, for all intents and purposes it begins with requests from government agencies to fund specific goods and services and programs*. Often, though by no means always, when the legislature decides what goods and services to purchase, it takes its cues from executive agencies, whose requests are embodied in the initial budget document (that is, the draft of the budget that the legislature first considers). Finally, *both the executive and legislative branches are intimately involved in government procurement*. The legislature must approve virtually all spending, but the executive branch figures prominently in the budgeting process.

Acquisition Procedures

After money is appropriated to purchase something, the procurement process moves into the *contracting* phase. Procurement expert Steven J. Kelman has written that "contracting involves (1) *structuring the business arrangement*, (2) *source selection*, and (3) *contract administration*."[6] At the federal level as well as in states and localities, all government purchases are structured by detailed regulations. For example, all federal government purchasing is governed by the Federal Acquisition Regulation (FAR), a mammoth document of more than 1,600 pages that details the rules of federal procurement.[7] Despite the existence of detailed regulations that apply to all procurements, many decisions about contracts are made by individuals and groups within the government agencies or entities making specific purchases.

Structuring the Business Arrangement: Contract Vehicles. The most important part of the first step – structuring a business arrangement between a government entity and a contractor – is choosing a contract vehicle. Contract vehicles come in many shapes and sizes.[8] Generally, contracts are either one-time-only purchase contracts (e.g., a government entity buys a specific product it needs) or "task order" or "delivery order" contracts by which a vendor is hired to provide a good or service for a specified amount of time. For example, a government entity might enter into a task order contract "with a software development contractor for writing customized computer security software the agency needs for five years, with specific assignments to be developed over the life of the contract."[9] A delivery order contract might be an agreement between an agency and a personal computer dealer to sell computers at a specified price for a specified period of time as the agency needs them. Often, "winning" a delivery order contract does not guarantee a business firm any sales. This is the case because more and more government entities throughout the country are using what are called "indefinite delivery/indefinite quantity" (IDIQ) contracts, which *allow* government purchasers to buy certain goods or services from certain vendors, but do not *require* them to do so. For example, a manufacturer of lampshades may win a contract to provide lampshades to several government agencies. If it is an IDIQ contract, the manufacturer's name is put on a list of contractors that are approved to sell lampshades (at a predetermined price) to the agencies, and agency buyers may or may not buy lampshades from that manufacturer.[10]

Source Selection: Choosing Who Gets the Contract. The second step is
source selection, which Kelman defines as "the process by which the government solicits and evaluates bids and selects a winning contractor."[11]
Generally, governments use two source selection methods: competitive
sealed bidding and competitive sealed negotiations. Competitive sealed
bidding starts with a public notice (such as an "invitation for bids" or
IFB) that specifies "work specifications, bidding procedures, contract terms
and conditions, and evaluative criteria."[12] For example, the federal government publishes IFBs for large procurements (those over $25,000) in
a publication called *Commerce Business Daily,* which is now available on
the Internet. It is not unusual for individual government agencies to
issue IFBs themselves as well, or to send IFBs directly to companies on
a list of preapproved vendors. After an IFB is issued, vendors submit
bids under seal. Next, the government opens all bids and determines a
winner.

Competitive sealed negotiations are different from competitive bids, and
are often used in complicated procurements in which the government
wants to receive a great deal of information about each bid and also wishes
to communicate with bidders after proposals are submitted. Competitive
sealed negotiations begin with a request for proposals (RFP) that specifies the good or service being purchased, as well as contract terms and
conditions. From here, the government evaluates each proposal, but also
negotiates with vendors to clarify each proposal and perhaps improve the
deal the government will get. The process ends when, after negotiation,
the government chooses a vendor based on price and on other information gathered during negotiations.[13] The advantage of competitive sealed
negotiations is that they allow government buyers to clarify proposals
and resolve problems therein, as well as negotiate for better prices and/or
terms.

Many people assume that on most purchases, government entities
award contracts to the lowest bidder after a standard "advertise, bid, and
choose" process. However, this is not usually the case. Today, most government purchasers use "best value" criteria to evaluate bids, which means
that they consider factors in addition to price, including a vendor's "financial capacity, plant capacity, skill, judgment, and integrity," as well as past
performance.[14] Kelman notes that best value purchasing is more complicated than straightforward lowest cost purchasing, as a government
agency (especially in large procurements) creates "a source selection team
to grade proposals."[15] Kelman continues: "Depending on the complexity of
the proposals, the team may be divided up into separate teams evaluating

technical, past performance, and cost criteria.... Depending on the size of the procurement and the agency, the final source selection decision is made by a 'source selection authority,' at a level above the evaluation team."[16]

Particularly important in best value purchasing is the past performance of government contractors. The Federal Acquisition Regulation emphasizes the importance of past performance in evaluating proposals:

> Past performance information is relevant information, for future source selection purposes, regarding a contractor's actions under previously awarded contracts. It includes, for example, the contractor's record of conforming to contract requirements and to standards of good workmanship; the contractor's record of forecasting and controlling costs; the contractor's adherence to contract schedules, including the administrative aspects of performance; the contractor's history of reasonable and cooperative behavior and commitment to customer satisfaction; and generally, the contractor's business-like concern for the interest of the customer.[17]

What this all adds up to is that government buyers throughout the country now tend to consider factors other than price during the source selection process.

Best value purchasing is designed to give government buyers flexibility that they otherwise would not have, and to ensure that government purchasers get quality goods and services. Indeed, the shift toward best value purchasing has occurred largely because government purchasers believed that under the old process quality often took a "back seat" to low price. The state of Kentucky (which is one of several states recently to move toward best value purchasing) notes that best value purchasing in the state took hold there because under the old system "purchase decisions were made on low price, without consideration for life cycle cost or long term benefit."[18] Unfortunately, "best value" evaluation and award practices raise the old bugaboos of subjectivity and corruption in purchasing. People who study federal government contracting, for example, acknowledge that "best value" purchasing leaves a great deal of discretion to the people within agencies who make source selection decisions.

Contract Administration. After a contract is awarded, the government implements and manages it. Kelman writes that contract administration comprises five basic activities: "(1) monitoring costs (for cost-reimbursement contracts), (2) monitoring performance, (3) contract modifications, (4) settling claims, and (5) contract termination or closeout."[19]

Costs and performance are monitored in a variety of ways, including active oversight by procurement personnel, cost or performance audits or inspections, and product testing.[20] As for who actually does the monitoring, there is no easy answer to this question. Many states have central purchasing offices that oversee contracts (even so, others are often included in the oversight process), whereas the federal government spreads this responsibility across several agencies. It is not unusual for a government entity to modify a contract after it has been awarded. Most federal government contracts, for example, contain a "changes clause" that allows the agency contracting officer administering the contract to negotiate a "change order" with the vendor. While a change order cannot radically alter the terms of the contract, it may change pricing or delivery specifications.[21]

Disputes over contracts are not uncommon. They are often about money. For example, a vendor may believe it is owed more money than the government has paid it for goods delivered or services rendered. Similarly, the government may believe that a vendor initially overpriced its goods or services and may seek a price reduction. Not all disputes are about money. Often, vendors may believe the government makes demands beyond those specified in a contract and file a claim to this effect. Similarly, the government may believe that a vendor has delivered shoddy work or product and file a claim to this effect. At the federal level, most claims are settled within the agency involved. However, if a vendor refuses to accept an agency's final decision concerning a contract dispute, the vendor has the choice of taking the dispute to either a Board of Contract Appeals or a U.S. Court of Federal Claims.[22] Many subnational governments have similar arrangements.

The final stage of contract administration is closeout or termination. Often, contracts simply expire after their terms have been met. When this occurs, contractors may still have business to conduct with the government. Kelman notes, for example, that after a contract has run its course, a contractor may still negotiate with an agency for a "final determination of contractor indirect costs."[23] Sometimes, however, contracts do not run their course, but instead are terminated. A contract ends badly when a government buyer cancels it in what is known as a "termination for default." A termination for default may occur when a contractor fails to "make delivery within the time specified in the contract," fails "to make progress so as to endanger the performance of a contract," and/or fails "to perform any provisions of the contract."[24] Before a contract is terminated for default, the government buyer generally gives the contractor the opportunity to remedy whatever problem is identified. Government buyers are often allowed to terminate a contract "for convenience." When a government buyer does so, it is not the fault of the vendor. Rather, the buyer may decide that it no longer needs or wants the products or services under contract. Before a buyer terminates a contract for convenience, it must issue a notice to the contractor that stipulates how the contract will be settled and when work is to stop. The big difference between termination for convenience and termination for default is that in the latter, the government buyer generally does not give the contractor notice of the impending cancellation.

A Word about Simplified Acquisition Procedures

Government procurement has changed substantially in the past 15–20 years. One of the most significant changes is a move toward simplified acquisition procedures, especially for relatively small government purchases. Though this is a bit of an oversimplification, I define *simplified acquisition procedures* as *procedures that do not require the government to go through the full acquisition procedure* described previously. The reasons for this shift are best summarized in the FAR, which notes that simplified acquisition procedures are used to "(a) Reduce administrative costs; (b) Improve opportunities for small, small disadvantaged, women-owned, veteran-owned . . . and service-disabled veteran-owned small business concerns to obtain a fair proportion of Government contracts; (c) Promote efficiency and economy in contracting; and (d) Avoid unnecessary burdens for agencies and contractors."[25]

The most obvious case in point of a simplified acquisition procedure is the use of government credit cards for small purchases. For example, many federal agencies issue government credit cards to certain employees, who then can use the cards to make small purchases. Of course, government employees who use small-purchase credit cards must abide by strict rules and regulations. Nonetheless, they may make purchases without the substantial red tape that accompanies many larger government purchases.[26]

Summary

Each year governments in the United States combine to spend over $1 trillion on goods and services. To put this figure in perspective, consider that Wal-Mart, the number one company in the Fortune 500, currently has a market capitalization of just over $200 billion.[27] To put it briefly, governments buy a lot of stuff.

Governments buy goods and services from the same entities we do – business firms big and small. However, governments seldom buy things – especially big and expensive things – the same *way* we do. Governments typically have complex and arcane procurement procedures that are designed to ensure accountability, fairness, and quality, and to limit corruption. In relatively large procurements, the process works as follows. A legislature appropriates funds for something, then an executive agency within the government purchases it. In most cases, after money is appropriated, a government purchaser advertises or otherwise publicizes its needs, receives offers from willing vendors, and then chooses a "winner" to provide the good or service in question. From here, the government enters into a contract with the vendor that specifies what is to be sold, when and how it is to be delivered, and at what cost. Recently, governments across the country as well as the federal government have moved to "best value" source selection methods and simplified purchasing methods designed to ensure quality and streamline the procurement process.

Unfortunately, my brief overview of the procurement process is of necessity incomplete. The FAR, to which I alluded earlier, is more than 1,600 pages long, and individual federal government agencies often have rules on top of those in the FAR. Moreover, the 50 state governments and more than 80,000 local governments in the United States have their own procurement rules. In short, a full rendering of the laws and rules governing procurement in the United States would be virtually impossible (not to mention excruciatingly boring). Here, I have attempted to give you a brief and *very* general overview of government procurement, the purpose of which is to allow you to understand where lobbyists fit into the overall procurement process.

PROCUREMENT LOBBYISTS: BACKGROUND INFORMATION

The data yield two important general findings about who procurement lobbyists are and whom they represent.

Most Procurement Lobbyists Represent Business Firms

First, the data suggest that almost all procurement lobbyists represent business firms. This is not surprising given that business firms are the primary entities in this country that sell to government. All but one of the procurement lobbyists I spoke to represents business firms almost exclusively.

Do other types of organized interests utilize procurement lobbyists? For the most part, the answer is "no." While it is not unheard of for trade associations to lobby on procurement matters, the data indicate that the vast majority of procurement lobbyists represent business firms when they lobby.

Many Procurement Lobbyists Are Contract Lobbyists

If you recall, in Chapter 2 I distinguished between in-house lobbyists (who work for and are employed by the organized interests for which they work) and contract lobbyists (who work for whoever hires them). My data suggest that most procurement lobbyists are contract lobbyists who are employed by consulting, law, lobbying, or public relations firms and are hired by business firms to lobby on procurement matters. Of the 15 procurement lobbyists interviewed, 12 are contract lobbyists.[28] I cannot say on the basis of my small sample whether or not this 12:3 ratio of contract to in-house lobbyists is reflective of overall trends. But it certainly is suggestive.

The prevalence of contract lobbyists among procurement lobbyists begs the following question: Why do so many business firms hire contract lobbyists rather than utilizing their own in-house lobbyists for procurement matters? The data suggest two answers. First, many business firms hire *outside* help because they do not have *inside* help. Many small businesses, for example, do not have their own lobbyists, *period*. Thus, if they wish to sell to government, they must hire outsiders. Lobbyist no. 26, a Washington contract lobbyist, told me about the owner of a small business who approached him about trying to market a storage rack to the army: "This guy, he invented and patented a storage rack. And he thought to himself, 'Maybe the army could use this on their Humvee.' So he hired me. He didn't know where to start. That's why he hired me." This business owner had virtually no experience lobbying government and did not want to hire a full-time, in-house lobbyist to work on this single project.

Second, some business firms hire contract procurement lobbyists because their inside lobbyists do not know very much about procurement. In other words, many business firms that do have their own in-house lobbyists nonetheless hire outside procurement lobbyists because procurement lobbying is different and more complex than public policy lobbying, which is the specialty of most in-house business firm lobbyists. Lobbyist no. 33, a Washington contract lobbyist, described how one of the largest construction and engineering equipment firms in the United States – a firm with many in-house lobbyists – came to him when it first became interested in selling to the federal government. The company had its own lobbyists, he reported, but none had any expertise in government procurement. "The company," he said, saw "a possibility" of selling some of its construction vehicles to the Pentagon. The problem, according to Lobbyist no. 33, was that the company "didn't have a clue" about how to do this:

> Here's this large, well-known, reputable, tremendously respected company, [and they're thinking] "Should we or should we not get into the defense business?" But none of them [company lobbyists] do defense work. We're like geniuses compared to anything they've got.

In sum, many business firms with in-house lobbyists hire outside procurement lobbyists because their in-house lobbyists are ill-equipped to lobby on procurement matters.

Perhaps surprisingly, even business firms with their own in-house procurement lobbyists rely heavily upon outside lobbyists. Why? According to my respondents, procurement rules and regulations – like land use rules and regulations – vary from place to place (e.g., from city to city or state to state) and from government agency to government agency. As such, any time a business firm – even one with extensive procurement experience – wants to move into a new jurisdiction or sell to a new agency, it may need outside help to do so. Lobbyist no. 32, for example, who lobbies in Washington, DC, said that many companies with their own procurement lobbyists hire him when they get started in defense procurement lobbying: "Some of the larger firms I represent know that I have a great relationship [with bureaucrats at the Department of Defense] and on the Hill as well. So they leverage that. They know certain things about the little things I can do and help make happen." Lobbyist no. 13, a contract lobbyist in Chicago, said that even huge companies with their own in-house procurement lobbyists often hire him when they first enter the Chicago government market because each local government is slightly different, and no single inside lobbyist is familiar with the workings of every local government: "If it's a Bechtel [the massive global engineering and construction firm] of the world and they go into a new jurisdiction, they realize they are going to have to get local players to figure out how to work their way through the system." Lobbyist no. 15, a contract lobbyist who works in Los Angeles occasionally, told a similar story about how a very large company with offices throughout the United States and several staff lobbyists might nonetheless need a little extra help when it moves into a new government market:

> A corporate lobbyist will cover a territory...not just L.A., but also...Burbank, or Pasadena, or they could even have Northern California.... So that person would say, "Look, there's no way I can really understand the beast in L.A....and quite frankly, since I can't put in as much time, I have to find somebody else who literally is there day in and day out and knows all the ins and outs."

In sum, the data suggest that like land use rules and regulations, procurement rules and regulations are highly localized. Procurement rules and regulations are highly *particularized* as well; that is, they vary from agency to agency even within the same local, state, or national government.

Summary
The data illustrate two important general points about procurement lobbyists. First, most procurement lobbyists represent individual business firms. This is not surprising given that most vendors who sell to government are business firms. Second, many procurement lobbyists are contract lobbyists.

WHAT PROCUREMENT LOBBYISTS DO OTHER THAN LOBBYING

The rest of this chapter describes the results of my analysis of procurement lobbying, beginning with an overview of the nonlobbying activities of procurement lobbyists.

Procurement Lobbyists Help Business Firms Understand and Navigate the Procurement Process
Selling to government is not easy. In order for a business firm to sell to government, it must navigate a labyrinth of baffling rules and procedures. If you managed to read the first section of this chapter without falling asleep, you know that the process by which governments purchase goods and services is perplexing. Surely there are *some* business firms out there that thoroughly comprehend this process, right? Not really.

Getting Started in the Government Market. For firms that are entering the government market for the first time, the procurement process is nothing short of incomprehensible. Not surprisingly then, many procurement lobbyists are hired to get business firms up to speed on the procurement process so that they can get a toehold in the government market. Lobbyist no. 25, a Washington contract lobbyist, related a story that nicely illustrates how procurement lobbyists are often called upon to explain and navigate the labyrinthine system of government procurement to the firms that hire them:

> I had a client, [called] Computer Business Inc.[29] Well, they came to me about a year and a half ago and said, "We want to get into the federal space. We've been in the staffing business. We've done well. [Because of] Y2K [the feared millennium computer problem], we blew up from a $50 million company to a $200 million company....But then staffing started to go badly and it kind of went downhill after that."... That client didn't have a clue [about how to get into the federal government market], and they let me do it from nuts to bolts to everything.

Later, this lobbyist put it more succinctly when she said: "Companies pay me – small, medium, and large – [to help them understand the process]. They say, 'What do I need to do [to get government to work]?'"

Lobbyist no. 13 told me that many business firms with no previous procurement experience naively think they can quickly and easily enter the government market. It does not take these firms long to realize that the procurement business is "hyper-technical" and often requires the expertise of a seasoned procurement lobbyist. According to this lobbyist: "There are people who say, 'Oh gee, it would be nice to get some government work.' Or their revenue is down and they're looking for other sources.... But they may not have had a government contract before," and soon after they start the process they realize that they are in over their heads. Similarly, Lobbyist no. 33 said that many firms new to the procurement business know nothing about it other than that they know nothing about it. Companies like this hire procurement lobbyists because they literally do not know where to start. These companies, Lobbyist no. 33 noted, "don't know what they don't know." These neophytes "see a possibility" to sell to government, but realize only that "they cannot do it by themselves."

Even the Experienced Need Help. Although many procurement lobbyists help firms that have never sold to government get started, it would be wrong to conclude that only greenhorns hire procurement lobbyists. Several respondents told me that even companies with decades of experience selling to government often need their help. For example, Lobbyist no. 32, a Washington contract lobbyist, said that even companies with long histories of success selling to government find procurement rules and procedures "mind-boggling." Few people, he said, truly understand all aspects of the procurement process. When companies get bogged down somewhere in the process, they call Lobbyist no. 32 or others like him – seasoned professionals with expertise and time and connections.

Sometimes even firms with loads of procurement experience face obstacles to selling to government. Lobbyist no. 16, a Washington contract lobbyist, said that he is often hired by companies that are actively engaged in attempting to obtain a specific government contract and get stuck somewhere in the process: "They come to us saying, 'Look we don't think we're being treated fairly in this situation.'" One client business that had repeated dealings with a specific government agency told this lobbyist that it was tired of losing contracts to one of its competitors. The firm believed that the agency was predisposed against it. Frustrated after years of missing out on lucrative federal contracts, the firm hired Lobbyist no. 16 to help ensure that the agency gave its proposals serious consideration. The firm, he said, did not "believe that the competition [for contracts was] fair and open." He therefore worked in a number of ways (e.g., he contacted the congressional committee charged with overseeing the agency and told them he had concerns about the way the agency awarded contracts) to make sure his client got a fair shot at the agency's contracts. Frustrated companies trying to sell to government, he said, are a large part of his clientele.

Procurement Lobbyists Monitor Government

Procurement lobbyists monitor government by gathering information about what government is doing or planning to do in the future. As Lobbyist no. 13 put it:

> Knowledge is power. I get the *Wall Street Journal*, I get the *Washington Post*, and I get the *Washington Times*. Somewhere in the middle there is the truth. I go through them real fast, and it's amazing . . . the different text in the stor[ies]. Okay, so I'm up on current events. And then I'll hit the Internet and other information as well. But to stay up on top of what is important to everybody and what is going on is so doggone important . . . you've got to be knowledgeable, and when you fail that test, you're failing your customer.

It is not immediately obvious what kinds of information procurement lobbyists seek when they monitor government. After all, newspapers like the *Wall Street Journal*, the *Washington Post*, and the *New York Times* do not cover government procurement to any significant extent. So what exactly are procurement lobbyists looking for when they monitor government? First, the data suggest that procurement lobbyists want to learn about broad trends in government purchasing and spending. For example, Lobbyist no. 5 told me: "I do . . . market analysis for our company – where the trends are, where the programs are, where the future funding is going to be and what the business climate is going to be like in [specific] agencies and programs." Lobbyist no. 5, who works in Washington for a large architecture, engineering, and consulting firm, went on to explain that he valued information about the general direction of government. Are Congress and the president looking to increase defense spending? Are they looking to decrease it? Are agencies being told to tighten their belts, or to be ready for expansion? What are the government's spending priorities? These are the sorts of answers that Lobbyist no. 5 wants.

In addition to information on broad trends in government purchasing, procurement lobbyists seek information on what specific government agencies are up to. This type of information gives lobbyists an idea of what specific agencies are buying and are likely to buy in the future. To paraphrase several respondents, "only through monitoring can a lobbyist become aware of where the selling opportunities are." Lobbyist no. 31, a big-city contract lobbyist from Los Angeles, used the following hypothetical example to explain why monitoring is so crucial. Imagine, he explained, that through aggressive monitoring you learn that the local airport authority is under court order "to try to increase noise abatement in and around the airports." This development would probably not be front-page news, but, he noted, you have a client that sells "a new type of glass that's soundproof." This is the type of glass "that you want to put in [or] near the airports." From here, Lobbyist no. 31 said, he would go to the airport authority and tell them, "Install this on 10 houses and see if it works." "You give it to them," he continued, and they find out that "by God it works." All of this happens before the airport authority ever issues a solicitation for soundproof windows – at this point, they are only exploring ways to reduce noise. After a successful demonstration of the windows, the agency requests money to buy the windows, it issues a solicitation, and the window maker "get[s] the award."

Monitoring allows procurement lobbyists to react to events in the political world and to improve their clients' chances of winning government contracts. Monitoring, for example, enabled Lobbyist no. 34, who is a Washington contract lobbyist, to learn that in the aftermath of 9/11, several agencies of the federal government were going to be asked by Congress to compile data on suspected terrorists and criminals. This, he knew, would require computer software capable of compressing large amounts of data. As such, he began lobbying several federal agencies by singing the praises of his client's compression software and trying to convince agency computer users that the software was far superior to the software they were currently using. Lobbyist no. 34 went to agency officials and said:

> Hey, we know that you guys are going to have a serious need for this, and we have taken a look at the legislation that is coming down the pike, and we know that you guys are going to have demands on you that your current technology can't meet. We have a technology, out of the box, it's ready to go. You just have to apply it to your current system, and here's what our technicians tell us about our ability to mesh with the systems you already have.

Lobbyist no. 34 described what happened next:

> So we try to show them that it's not going to take them a lot of time to install. We try to show them that it has been tested in Europe [and] it already works for them.... We show them, we bring in basically a presentation, to the "tech" people, within the given agencies... and say, "Here's out PowerPoint presentation, here are our specs, so bring your people in."

Monitoring allowed this lobbyist to learn about the needs of the federal government (e.g., the need for compression software), and about specific agencies that were likely to purchase compression technology in the future. These two pieces of information were crucial to Lobbyist no. 34's lobbying campaign.

As for where procurement lobbyists look when they monitor, my respondents mentioned newspapers, magazines, specialized political publications (e.g., *Roll Call, Congressional Quarterly Weekly*), television news broadcasts, and of course people as important sources of information.

Summary

Procurement lobbyists do two main things in addition to lobbying. First, many spend substantial time helping businesses that sell to government understand and navigate the procurement process – a very complicated process. Businesses that are new to the world of government procurement are especially dependent upon the expertise of procurement lobbyists, but even experienced companies sometimes require their help. Second, procurement lobbyists monitor government to learn about broad trends in government spending and purchasing, as well as to keep abreast of the needs of specific government agencies.

LOBBYING TO AFFECT PROCUREMENT DECISIONS

Thus far I have examined who procurement lobbyists are and what they do other than lobby. In this section, I examine how procurement lobbyists attempt to affect government procurement decisions, beginning with a discussion of how and why procurement lobbyists lobby executive agencies. From there, I examine how and why procurement lobbyists lobby the legislature.

Lobbying Executive Agencies

Despite their interest in helping businesses understand the procurement process, the ultimate goal of most procurement lobbyists is to help specific business firms get government contracts. After all, the businesses that care about government procurement care about it because it affects their ability to make money – to sell their goods or services to the government at a profit.

Individual government agencies – the end users in government – are at the heart of the procurement process, especially at the federal level. In fact, *my data suggest that executive agencies are the locus of most procurement lobbying*. This is the case for two reasons. First, at all three levels of government, individual agencies play a dominant role in source selection (i.e., who gets the contract to provide a particular good or service). At the federal and state levels, for example, individual agencies almost always make final decisions regarding source selection. At the local level as well, to varying degrees depending on the jurisdiction, agency officials play a large role in determining which vendors receive government contracts. Second, at all three levels of government, individual agencies play a major role in determining what goods and services and programs the government funds. As mentioned earlier, the budget process begins with requests from executive agencies. The legislature and the chief executive, of course, do not always give agencies what they want. But they do seriously consider agency requests when they make their final budget decisions. In sum, executive agencies, though they do not make final spending decisions (legislatures and chief executives do), are the targets of a great deal of procurement lobbying because they are integral in the procurement process.

In this subsection, I examine how procurement lobbyists attempt to affect the decisions of executive branch officials, beginning by describing the ways in which procurement lobbyists lobby executive agencies to affect source selection. Next, I examine how procurement lobbyists attempt to affect what executive agencies ask for when they submit their budget requests to the chief executive.

Lobbying to Affect Source Selection 1: Preparing Effective Proposals. One of the ways that procurement lobbyists lobby to affect source selection decisions is by helping business firms prepare winning proposals in response to government solicitations (e.g., RFPs, IFBs). To recap, after an agency receives money to buy something, it must decide which vendor (seller) to buy that something from. An agency does this by issuing a solicitation (e.g., RFP, IFB), collecting proposals, and then choosing a winning vendor.[30] Not surprisingly, many procurement lobbyists help business firms write effective proposals. Lobbyist no. 15, a contract lobbyist in California, explained in some detail what he does for his clients that ask for help in responding to RFPs from city governments in his area:

> Where we get involved is in the competitive requests for proposals that have an evaluation that is, [for example], sixty percent on price and forty percent . . . on qualifications, [such as] number of years experience, the people that you are proposing to be, say, project managers. . . . So then you get into some subjective [things], not just objective or hard numbers. . . . We assist [the client] in the response process. Once they hire us we give them what our read is on this entity in which they're responding to . . . what the likes and dislikes may be. Ultimately, we want to get them to a spot where they've thought of everything, that they understand the target – the government entity as best they can. . . . My job is to prepare these documents to make them obviously as effectively as possible for [my] clients.

Lobbyist no. 15 noted that the firm from whom an agency chooses to purchase something often comes down to personalities. "Everyone [at the agency] has to assume that you can do [the job in question]," he said, and thus technical aspects of a specific proposal are generally not the determining factors in who wins and who loses. Rather, it comes down to crafting the type of proposal that the specific decision-making individuals within an agency will respond positively to. And lobbyists, especially experienced lobbyists, are the people who know what kinds of arguments appeal to what people.

What might a procurement lobbyist insert into a proposal that would improve it? Lobbyist no. 31 told me about a recent case in which he helped an out-of-town contractor craft a proposal that would be successful in Los Angeles. The client, he said, was "not from Southern California" and did not understand the city's goals concerning minority outreach in government contracting: "In L.A. you can't have mandated [minority] set-asides. So L.A. now has goals." He explained to the client "the importance of certain components of their proposal regarding minority outreach." In short, Lobbyist no. 31 told his client the rules of the game in Los Angeles, and advised the company to cover the issue of minority outreach in its proposal. He concluded by telling me: "I've seen procurements where some of the biggest corporations in America are bidding [on] technology [contracts], and at the end of day it's not about their technology, it's about which minorities are on their team."

Lobbyist no. 5, an in-house Washington lobbyist, said that he is heavily involved in crafting proposals for his company:

> There are [two] pieces basically of any presentation or any proposal. First is the experience of doing work that's similar to the project that's contemplated. Secondly and increasingly important is the team that's actually going to do the work. You don't really hire a firm. You hire a group of people who are actually going to produce the products.

He said that his expertise and experience working with specific individuals within agencies allowed him to create good proposals – proposals that appealed to the specific individuals making source selection decisions.

Many procurement lobbyists help business firms prepare "bid documents." Indeed, one of the reasons procurement lobbyists are valued is that they understand the criteria specific agencies use to evaluate proposals, and they help businesses craft proposals accordingly.

Lobbying to Affect Source Selection 2: "Talking Up the Product." Procurement lobbyists also lobby the executive branch to affect source selection by "talking up the product" they are selling. An interesting finding from the data is that much of the procurement lobbying aimed at executive branch agencies is *not* related to a specific procurement, but rather is akin to marketing and advertising, and is designed simply to draw attention to a particular good or service. Several respondents pointed out that many government agencies contract for the same goods or services over and over again. To use some mundane examples, agencies purchase copiers, computers, and office furniture repeatedly. Similarly, agencies of all kinds continually buy information technology (IT) services. Because government agencies are repeat buyers, many procurement lobbyists try to convince agencies that *their* product or service is preferable when they are in the market for a particular good or service.

What does this mean exactly? In the simplest terms it means familiarizing agency personnel with your good or service. And it means convincing agency officials that the business firm you represent is a good and effective and reliable supplier of that good or service. If a procurement lobbyist is successful at pitching his or her wares, an agency will choose the lobbyist's product when the time comes to make a purchase. Lobbyist no. 5 explained that in many cases, even before a specific solicitation has been issued, he spends time with the agency personnel involved in source selection:

> What you try to do, is you try to get to know them and get them to know you before [a solicitation comes out]. [I try] to get as much advance intelligence as possible about when contracts are likely to come out, when solicitations are likely to come out, and to meet as many of the people that are likely to be part of the selection panel, so that when they actually see your proposal and then your presentation, they know a little bit more about you than just what's on the paper or what's on the PowerPoint.

Several respondents told me that this "background lobbying" (as I call it) is especially useful now that so many procurements are negotiated and that best-quality purchasing is becoming the rule rather than the exception. According to Lobbyist no. 16, a Washington contract lobbyist, the reason companies like Halliburton and Bechtel get such huge and lucrative contracts is not necessarily that they are favored by legislators and executive branch luminaries, but rather because they have a reputation for being able to do complex things. "Within the government agencies" that award contracts for work in Iraq, for example, "these are the guys that are known," noted Lobbyist no. 16. "If you're looking for somebody to set up your information technology service in Baghdad, you're going to look to a couple of specific [firms]." The way agencies know *which* businesses to look to is through constant communication with procurement lobbyists working for such businesses. Lobbyist no. 5 said that his job is to be such a presence in the executive agencies he targets that when an agency even *thinks* of issuing a solicitation, his client's name pops into agency people's heads: "I just sort of plant the seed in their head that [my client is] a company that can do basically a certain number of things."

Sometimes background lobbying is designed to show executive agency officials that a particular supplier of a good or service not only is reliable and capable of delivering a good product but also has other qualities that make the supplier attractive. For example, Lobbyist no. 31 said that these days, many governments like to award contracts to women- and minority-owned businesses. Thus, when he was hired by a woman-owned firm to pitch the firm's conveyor belts[31] – conveyor belts the likes of which you see in virtually every airport in the country – he saw an opportunity to inform governments all over the country that he had a vendor they should think seriously about:

> Well, [I worked for] this company [that] doesn't exist anymore [it made conveyor belts]. [The owner of the company] was responding to an RFP for [a huge international airport] for conveyor belts – you know, [conveyor belts] that you see all over the airport. She'd just formed her company, created some new technology, and she bid on it. And we won with a three-to-two vote, displacing the incumbent company. [She was] the one and only [maker] of these things anywhere in the world and she didn't have any contracts, OK. This was her first. I now went around the country, I went to a number of jurisdictions and said, "You have your existing operator, but don't you *really* want to do business with a woman-owned company?" So in five years she went from zero contracts to 25 contracts. It was a real tough detail having to go to Hawaii! But I had to do it. So this is the type of thing we did. . . . What ended up [happening] with her is the other big company [that makes conveyor belts] just got tired of losing and so they bought her out for a fortune.

For several months, Lobbyist no. 31 went all over the country familiarizing airport authorities and other local governments with his client's product. Eventually, all this background lobbying paid off, as governments began to award his client contracts when they were in the market for new airport conveyor belts, many because doing so increased the diversity of their "vendor pool."

The key to this sort of background lobbying is building and maintaining personal relationships with agency officials. Lobbyist no. 12, a Washington contract lobbyist, said that agency personnel interact with procurement lobbyists constantly, because "a certain part of an agency executive's job is interacting with agency stakeholders." Lobbyist no. 32, a Washington contract lobbyist, explained:

> Over time you develop relationships with people. My job is relationships, relationships, relationships. Relationships come in handy [when] you've got. . . . an agency [that] is going to do something. The agency's job is to marry up the need with somebody that can fill that need.

This lobbyist went on to say that when they decide who to award contracts to, agencies choose people they respect and people they know are trustworthy. Lobbyist no. 25, a Washington contract lobbyist, candidly admitted that having close relationships with source selection teams or individuals helped her clients win contracts. She cultivates and nurtures these contacts, she said, because when contract award time rolls around, she wants her clients to be well positioned in the competition. She was blunt:

> If I'm [Lana Feldman[32]], for example, at [a large federal government agency]; well, Lana gets probably ten to twenty projects a year that she will have that are anywhere from small to large in size. And she's pretty much the sole decision maker over who gets these [contracts]. Well, nine times out of ten she's going to go to vendors that she knows that she trusts, right? So, what are the odds of a new guy getting in the door to even be heard when a lady like that gets about a hundred calls a week literally from all over the country saying, "Let me talk to you. Let me see you"? She doesn't return any of those calls.

While I am on the subject of background lobbying, it is important to note that such lobbying is crucial to a procurement lobbyist's success because in many cases, lobbying a source selection team *after* an agency has issued a solicitation is against the law. This, of course, does not preclude procurement lobbyists from helping businesses prepare effective bid documents. Nor does it stop procurement lobbyists from negotiating with agencies during negotiated procurements or providing a source selection team with information about a good or service if the team asks for it. But in many cases the law is very clear: After a solicitation has been issued, lobbyists are not allowed to try to persuade source selection personnel to choose one good or service over another. Thus, it is absolutely crucial for procurement lobbyists to "get their licks in" *before* an agency issues a solicitation. In a way then, the term *background lobbying* is a bit of a misnomer; there really is no such thing as "foreground" or "upfront" lobbying in the world of procurement because lobbying source selection personnel after a solicitation has been issued is off-limits. Lobbyist no. 16, a Washington contract lobbyist, said that because "lobbying government officials during a competition [for a government contract] is illegal," background lobbying is absolutely crucial to winning government contracts.

The ultimate background lobbying triumph for the procurement lobbyist is a case in which a government entity designs a solicitation with a single specific business in mind. For example, a government agency that wishes to purchase a sophisticated computer software package may write a solicitation that contains very detailed specifications – specifications that are virtually unique to one product. Or the Defense Department may write a solicitation for a piece of equipment that virtually disqualifies all but one defense contractor. According to Lobbyist no. 16, a Washington contract lobbyist:

> Helping clients pitch their products prior to the release of the [solicitation] can actually influence the scope of the [solicitation], and officials may include a specific requirement in [the solicitation] that benefits your client. For example, a lobbyist may convince [a government agency] that [it] only [wants] to purchase Vendor Y's information technology equipment because they learn from the lobbyist that [Vendor Z] – the competitor's equipment – cannot interface with [the equipment the agency currently uses]. The agency then writes into [the solicitation] that the information technology equipment must be able to interface with existing agency equipment, and therefore Vendor Z can no longer compete.[33]

How common is it for a government entity to write a solicitation with a specific business in mind? The answer, my respondents agreed, is *very common*. Indeed, several respondents implied (though did not explicitly state) that on a really big procurement, it is unusual for a government entity *not* to have a specific business or two in mind when it writes a solicitation. It is impossible to overemphasize how important "advantageous solicitations" (as I will call them) are to procurement lobbyists and the business firms they represent. Indeed, all of my procurement lobbyist respondents told me that affecting the content of a solicitation is often the key to successful procurement lobbying.

To some observers, the government practice of issuing advantageous solicitations may appear unseemly. How can this practice be defended? My respondents came up with two (admittedly self-serving) answers. First, several respondents pointed out that advantageous solicitations are often written to benefit firms with excellent track records. It is only natural, they noted, for a government agency to bring repeat business to firms that perform well. Second, advantageous solicitations are often written for products or services that government entities already have used. For example, an agency may write an advantageous solicitation for a software package after the agency has tested the product and found that it works. This, according to my respondents, is good business. All of this notwithstanding, the practice of issuing advantageous solicitations is controversial in some quarters.

Lobbying to Affect Source Selection 3: Unsolicited Proposals. When agencies issue formal solicitations for a particular good or service, the procurement lobbyists' job is to help their clients or employers get the contract to provide the good or service. However, in many cases, agencies do not issue formal solicitations, but rather publicize "broad agency needs." For example, the Department of the Navy might publicize the fact that many of its bases are polluted and that it would like to fix the problem. Similarly, a local or state agency might publicize that its computers are slow and that it would like to find a way to make them faster. In response to such needs, which are often publicized in documents called "broad agency announcements," procurement lobbyists may submit unsolicited proposals. An unsolicited proposal is defined as "a written offer submitted to" an agency "on the offeror's initiative to obtain a government contract."[34] Several of my respondents say that they submit unsolicited proposals to agencies. Lobbyist no. 25, a Washington contract lobbyist who represents a number of medium-sized business firms, often submits unsolicited proposals to agencies:

> So essentially our job is to utilize our relationships and contacts and get access for the client to show off his/her capabilities in front of [executive agency] decision makers. And if they set themselves apart and they distinguish themselves. . . . Let's say, for example, you've got a project in mind that you would like to get funded. Well what usually happens then is you submit some type of unsolicited proposal and if the powers that be like it and think it's good . . . it turns into a statement of work or an RFP which then becomes a contract of work. Now obviously, if you're the guy that's written the document, you've got a real good chance of winning it when it comes bid time. Am I right? Because you already have the jump on everybody else.

Unsolicited proposals are common, especially when agencies face new challenges and procurement lobbyists believe they can help them meet them. Lobbyist no. 25 told about the frenzy of unsolicited proposals that inundated the Department of Homeland Security shortly after it was created:

> It was chaos after 9/11. Everybody and their mother was trying to market themselves as a "Homeland Firm." . . . They all started to kind of rearrange things and say, "Oh, we've got this new software, or we've got this water treatment system in case they attack the water supply," or whatever they did. And so in that case, you had a lot of small companies, which is [*sic*] always the engine of growth in this country. I mean, there was one guy who came out with what they call, I forget what kind of train it was called, but let's say that they nuked D.C. completely and they had to try to get supplies up to what was left out into the suburbs of Virginia and Maryland. They had like this supply train that could go through nuclear stuff and whatever – rain, terrain, water – and get food and materials to

the wounded folks. So, you know [the Department of Homeland Security] and the Department of Defense . . . had a free-for-all . . . of unsolicited proposals. They probably got like 12,000 the first month.

When procurement lobbyists help business firms draw up unsolicited proposals, they do the same sorts of things they do when they help business firms draw up solicited proposals. Specifically, they give business firms advice on how to craft their proposals.

Lobbying to Affect What Executive Agencies Want and Ask For. Procurement lobbyists lobby executive agency officials in yet another way. Specifically, they often try to influence what executive agency personnel ask for when they submit their budget requests to the chief executive. In other words, procurement lobbyists often try to convince executive agency officials that they need the type of product or service the lobbyist is selling. If a procurement lobbyist can convince an agency that it needs a particular type of good or service, the agency will then request that the legislature appropriate money to buy that good or service. Not surprisingly, if a procurement lobbyist successfully convinces an agency that it needs a particular good or service, the agency will then be inclined to award the contract to the lobbyist's firm.

So how do procurement lobbyists go about convincing executive agency officials that they need to purchase a specific type of good or service? Most commonly, procurement lobbyists meet informally with agency personnel. Lobbyist no. 33, a Washington contract lobbyist who often lobbies for defense companies, said that a few years ago, a large company hired him to convince the Department of Defense that it needed a certain type of vehicle produced by the company. Through his constant monitoring, he had learned that the department was considering a replacement for one of its staple vehicles.[35] His job was to convince the officials that the type of vehicle his client's company produced was "the right one for the job," and that the department should, in its annual budget request, ask Congress to appropriate some money to buy one like it. Lobbyist no. 33 described what he did:

We [the company] brought this piece of equipment to the military. In this particular case it was a [very high ranking officer] in charge of [a specific army unit]. In most cases . . . it's much more complicated. [But in this case], he ran his own ORD [Operational Requirement Document] where he told his people, "Go out and develop a requirement [for a new vehicle]."[36] This one was one that we saw a niche [and we] pushed the piece of equipment. We had to take the vehicle . . . we gave it to them [an army unit] for almost six, seven, eight months. They evaluated it. They threw it out of planes. They slung it under helicopters. Oh yeah, they did everything that the army would do on a new piece of equipment. But they really wanted it, and they did it, you know. . . . They proved to themselves that this piece of equipment worked.

Lobbyist no. 33 reported that after testing the vehicle, the army was convinced that it needed one like it. Just as he had hoped, the army eventually asked Congress for money to buy a vehicle like the one his client manufactured.

Lobbyist no. 33 told a similar story. By monitoring the Defense Department, he learned that a number of military bases throughout the country had pollution problems caused by hazardous waste materials they were having trouble getting rid of. He also had a client who manufactured environmental cleanup technology. Here is what he did: "I went to the agency. [I said], "You've got a [need] out here . . . and here's how I can solve it for you." His goal was to convince the Defense Department that it needed the type of technology his client's firm produced. If he could do this, he told me, the department would ask for money to buy the cleanup technology in its annual budget request to Congress.

Summary. Procurement lobbyists at all three levels of government target executive agencies extensively when they lobby to affect procurement decisions. They do so by helping business firms formulate proposals, "talking up products" in informal meetings with agency officials, submitting unsolicited proposals, and trying to convince agency officials that they need certain goods and/or services.

Lobbying the Legislature

Procurement lobbyists lobby the legislature as well as the executive branch. This is not surprising given that legislatures have the power of the purse. In this section, I examine how and why procurement lobbyists lobby legislators.

Lobbying the Legislature for Appropriations. As mentioned earlier, the procurement process officially begins when the legislature appropriates money to purchase something. Thus, procurement lobbyists lobby the legislature to affect what the legislature spends money on, in other words, to affect budget decisions.

In some cases, procurement lobbyists lobby to ensure that the government funds the types of goods or services they are selling. A lobbyist for a landscaping firm, for example, might lobby a local legislature for increased spending on parks. Similarly, a lobbyist for a civil engineering firm might lobby a state legislature for increased spending on bridge repairs. Lobbyist no. 16, a Washington contract lobbyist who represents a company that sells information technology services, regularly lobbies Congress for increases in federal IT spending:

> It [all] goes back to, really, the regular budget cycle. You want your product or service or the generic account that you're going after [to be included in the budget]. For example, [one of my clients provides IT services for the] Border Patrol. You want to make sure that [the technology] initiative is funded at a level where it makes sense for you as a vendor to compete for that contract.

Lobbyist no. 5 told a similar story. He recently lobbied on behalf of his company, which hoped to get a large federal government contract to repair roads and bridges:

> One of the biggest projects [we] are working on right now is the reauthorization of the Surface Transportation Act. The real issue there is how much total money is going to be involved. And we're all pushing for the bill that the House Transportation Committee has been talking about – 375 billion dollars over six years, with an increase in the gas tax and an indexing of the fuel tax revenues.... We're looking right now to go after some of the roadways around [a Washington, DC, landmark].... So that's a separate piece of that bill.... We also do transit work and railroad work, so the elements of that bill that relate to transits and railroads, grate separation and things like that, are also of concern.

In short, Lobbyists no. 16 and no. 5 lobbied the legislature for increased funding for IT services and for highways and transportation, respectively, because they were quite confident that the companies they represented would get a piece of the pie when the money was spent.

Despite the accounts of Lobbyists no. 16 and no. 5, most procurement lobbyists do not like to waste time lobbying for appropriations unless they are certain they will get some of the action. Lobbyists for defense contractors, for example, will typically not go out of their way to lobby Congress for a huge increase in defense spending unless they are certain that their companies will get a contract to provide some of the goods and/or services funded by the spending increase. Lobbyist no. 32, for example, told me: "I am not going to waste my time lobbying for a huge defense increase unless I am absolutely sure my client is going to get some of that money." So how can procurement lobbyists be certain that companies they represent will get a piece of the pie when the legislature appropriates money? One answer is to lobby the legislature for things that agencies already buy. After a particular business firm has won a contract to provide a good or service to an agency, it is not unusual for the agency to ask for more of that good or service. Let's say an automobile manufacturer wins a contract to provide cars to an agency in Year 1. The agency may then ask the legislature for money to buy more cars in Year 2. When this happens, the automaker's procurement lobbyist will lobby the legislature heavily in support of the agency's request.

The case of Lobbyist no. 33, who convinced the army that it needed a vehicle his client produced, nicely illustrates when and why procurement lobbyists turn their attention to the legislature. He began his lobbying effort, as I mentioned earlier, by trying to convince the army that it needed the vehicle: "After the army decided it needed [the vehicle]," he told me, "it requested some money to buy some of them. We lobbied Congress hard to make sure they provided the money to buy them." Congress initially provided a small amount of money to the army, which then issued a solicitation for the vehicle. Not surprisingly, Lobbyist no. 33's client won the contract to sell the vehicle to the army, which was so happy with the performance of the vehicle that in several subsequent years, it asked Congress to fund the purchase of more and more of them. Every time the army made a budget request to Congress, Lobbyist no. 33 lobbied hard in support of the request: "In year one, we were modestly successful. [In] year two we started to get a little more successful. And if you fast-forward to where we are now, we . . . got money for one thousand." This lobbyist continues to lobby the army, telling army personnel that the vehicle is performing well in Afghanistan and Iraq and that they should consider asking for more in their annual budget requests. However, now that his client has a contract to provide the vehicle, he focuses primarily upon Congress, trying to convince legislators that the army needs money to buy more vehicles.

This kind of lobbying – in which procurement lobbyists lobby the legislature to buy more of something that their clients already have a contract to provide to an agency – is especially prevalent among defense company lobbyists. The data suggest that lobbyists for large defense contractors spend more time lobbying the legislature than lobbyists for most other types of companies because, as Lobbyist no. 34 explained, "Congress . . . is much more involved, especially when it comes to large [defense] contracts." It is not unusual, for example, for a defense contractor who has won a contract to provide a ship or an airplane to the Defense Department to ask Congress to buy more of them.

Although several respondents told me that they seldom lobby the legislature for money to buy things that agencies do not want or have not asked for, the practice is not unheard of. For example, the legislature sometimes appropriates money for very specific projects that are not included in the initial (e.g., chief executive's) budget. Generally, these "earmarked" funds are not earmarked for a specific vendor, but they are allotted for a specific project that will almost certainly go to a specific vendor. According to my respondents, at the federal level these earmarked funds are especially prevalent in the Departments of Defense and Homeland Security. Lobbyist no. 25, a Washington contract lobbyist, told me:

> [As] far as the Congress goes, there's a whole "nother" process. . . . Let's say I am in a district in Indiana and my Congressman is, we'll just say Dan Burton, for example. . . . [He's my] Congressman [and] I'm a big company or big employer or small business even. I go to that member of Congress and say, "Look I've got a unique technology. I've got something here, but I need it funded." Well, members have a lot of prerogative and privileges particularly if they've been around for a while and if they're senior members of committees, chairmen, etc. They can do what's called a CA – that's a congressional "add" or an appropriations "add" which is kind of like a rider that's attached to a bill that says, "You know, ABC Corporation gets two million dollars for the next four years, and it's attached to this farm bill here to study the way that frogs fly through the mud and how that impacts the agriculture of America."

Lobbyist no. 13, who works primarily on local procurement matters but nonetheless has some experience with the Illinois state legislature, told a similar story about legislative earmarks in his state:

> Some legislators have blocks of money for different projects. It's what they call legislative initiatives. There's a part of the budget that the legislature – it's their play money, their pot of gold – they can designate to particular projects within their districts. If a state legislature has that kind of arrangement then people will lobby the powerful leadership in the state legislature to have money granted for their particular organization . . . or their particular community.

Lobbying the Local Legislature for Source Selection. At the state and federal levels of government, the legislature is not typically involved in source selection. In other words, state legislatures and Congress typically appropriate money for certain goods and services but are seldom involved in choosing specific contractors to provide these goods and services. At the state and national levels these source selection decisions are left to executive agencies. However, at the local level, legislatures are heavily involved in source selection. Therefore, local procurement lobbyists lobby the legislature not just for appropriations but also to affect source selection. Lobbyist no. 15, a contract lobbyist in California who works at both the state and local levels, summed up the rules that govern source selection in one of the cities he works in:

> [The city] charter states that . . . if a [contract is] over one million dollars, I believe, or over a three-year time period . . . it must get council and mayor approval. So in other words, you can buy your papers and pencils and other machinery you need on a daily basis [and] we won't micromanage you. But anything above that, we're going to [be involved].

Most local governments have similar rules – rules stating that large contracts must be awarded by the legislature.

In most local jurisdictions, the legislature holds a simple majority vote on source selection, usually after a source selection team from the agency purchasing the good or service has made a recommendation. Because legislators are intimately involved in source selection at the local level, they attract a great deal of attention from local procurement lobbyists. Lobbyist no. 28, a contract lobbyist in Los Angeles, related his experience lobbying for a company that wished to sell rail cars to the local transportation authority:

> The transportation authority [was] procuring rail cars. And there was no prequalified list. So an RFQ [request for qualifications] was sent out, and they may have limited the list to five or eight companies. Then they put out the RFP, with specifics as to dollars and cents. And there was a tremendous amount of lobbying to get qualified and then to have your bid accepted. There was a tremendous amount of lobbying going on. You are trying to convince the decision makers – and for large procurements, it's the legislative body that makes the decision. They will get a recommendation from staff. Basically, you are going to those people and those decision makers and telling them, "My client has a much better product [than the other company]." [And if the staff suggests to them the other company, I say], "The staff is wrong. The cost of [our] vehicles may be more up front, but if you look on the operational side it's pennies on the dollar compared to this other product. The history is much more well established . . . reliability, and all these other things." So you're like a car salesman trying to sell somebody a car.

Lobbyist no. 15 concurred with Lobbyist no. 28, and said that on most of the large local government procurements for which he lobbies, he focuses on legislators: "[I'll lobby] the City Council.... You know, [I'll] do the committee level, which is three out of the fifteen members ... and then ... the full council." In many cases, local procurement lobbyists lobby legislators at the same time they lobby executive agency officials. Lobbyist no. 15, for example, said that recently he had helped a client who wanted to win a contract to repair a large sewer plant:

> [Let me give you] a classic example – [the] Public Works [Department] – because they do the most. You know, we have a big sewer plant, Hyperion. I mean that's where all the you-know-what flows, and it's a big city! The roads constantly need fixing, and they always need equipment. So our Public Works [Department] is made up of seven bureaus or nine bureaus; the Bureau of Street Services, Street Lighting, Sanitation, those sorts of things. The client will have been working at that level to hear about the opportunities [for contracts], because that's what they do, so they're going to gravitate to that level of the government – the staff level. Then in L.A ... we have commissioners [on the Board of Public Works]. They're appointed by the mayor's office and confirmed by the city council. They will oversee [projects] and have the general managers of the various bureaus report to them. So at one point, we'll be lobbying those commissioners on behalf of [our client]. Then the commission [makes a recommendation that] would go to a committee of council members ... a public works committee which typically sees all the public works items. [Then a large contract] must get council and mayor approval. [So in the end] I'll be knocking on different doors, different levels, various levels, depending on where [I am] in the process.

Lobbying the Legislature to Oversee Executive Branch Actions. While procurement lobbyists often lobby legislators to affect appropriations, they also occasionally lobby to get them to exercise legislative oversight of executive branch agencies. *Legislative oversight* is defined broadly as *the process by which the legislature reviews and studies and monitors the performance of executive agencies.* Procurement lobbyists see legislative oversight as an important way to ensure that the business firms they represent get a fair shake in the procurement process. If they believe that a business firm they represent is getting treated unfairly (especially during the source selection process), they may ask the legislature to intervene on their behalf. Lobbyist no. 16, a Washington contract lobbyist, reported that a large part of his job is lobbying Congress to exercise its oversight duties to ensure that his clients were getting treated fairly by executive agencies:

> There are situations where there is not a level business playing field within the agencies. There may be a potential bias against a company that comes into play. For example, we had a client [and] there was an incumbent contractor that had held onto a contract for many years. [The client felt that] there was certainly, clearly, a bias toward retaining the incumbent contractor, and it essentially required political, I guess I would say, over-sight to ensure that our client had the opportunity to compete for that contract despite the agency's position on the procurement.

He said that he never wants to go over the head of an agency's procurement personnel. However, sometimes doing so is necessary. The goal here is to convince the agency that it must do a better job of ensuring equal treatment for all potential vendors. And there is no better way to convince career bureaucrats to reconsider some of their actions than to apply congressional pressure. Lobbyist no. 16 put it tactfully but force-fully: "You know, you raise a level of interest or level of concern at the programmatic level when they believe that there is going to be additional oversight . . . from Congress as to the actions of that particular division or department." Ultimately, he hoped to "open the minds" of the bureaucrats at the agency in question so they would consider his client's proposals more seriously in the future.

Lobbyist no. 5 said that though convincing Congress to exercise more oversight of agency purchasing was not a large part of his job, he did do it occasionally:

> [Congressional committees] do oversight sometimes if there's some kind of question about whether or not [a specific procurement] was prop-erly done. There are oversight hearings, or the GAO gets involved. The GAO [Government Accountability Office] is an arm of Congress that does studies all the time. [They might] ask: What happened? Where'd the money go? [Was] the law . . . followed? Were the fiscal and other kinds of accounting controls implemented?

Lobbyist no. 12, a Washington contract lobbyist, told a similar story about a recent experience he had had with a large federal government agency:

> I had information that [the agency] had a bias. The process was stacked [in favor of a certain contractor]. The agency had an agenda. And it always chose [a specific contractor]. So on behalf of [a competitor], I collected information. I collected data on their performance. And then I

took it to the Hill. I told [some members with oversight of the agency] that awarding these contracts the way the agency did was a huge mistake. I say, "Hey, you need to look what's going on." I won. I got the chairman of the committee to write a letter to the agency to force them to tell him what was going on.

Lobbyists no. 16, no. 5, and no. 12, all of whom who work in Washington, agreed that sometimes it is necessary to get Congress involved simply to ensure that a client gets a fair shake when it competes for contracts. The line between lobbying for legislative oversight of agency purchasing and lobbying an agency to purchase a specific good or service is not as clear in local government as it is at the federal level. This is the case because as mentioned, most specific large local government procurements must be approved by the legislature. States have varying levels of legislative involvement in large procurements, and at this point, my data do not allow me to reach any one-size-fits-all conclusions about state legislative oversight of agency purchasing.

Sometimes disputes go beyond legislatures and find their way into court. Lobbyist no. 13, a contract lobbyist in Chicago who works on a lot of contract disputes, said that he sometimes has to resort to lawsuits:

Let's say [that in] the city of Chicago, or Cook County, or the state of Illinois, [a client] feels that the bidding process or the RFP process or RFQ process has not been followed, and they are looking for help. I represent them before the agency, [or] sometimes we sue the agency. Sometimes we will file suit against either the agency or the municipality. A typical dispute may be a change order dispute, or what they call "extras" – a contractor has been told to do something outside the contract, and told they were going to be paid for those extras, and then of course they don't get paid. So oftentimes a contractor will have a dispute with a municipality, governmental agency, or the state, and they'll call me to interface with the procurement people and oftentimes their attorneys to try to resolve the matter.

Summary

The ultimate goal of procurement lobbyists is to get the government to purchase whatever they sell. Despite the fact that the legislature (in combination with the chief executive) has the power of the purse, procurement lobbyists spend considerable time lobbying the executive branch – executive agencies in particular. In fact, the data suggest that executive agencies attract as much (if not more) lobbying attention as the legislature. Procurement lobbyists lobby the executive branch by helping business firms prepare effective proposals, talking up a particular good or service, submitting unsolicited proposals, and trying to influence what agencies ask for. Procurement lobbyists also lobby the legislature. They do so to try to affect what the legislature appropriates money for and to convince legislators to oversee agency actions.

WHAT DOES PROCUREMENT LOBBYING LOOK LIKE?

Drawing upon the data I presented in the previous sections, I ask: *What does procurement lobbying look like?* As with the questions at the ends of Chapters 4 and 5 about public policy lobbying and land use lobbying, the answer requires a series of other questions.

Where Does Procurement Lobbying Take Place?

While land use lobbying is conducted almost exclusively at the local level of government, procurement lobbying, like public policy lobbying, takes place at all three levels of government. Governments and government agencies of all kinds, regardless of what they do or where they do it, must procure goods and services. Wherever governments and government agencies procure goods and services, lobbyists are working to influence purchasing decisions.

Who Lobbies?

My data suggest that most procurement lobbying is done by lobbyists representing business firms. All of my sample procurement lobbyists spend the bulk of their time representing business firms that sell things to government. Some procurement lobbyists are in-house lobbyists who are employed by business firms that sell to government. Others are in-house lobbyists who are employed by trade associations that consist of firms that sell to government. But the data suggest that many (perhaps most) procurement lobbyists are contract lobbyists who work for public relations, consulting, law, or lobbying firms, and are retained by businesses that sell (or want to sell) to government. Unfortunately, it is difficult to generalize about what types of firms sell to government (and thus retain procurement lobbyists) because governments in the United States purchase so many different things. Among the firms represented by sample lobbyists are manufacturers of chemical decontamination equipment, information technology, laser guidance components, military transport vehicles, recycling bins, and trash receptacles; and firms that offer architecture, engineering, and landscape design services. Procurement lobbyists represent a vast array of business firms that sell to government. The other types of organized interests mentioned in Chapter 2 – trade associations, professional associations, citizen groups, labor unions, governmental entities, think tanks, charities, universities and colleges, coalitions, hospitals, and churches – are only sporadically involved in procurement lobbying, if they are involved at all.

What accounts for the dominance of business lobbyists in procurement politics? The answer is simple: Business firms are the primary entities in the United States that provide (i.e., sell) goods and services. While they are not the only entities in this country that provide goods and services (charities, for example, provide a wide variety of services for people in need), they are the most plentiful. As such, when governments seek to purchase goods or services, they rely primarily upon business firms.

What Nonlobbying Activities Do Procurement Lobbyists Engage In?

Procurement lobbyists spend substantial time on nonlobbying activities. First, the data show that procurement lobbyists take time to explain the procurement process to their clients. As the opening section of this chapter attests, procurement regulations and rules are complex and difficult to understand. Companies that are new to the "government market" often understand very little about how to get started. Moreover, even companies with vast experience selling to government often need help understanding mind-boggling rules and procedures, especially since these rules vary from place to place and agency to agency, and change from time to time. In short, even experienced companies occasionally need the help of a seasoned procurement lobbyist to help them get up to speed on new rules and regulations. Second, the data show that procurement lobbyists continually monitor government. They do so to detect broad trends in the direction of government and to learn about the specific needs and proclivities of individual government agencies.

Whom Do Procurement Lobbyists Target?

To repeat, government purchasing begins with a grant of money from the legislature. It is perhaps a bit surprising then that procurement lobbyists target executive agency officials (i.e., bureaucrats) extensively. My data suggest that at all three levels of government (and especially the federal level), executive agency officials receive as much (if not more) attention from procurement lobbyists as legislators do. Moreover, it is not just the higher-ups in agencies that receive lobbyist attention. Lower-level bureaucrats also receive just as much attention from procurement lobbyists.

The Bureaucracy. Why do procurement lobbyists target executive agency personnel to such a large extent? The data suggest two main answers. First, bureaucrats have considerable discretion in determining which firms win government contracts. In other words, bureaucrats are prominent players in source selection. At the federal level (and in some cases at the state and local levels as well), after money has been appropriated or pledged and a solicitation has been issued and proposals have been received, an agency puts together a source selection team that consists of bureaucrats from within (and occasionally from outside) the agency. In many cases, these bureaucrats have final say about the company that gets the contract. As such, they are very powerful. Often, lobbyists are banned from lobbying source selection teams while they are actively considering proposals. However, as the data make clear, procurement lobbying does take place before a specific solicitation has been issued. Procurement lobbyists hope that their constant wooing of bureaucrats pays off when source selection time rolls around.

Second, procurement lobbyists lobby executive agency personnel because they are often the driving forces behind new government purchases. Time and again, my respondents told me that the impetus for government purchases of goods and services often comes from within government agencies. To put it briefly, the budget process begins with agency requests for funds – funds for certain types of goods and services. In essence, this means that every year, bureaucrats make "wish lists" that they submit to the chief executive (or whoever formulates the initial budget) and are then passed on to the legislature. Procurement lobbyists know that executive agencies play an integral role in the budget process, and they try hard to affect what bureaucrats and their agencies put on their wish lists. Several respondents said, in fact, that the key to winning a government contract is to get a client's product on one of these wish lists because they often lead to appropriations, then solicitations, and then purchases.

Nowhere are these lists more obvious and important than in the area of defense procurement. Lobbyists no. 32 and no. 33, both of whom lobby on defense procurement, said that all the armed services have what are called "unfunded requirements," which essentially are things that the armed

forces want that they most likely will not get immediately. According to
Lobbyist no. 33, who represents several defense companies:

> [Every year], the service chiefs, by direction of Congress, are required to
> put an "unfunded requirements" list together. In other words, [Congress
> says to the service chiefs], "If there was unlimited money here, Mr. Chief
> of the Army, what other types of equipment and things would you need?"

The key to getting a defense contract, Lobbyist no. 33 said, is getting a
client's product on someone's unfunded requirement list. Congress often
looks at this list to determine which new programs it will fund. Not all
agencies have such lists. But many, at all three levels of government, have
something approximating them.

All of this leads to the following question: How do lobbyists get their
clients' products on an agency's "wish list"? The key, according to my
respondents, is convincing agency personnel that they need a certain product to do their jobs. Essentially, it comes down to learning about what agencies do and trying to introduce them to products and services that can help
them do their jobs better. It is important to remember, as many respondents pointed out, that agencies are virtually always open to unsolicited
proposals, some of which turn into RFPs and then contracts for work.

Other Targets. In sum, executive agency personnel are prime targets for
procurement lobbyists at all levels of government. This does not mean,
however, that procurement lobbyists ignore legislators. The data suggest
that at all three levels of government, they lobby legislators to appropriate
money for programs and projects. As I have pointed out, procurement
lobbyists often lobby legislators to ensure that the goods or services they
sell are supported in the budget. This sort of lobbying is especially common
in national defense and homeland security, where the money involved is
substantial. In addition, procurement lobbyists ask the legislature for earmarked funds that are reserved for specific companies and projects. Many
federal procurement lobbyists also lobby legislators to increase agency
oversight. The data suggest that agency oversight is an indirect way for
procurement lobbyists to help clients sell their products to government.
Finally, at the local level, legislators loom even larger in the procurement
process because they must approve large purchases. Not surprisingly then,
the data suggest that legislators are targeted heavily by local procurement
lobbyists.

Before leaving the subject of the targets of procurement lobbyists, it
is worth mentioning that two targets are more or less ignored by these

lobbyists. First, there is the public. The public, my respondents told me, is simply not involved (or interested) in procurement decisions, and as such does not attract much lobbying attention. Second, my data indicate that chief executives also receive little attention from procurement lobbyists.

Which Techniques Do Procurement Lobbyists Use Most?

The data suggest that for procurement lobbyists at all three levels of government, the most common lobbying techniques are meeting personally with executive agency personnel and meeting personally with legislators and/or their aides. In addition, at all three levels, procurement lobbyists often make oral presentations before agency committees. At the local level, they on occasion make oral presentations before legislative committees (or the entire legislature). These oral presentations – which are part of the source selection process used by many agencies and some local legislative bodies – are akin to congressional and agency testimony, and are basically "sales pitches" in which procurement lobbyists and/or their clients try to convince source selection teams to buy their products or services.

The Rare Techniques. If you take a look back at Table 2 (in Chapter 2), you will notice that entire categories of techniques are more or less eschewed by procurement lobbyists. Specifically, procurement lobbyists do not rely upon direct democratic techniques, electoral techniques, or grassroots lobbying techniques to any extent. And only one of my sample procurement lobbyists mentioned lobbying the judiciary. Moreover, even within the two categories of techniques mentioned often by respondents – executive branch and legislative branch techniques – the number of techniques that respondents mentioned is severely limited. Why do procurement lobbyists use so few techniques? The data suggest that many are simply not relevant to the procurement process. For example, grassroots lobbying techniques are seen as mostly irrelevant by most procurement lobbyists because the public plays a limited role in government procurement.[37] About the only scenario under which these lobbyists consider engaging the public is when the government considers increasing or decreasing appropriations substantially, potentially affecting their ability to sell to government. Defense procurement lobbyists, for instance, might use grassroots techniques when major increases or decreases in defense spending are under consideration by Congress. Direct democratic techniques are also irrelevant because initiatives and referenda seldom concern government purchasing. Finally, procurement lobbyists generally eschew electoral techniques because many of the most important decision makers in the procurement decision-making process are bureaucrats, and they do not run for election.

In all, the data suggest that procurement lobbyists rely primarily upon a small array of lobbying techniques. Specifically, they rely heavily upon meeting personally with bureaucrats and legislators. Perhaps this is not surprising. Procurement lobbying has more than a little in common with private sector sales, and sales is a "people business." And like sales and marketing people in other industries, procurement lobbyists rely largely upon face-to-face meetings with buyers when they lobby.

Which Techniques Are Most Effective?
Because the repertoire of procurement lobbyists is so limited, answering this question is not particularly difficult. The data show that meeting personally with legislators and meeting personally with agency personnel are the most effective procurement lobbying techniques.

Meeting personally with government officials and their aides is effective for three reasons in particular. First, whether the officials are bureaucrats or legislators (especially at the local level), a personal meeting is the only way to demonstrate that a client's product or service actually works. Several respondents told me that they often set up meetings in which their clients demonstrate products, just as salespeople do in the real world. Lobbyist no. 31, for example, set up meetings with local bureaucrats and legislators to demonstrate how well a client's luggage cart worked, compared to the cart that was currently being used by the local airport authority. He described a comical scene in which he piled 10 pieces of luggage on the competitor's cart and 10 pieces of luggage on his client's cart and demonstrated both products. "They had a ... cart that you pulled instead of pushed," he said, "so when the baggage fell off the cart, you didn't even know it was off the cart." When he demonstrated his client's cart, he was able to show local government officials that "it [the luggage] was always in front of you." Lobbyist no. 33, the defense lobbyist cited earlier, set up meetings with army personnel to demonstrate how versatile and useful his client's vehicle was. Stories like these are not unusual. Procurement lobbyists regularly set up meetings with bureaucrats (and in localities, legislators) to demonstrate their products.[38] While brochures, product flyers, and telephone conversations can familiarize government officials with a product or service, only personal meetings allow procurement lobbyists and/or their clients to *demonstrate* them in action.

Meeting personally with government officials is also effective because government officials like it. Lobbyist no. 34 pointed out that government officials – especially bureaucrats – like to meet with procurement lobbyists because doing so "makes them feel important." Bureaucrats, as any observer of American politics knows, are often assailed for their laziness, ineptitude, and truculence. The data suggest that because bureaucrats are generally vilified, many welcome the wooing they receive from procurement lobbyists. Not surprisingly, it appears that these bureaucrats remember their suitors when it comes time either to write a solicitation or to choose a vendor for a particular good or service.

Finally, meeting personally with government officials is effective because it allows procurement lobbyists to "connect" with government officials and build or maintain personal relationships with them. Without putting it in such bald terms, my respondents implied that government agencies are more likely to buy products from people they like than from people they either do not know or do not like. As Lobbyist no. 15 put it: "I think elected officials or general managers who make these sort of decisions . . . they like to know the people they are working with." In many cases, the products or services pitched by procurement lobbyists are not that different from other products or services. Given the choice between buying a product or service from a company represented by an unknown and buying a similar product or service from a company represented by a well-known and well-liked procurement lobbyist, government officials will often go with the latter. As Lobbyist no. 32 noted, procurement lobbying often comes down to "relationships, relationships, relationships."

On the whole, the data suggest that personal meetings are the most efficient and most effective way for procurement lobbyists to deliver information to government decision makers. Personal meetings are so effective and so prevalent, in fact, that procurement lobbyists tend to eschew most other lobbying techniques.

Which Types of Information Do Procurement Lobbyists Provide?

In Chapter 2 I noted that lobbyists provide three types of information to government officials (and/or the public) when they lobby: political information, career-relevant information, and policy-analytic information. This threefold classification is not particularly useful for understanding procurement lobbying because the data show that the most important type of information procurement lobbyists provide government decision makers is what I call *product information*. However, policy-analytic information and career-relevant information do have their uses.

Product Information. Product information, as the name implies, is simply information about the specific product or service the procurement lobbyist is selling. Two types of product information are particularly important, according to my respondents. First, there is price. They reminded me repeatedly that while procurement rules in most places do not require government purchasers to award contracts to the lowest bidder, price is always an important consideration. Second, there is performance. Government buyers want information about how well a product or service is likely to perform. One indicator of future performance, a number of respondents indicated, is past performance. Thus, one way they demonstrate the effectiveness of the things they sell is by referring to past successes. For example, Lobbyist no. 34 said that when he tried to convince several federal agencies that they needed his client's software, he told them that "[the government] of Ireland uses this... technology. It already works for them. The Irish government has had good luck with this firm." Another way to provide performance information is through oral presentations and product or service demonstrations about the product or service the lobbyist is selling – which are often part of the formal procurement process. These presentations may entail slide shows, actual "hands-on" demonstrations (as in the case with the luggage carts demonstrated by Lobbyist no. 31), or data on the usefulness of the product or service in question. The specific nature of the product information depends upon the type of product or service in question, as when Lobbyist no. 33 demonstrated his army vehicle's versatility by having it tossed out of planes.

Policy-Analytic Information. In addition to product information, the data indicate that many procurement lobbyists provide policy-analytic information to government officials, although it is often information about the firm that sells a product or service, rather than about the product or service itself. If you recall, policy-analytic information was defined in Chapter 2 as information about "the likely economic, social, or environmental consequences" of a particular course of action.[39] I was surprised to learn that procurement lobbyists often tout the desirable qualities of *their clients* when they sell products and services to the government. In a perceptive article on government procurement in the United States, political scientist Khi V. Thai has noted that throughout the country, government procurement is "utilized as an important tool for achieving economic, social and other objectives."[40] The federal government, for example, uses procurement to advance women's business ownership, minority business ownership, and small business success. Currently, for instance, the federal government requires the adoption of yearly government-wide contract-award goals (in 2003, for example, the goals aimed to award "23 percent of prime contracts [to] small businesses," "5 percent of prime and subcontracts . . . [to] woman-owned businesses," and "3 percent of prime and subcontracts . . . [to] service-disabled veteran-owned small businesses.")[41] Federal government buyers also must abide by a law called the Buy American Act of 1933 (still in effect) that requires federal agencies to buy American-made goods whenever possible.[42] Many state and local governments have similar rules on minority outreach and American-made goods and services. Because governments have policies designed to serve certain economic and social goals, procurement lobbyists often emphasize the economic and social aspects of the clients they represent. Numerous respondents told me that they talk up the unique qualifications of their clients when they lobby, as Lobbyist no. 31 did when he parlayed the fact that one of his clients was a woman-owned business into several government contracts. Similarly, Lobbyist no. 25 said that she often works with small businesses, and that a business's status as small is helpful in winning government contracts.

Some procurement lobbyists provide more straightforward policy-analytic information about how the product or service they are pushing will be good for the economy, society, or the environment. For example, defense lobbyists often tout the economic (not to mention national security) advantages of funding large and expensive defense programs. A lobbyist for Boeing, for example, will tell a member of Congress that building 10 more airplanes is good for the economy (and national security). Similarly, lobbyists for all sorts of products will tout the societal benefits of their products. They often do so by referring to vague goals, such as "environmental protection" or "national security" or "efficient government." In many cases, product information overlaps with policy-analytic information, as procurement lobbyists use product information to tout the societal benefits of their products or services. Lobbyist no. 24 said that his organization (which represents firms that manufacture building materials) works hard to convince government buyers that his firms' building materials are not only as good as but also more energy efficient than other types of building materials.

Career-Relevant Information. Finally, the data suggest that procurement lobbyists provide career-relevant information to government officials – that is, information about the implications of particular courses of action for officials' job prospects. What kind of career-relevant information do procurement lobbyists provide? First, they provide legislators (who are important for procurement decisions at the local level and for large ticket items at the state and federal levels) with basic information about how support for the purchase of a certain good or service might serve the legislator well during election time. This information is usually general in nature. For example, a defense lobbyist who asks a member of Congress to support a bill that would provide money to build new tanks for the army will tell the legislator that the public is worried about national security, and that a "yes" vote will appeal to these voters. Similarly, at the local or state level, a procurement lobbyist may tell a legislator that supporting the purchase of a new computer system for government agencies will increase government efficiency and reduce the need for new taxes.

Second, procurement lobbyists provide bureaucrats with information, that to paraphrase Lobbyist no. 34, "makes them look good." As I have pointed out repeatedly, procurement lobbying often starts with a visit to an agency during which the lobbyist tries to convince agency officials that they need a particular good or service. To paraphrase this lobbyist further, procurement lobbyists often appeal to bureaucrats' career ambitions by telling them that if they bring an exciting new technology or product or service to their bosses, they will "look good," which may eventually lead to a promotion.

In sum, the data suggest that procurement lobbyists provide two kinds of information mentioned in Chapter 2 – policy-analytic information, and career-relevant information. More important, however, is product information – a type of information that is unique to procurement lobbying.

What Determines Whether or Not Procurement Lobbyists Win?

Before answering this question, it is important to specify what "winning" is in the context of procurement lobbying. For the procurement lobbyist, winning is getting a government contract. So in that context, the question can be restated as follows: What determines whether or not procurement lobbyists are successful in winning government contracts for their clients? I should caution that this question is not an easy one to answer. The number of factors that enter into the decision to award a government contract to one firm rather than another is staggering. Moreover, because I spoke to the lobbyists who try to affect procurement decisions, rather than to the people who actually make government procurement decisions (i.e., government officials), I cannot reach definitive conclusions about why some procurement lobbyists are successful and others are not. Nonetheless, the data provide us with clues about variables that affect a procurement lobbyist's chances of winning.

Connections. First, the data suggest that one important determinant of a procurement lobbyist's success is *the extent of his or her connections*. Connections – that is, relationships with government officials – were cited by all of my procurement lobbyists as absolutely essential to winning government contracts. Why are they so important? It is not, the data suggest, simply that government officials who make procurement decisions like to award contracts to people they know (though this does appear to be the case). Rather, the data suggest that connections give procurement lobbyists access to the very government officials who make procurement decisions. Access enables them to meet personally with government officials; and as we learned earlier, meeting personally with government officials is the most effective lobbying technique in the procurement lobbyist's repertoire. As I tried to make clear in the previous section of this chapter, procurement lobbyists do much of their work before the government ever issues a solicitation for a specific good or service. In other words, procurement lobbyists "plant seeds" in government agencies that they hope will blossom into government contracts. The ability to plant seeds – to meet with government officials and convince them that they need a certain good and/or service, or that the specific brand of good or service a lobbyist is pushing is the best brand – is dependent on the ability to get a foot in the door. And lobbyists with connections have that ability. In short, connections with government officials are crucial to a lobbyist's ability to get meetings with government officials, and meetings are crucial to a lobbyist's ability to win government contracts.

The value of connections may lead you to wonder how procurement lobbyists develop connections with government officials. For many, the answer is that they don't. The data suggest that many procurement lobbyists come to the procurement lobbying profession from government. In other words, they show up with ready-made connections. Nine of the procurement lobbyists I spoke to spontaneously mentioned that they had worked in government before they came to the lobbying profession. Perhaps even more telling, the two lobbyists who lobby primarily on defense procurement – Lobbyists no. 32 and no. 33 – had impressive government careers before entering the lobbying profession: the first held the rank of general in one of the armed forces, and the second served as a legislative liaison for the secretary of one of the armed forces and then as chief aide for a senior member of Congress. While the literature on lobbying suggests (see the notes for Chapter 2) that most lobbyists have government experience, my data suggest that government experience is more useful for the procurement lobbyist than for either the land use or public policy lobbyist.

Connections lead to personal meetings, which are crucial to procurement lobbying success.

The Product. Even an ex-general cannot sell the U.S. Army a Hyundai Accent when it is looking for a new battle tank. So while connections are important, they are not the only determinants of a procurement lobbyist's success. The data suggest that another determinant is *the nature of the product he or she is trying to sell*. In other words, some products are easier to sell to government than others. Two types of products in particular are relatively easy to sell to government. First, there are products and services that governments use every day – things like paper, computer software, and engineering services. Because governments buy them on a regular basis, they are easier to sell to government than, say, golf clubs, Gucci handbags, or Rolex watches. This is a simple point, but it bears mentioning. Second, certain hugely expensive and complex products or services are provided by only one or a small handful of companies. Several respondents told me that for behemoth businesses like Halliburton (which has contracts in Iraq to, among other things, fight oil well fires and provide food and housing for U.S. troops) and Bechtel (which has contracts in Iraq to rebuild power plants, electrical grids, and sewage facilities), it was not so much lobbying that won them lucrative contracts but, rather, the fact that they were two of the only business firms on the planet with the capacity to do the work the federal government wanted. Similarly, while defense contractors, such as Lockheed Martin and Boeing, lobby extensively, their ability to secure government contracts is significantly enhanced by the fact that they have very few competitors.

Track Record. Another determinant of success is *the track record of the service or product the lobbyist is trying to sell*. Several respondents said that an "incumbent business firm" – that is, a business firm that already has a government contract to provide a specific good or service – has a higher chance of success than a neophyte. The data suggest that if government buyers are reasonably happy with a particular firm's good or service, they are hesitant to try a competing firm's good or service. Moreover, for some goods and services – again, think expensive defense purchases – the legislature can order more after a firm wins an initial contract to provide a certain quantity. Therefore, in some cases, winning the initial contract to provide a good or service can substantially increase the probability of getting further business.

Knowledge. Another determinant of a procurement lobbyist's success is his or her *knowledge of the procurement process.* On the whole, knowledgeable procurement lobbyists tend to win more than the less knowledgeable do. The procurement process, as I have pointed out repeatedly, is arcane and complex. Knowing the ins and outs of the process is crucial to a procurement lobbyist's success. In fact, procurement lobbyists have virtually no chance of success if they do not thoroughly understand the process. Completing paperwork incorrectly, not knowing where to look for contract opportunities, and not understanding what types of information to put in proposals (among other things), can all seal a procurement lobbyist's fate. In addition, as simplified acquisition procedures have become more common, receiving a government contract is requiring a thorough knowledge of the process by which a seller becomes eligible to get government contracts. In short, procurement lobbying is a specialty where the generalist (that is, a lobbyist who works on a variety of things) is at a decided disadvantage.

Attaching Solutions to Problems. A final important determinant of success for the procurement lobbyist is *the ability to convince government buyers that a product or service can help solve a problem.* One of the most striking things about my data is that they reveal a system of government buying in which "push-selling" is prevalent. In other words, selling to government entails more than simply responding to government solicitations and working hard to garner contracts. It also entails trying to convince government buyers that they need certain goods or services.

My respondents told me repeatedly that push-selling often begins within government agencies. The process works something like this. First, a procurement lobbyist uses connections to learn as much as possible about a particular government agency (or several agencies). Specifically, the lobbyist is on the lookout for problems and difficulties within the agency. Lobbyist no. 33, for example, learned from his numerous contacts in the U.S. Army that a certain vehicle was rapidly falling into disfavor among operational personnel. Second, the procurement lobbyist offers agency personnel solutions to their problems, which, not surprisingly, are a client's goods or services. To continue with the example provided by Lobbyist no. 33, after he learned that the army was encountering problems with one of its vehicles, he convinced army personnel to take a look at his client's vehicle. He then brokered an arrangement whereby his client provided the army with some of them. Third, agency personnel, convinced that a product or service can help them, request money from the legislature to buy that product or service. In this case, the army told Congress, "we would like to purchase some of these vehicles." Finally, Congress appropriates money for the purchase of the product or service. At this point, the agency issues a solicitation, and the procurement lobbyist's company competes for the contract to provide the product or service. In our sample case, Lobbyist no. 33 said that his company was virtually assured the contract because the solicitation was written with his client's vehicle in mind. Moreover, because he had been in close contact with army personnel for years before the final solicitation was issued, the source selection team was familiar with his client's vehicle. Not surprisingly, Lobbyist no. 33's client won the contract to provide the army with several vehicles, and was subsequently asked by Congress to provide even more vehicles.

Before leaving the topic of attaching solutions to problems, I want to point out that according to respondents, monitoring agencies closely is absolutely crucial to the ability of a procurement lobbyist to learn about the problems that plague agencies. In short, the process by which procurement lobbyists push-sell begins with knowledge of agency needs.

In sum, the data suggest that a number of factors determine whether or not a procurement lobbyists win. Among the factors are their connections, the nature of the products or services they sell, the track record of the product or service they sell, their knowledge of the procurement process, and their ability to convince agency officials that a particular product or service can help solve an agency's problems.

CONCLUSION

Each year, governments in the United States spend over $1 trillion on goods and services. Many businesses are eager to tap the government market – a market that is large and seemingly always growing. Businesses that wish to sell to government, as well as the organizations that represent them, often require the help of procurement lobbyists. In this chapter, I have explained where procurement lobbyists fit into the procurement process. I began with a brief description of the process by which governments buy goods and services. At all three levels of government, both the legislature and the bureaucracy are involved, and both branches of government attract attention from procurement lobbyists. I then summarized what the data indicated about who procurement lobbyists are and what types of organized interests they represent. Two findings in particular stand out: (1) Most procurement lobbyists represent business firms, and (2) many procurement lobbyists are contract lobbyists.

The bulk of the chapter described what procurement lobbyists do. I found that they help business firms navigate the procurement process, monitor government, lobby to affect legislative appropriations, lobby to affect source selection, and lobby to convince legislators to oversee agency actions. I concluded with a brief rendering of the kind of lobbying that accompanies procurement decisions.

In closing, I wish to reiterare a few general points about procurement lobbyists and lobbying. First, the data show that procurement lobbyists do a lot of things other than lobby. Specifically, they continually help clients respond to solicitations, counsel businesses on how to craft effective bid documents, and help businesses understand the complicated world of government procurement. Second, procurement lobbying bears a striking resemblance to marketing. Executive agencies – the end users in government – are at the center of the procurement process, and they attract the attention of procurement lobbyists, whose job includes convincing agency personnel that they should buy or consider buying a specific good or service. Third, the data suggest that procurement lobbying often rests upon relationships. Several respondents noted that the key to effective procurement lobbying is maintaining access to decision makers who make procurement decisions. Fourth, the procurement process, despite what one respondent called "firewalls" designed to shield it from political pressure, is a startlingly open process. Despite rules and regulations, procurement lobbyists have a great deal of freedom to pitch their wares to government buyers.

Are procurement lobbyists influential? I cannot pretend to answer this question definitively. Nonetheless, my data suggest that procurement lobbyists often bring good ideas to government, and that government officials often seize upon these ideas and make them their own. If having a great deal of information about a wide variety of goods and services makes one a better shopper, then procurement lobbyists play a positive role in helping governments in the United States be better shoppers. The relative ubiquity of procurement lobbyists has a potential dark side, however, and it involves money. Some business firms do not have procurement lobbyists, and thus are arguably less able to sell to government. While I am unable to point to a particular factor that determines whether or not a business firm hires a procurement lobbyist, I would guess that money is the crucial determinant. If this is true, small companies are at a decided disadvantage in selling to government. And if this is true, the government may not be getting either the best deal or the best goods or services available.

Our tour of the universe of lobbying is now over. In the preceding chapters, I tried to paint broad portraits of public policy lobbying, land use lobbying, and procurement lobbying, respectively. I cannot pretend that I have told you everything you need to know about lobbyists and lobbying. However, I hope that I have been able to convey to you a basic sense of who lobbyists are, what types of interests they represent, what they want, and how they try to get it. All that is left now is to wrap things up.

7 Recap and Final Thoughts

The primary objective of this book was to paint a broad picture of what lob-byists in America do. To serve this objective, I divided lobbying into three categories – public policy lobbying, land use lobbying, and procurement lobbying – and examined each category in detail. Specifically, I examined public policy lobbying in Chapters 3 and 4, land use lobbying in Chapter 5, and procurement lobbying in Chapter 6. These substantive chapters were designed to present detailed information about who lobbyists are, what interests they represent, how they do their jobs, and to what extent they affect government decisions. Here, I want to recap my findings by address-ing the same set of questions I addressed at the end of Chapters 4, 5, and 6. I conclude with final observations about lobbying and lobbyists in the United States.

RECAP OF SUBSTANTIVE FINDINGS

Public policy lobbying, land use lobbying, and procurement lobbying have a lot in common. In many ways, however, they are different, as you have learned.

Where Does Lobbying Take Place?

As Chapters 3–6 demonstrate, lobbying takes place at all three levels of government – local, state, and national. As I pointed out in Chapters 1 and 2, journalists and scholars alike tend to focus their attention on Wash-ington lobbying, rather than on state or local lobbying. This Washington-centric bias notwithstanding, the data clearly show that lobbying in Amer-ica takes place wherever government decisions are made – in Washington, in state capitals, in cities, in towns, in counties, and in villages.

Does the fact that lobbying takes place at all three levels of government mean that local, state, and national lobbying look similar? The answer to this question is "yes and no." On the one hand, to a large extent lobbying looks the same across levels of government. I say this because the data demonstrate that when it comes to procurement and public policy lobbying, local, state, and national lobbying look quite similar. On the other hand, lobbying looks somewhat different across the three levels of government. Specifically, the data show that local lobbying is quite different from state and national lobbying in that it principally concerns land use. As Chapter 5 shows, the lobbying that surrounds land use decisions is in many ways different from the lobbying that surrounds procurement and public policy decisions. Because land use lobbying is almost entirely a local government phenomenon, local lobbying, therefore, differs from state and national lobbying.

Who Lobbies?

Chapter 2 contains a list of the manifold types of organized interests that lobby in America. While all 12 types of organized interests actively lobby in the United States, some organized interests are more active than others. Which types? One answer is business firms. The data clearly show that business firms dominate land use lobbying and procurement lobbying, and they are also very active in public policy lobbying. Overall, the data show that business firms are the most active types of organized interests in America.

As for other types of organized interests, the data show that who lobbies depends upon what type of lobbying we are talking about. For example, Chapters 3 and 4 show that professional associations, labor unions, citizen groups, governmental entities, think tanks, coalitions, trade associations, universities and colleges, hospitals, charities, and churches – that is, virtually the full assortment of organized interests – are regular players in public policy lobbying. In contrast, Chapter 5 shows that land use lobbying is largely the purview of business firms and citizen groups (neighborhood associations, in particular), with intermittent participation from charities, universities and colleges, hospitals, and churches. Finally, Chapter 6 shows that procurement lobbying is almost entirely the bailiwick of business firms.

What Nonlobbying Activities Do Lobbyists Engage In?

The reason political scientists study lobbyists is because they lobby – that is, they try to affect what government does. The data clearly support the notion, however, that lobbyists do other things as well. I cannot say for certain on the basis of my data what portion of their time lobbyists spend on nonlobbying activities, but my guess would be between 10 and 50 percent, a rather wide range. So what nonlobbying activities do lobbyists engage in? The data show that the answer differs substantially across the three kinds of lobbying. Specifically, Chapter 4 shows that public policy lobbyists monitor government and manage clients. Chapter 5 shows that land use lobbyists advise and counsel clients on what they are allowed to do with their land, make recommendations to clients about how to proceed with development projects, consult with local government bureaucrats, and fill out papers. Finally, Chapter 6 shows that procurement lobbyists explain the procurement process to business firms that wish to sell to government, and they also monitor government. The data show that virtually all lobbyists spend substantial amounts of time on nonlobbying activities.

Whom Do Lobbyists Target?

When they lobby, lobbyists have many choices about whom to target. Just as previous studies suggest, my data show that lobbyists target government decision makers across all three branches of government, as well as the public. The data also show that different types of lobbyists target different decision makers to varying degrees. For example, Chapter 4 shows that public policy lobbyists target legislators and/or their aides primarily and executive agency personnel and the public secondarily. In contrast, Chapter 5 shows that land use lobbyists primarily target executive agency personnel (e.g., planning staffers and planning commissioners), but they also regularly target local legislators and the public. Finally, the data suggest that procurement lobbyists target executive agency personnel primarily and legislators and/or their aides secondarily.

Overall, my findings point to three general conclusions. First, the judiciary attracts far less attention from lobbyists than either the legislative or executive branch. This is hardly a novel conclusion – most surveys of lobbying activity reach a similar conclusion. But it is worth reiterating. Second, contrary to much of the conventional wisdom, it is not the case that legislators attract more lobbying attention than officials in other branches of government. While it is true that legislators and/or their aides are the primary targets of public policy lobbyists, it is not true that they are the primary targets of land use and procurement lobbyists. Land use lobbyists appear to target executive agency personnel as much as they target legislators and/or their aides, and many procurement lobbyists appear to target executive agency personnel *more* than they target legislators and their aides. Third, just as the conventional wisdom suggests, lobbyists target the public quite regularly. While ordinary citizens are targeted hardly at all by procurement lobbyists, they are primary targets for land use lobbyists, as well as occasional targets for public policy lobbyists.

What Techniques Do Lobbyists Use Most?

In Chapter 2, I presented an inclusive list (see Table 2) of lobbying techniques, which shows that some lobbying techniques are far more prevalent than others. Specifically, the data show that lobbyists of all kinds rely primarily on two techniques: meeting personally with legislators and/or their aides and meeting personally with executive agency personnel. In the end, despite all the techniques available to them, most lobbyists tend to come back to the "old favorites": meeting personally with legislators and their aides and with bureaucrats.

This said, these two techniques are far from the only techniques commonly used by lobbyists. Indeed, one of the more striking findings is that grassroots lobbying techniques are fairly common. Chapter 5, for example, shows that land use lobbyists rely quite heavily upon grassroots techniques. Specifically, land use lobbyists regularly meet personally with citizens in small groups, and they provide citizens with information through the mail, over the telephone, or door-to-door. One reason land use lobbyists rely heavily upon grassroots techniques is that the public is so heavily involved in land use politics (indeed, public hearings are mandated on most important land use decisions). Another (and perhaps more important) reason is that a lack of public opposition is often crucial to a land use lobbyist's success. As for public policy lobbyists, they too deploy grassroots techniques regularly. Specifically, Chapter 4 shows that public policy lobbyists frequently engage in e-mail, letter, telegram, or telephone campaigns, talk to the media, stage media events, and run advertisements in the media.

Two other common techniques are testifying before legislative committees, and testifying before executive branch agencies. Chapter 6, for example, shows that procurement lobbyists regularly testify at agency hearings and make oral presentations. Similarly, Chapter 4 shows that public policy lobbyists regularly testify at legislative hearings. Finally, Chapter 5 shows that land use lobbyists testify at both legislative and executive agency hearings on occasion.

What is perhaps most conspicuous about my findings regarding technique use is that so many of the techniques listed in Table 2 are more or less eschewed by most lobbyists. For example, while contributing money to candidates' campaigns is a widely known (and much feared) technique, it is surprisingly uncommon. Also more or less ignored are virtually all judicial techniques, direct democratic techniques, and electoral techniques. Of course, none of this means that these other techniques are unimportant or ineffective. Rather, it simply means that for most lobbyists most of the time – no matter where they work or what they want – lobbying entails meeting personally with legislators and/or their aides and meeting personally with executive agency personnel.

Which Techniques Are Most Effective?

As I have pointed out repeatedly, it is difficult to say for certain which lobbying techniques are most effective. Still, the data show that lobbyists themselves believe some techniques to be more effective than others. Specifically, they say that meeting personally with government officials is by far the most effective way to influence government decisions. For example, Chapter 4 shows that public policy lobbyists believe that meeting personally with legislators and/or their aides and meeting personally with executive agency personnel are the two most effective lobbying techniques. Why? They gave me two answers. First, face-to-face meetings allow them to forge personal relationships with government decision makers – relationships that can pay dividends down the line. According to my respondents, when government decision makers need help, advice, or information, they are much more likely to call upon lobbyists they know well. Second, personal meetings with government decision makers give public policy lobbyists the opportunity to listen as well as to talk. Listening allows a lobbyist to keep abreast of what government officials are up to and to head off any problematic policy proposals.

Land use lobbyists and procurement lobbyists are similarly sold on personal meetings. According to my land use respondents, meeting personally with decision makers allows a lobbyist to simplify complex matters and to capitalize on his or her connections. As for procurement lobbyists, personal meetings with government officials allow them to demonstrate their products (often necessary to make a sale), build important and lasting relationships with officials who make purchasing decisions, and lavish attention upon agency personnel who often appreciate such attention.

Several land use and public policy lobbyists also reported that grassroots techniques can be very effective. Indeed, land use lobbyists (unlike procurement and public policy lobbyists) reported that grassroots techniques are virtually always necessary to win pitched land use battles. Among the grassroots techniques available, land use lobbyists identified meeting personally with citizens in small groups as the most effective. According to my respondents, meeting with citizens allows a land use lobbyist to put a "human face" on large development projects (which, after all, are usually developed by large, faceless business organizations). It also affords land use lobbyists the opportunity to prove that they are reasonable and that they take citizens' concerns seriously.

What Types of Information Do Lobbyists Provide?

Overall, the data show that lobbyists rely upon all three types of information (i.e., political information, career-relevant information, and policy-analytic information) cited by the communications theory of lobbying (see Chapter 2). However, the data also show that the precise types of information that lobbyists provide depend heavily upon the kinds of lobbying they engage in.

Chapter 4 shows that public policy lobbyists provide several types of information when they lobby. First, when they lobby legislators and/or their aides, public policy lobbyists primarily provide background information – information about the organized interest(s) they represent and where and how they can be reached. Background information is important because it affords these lobbyists the ability to personally connect with government officials, many of whom call upon lobbyists for advice and other types of information subsequently. Second, when public policy lobbyists lobby bureaucratic agencies for permits of various kinds, they provide technical information. As for the three types of information discussed in Chapter 2, public policy lobbyists provide all three. First, they often provide policy-analytic information, especially to legislators and/or their aides and to the media. Second, they often provide career-relevant information, for example, when they engage in proposal-specific legislative lobbying. They provide this type of information to bureaucrats as well. Finally, they occasionally ply political information when they lobby. An interesting finding is that public policy lobbyists provide political information to the public more than they do to government decision makers.

Chapter 5 shows that land use lobbyists rely primarily upon policy-analytic and career-relevant information when they lobby. In the context of land use lobbying, policy-analytic information is generally information about how a proposed land use project will affect the economy, employment, the environment, noise, pollution, population density, property values, and traffic, among other things. Land use lobbyists provide policy-analytic information to both government officials and ordinary citizens. Land use lobbyists also provide career-relevant information when they lobby, especially when they lobby legislators. Local legislators (like elected officials everywhere) worry about reelection, and they look to lobbyists to provide them with public opinion data about the land use proposals that come before them. Finally, land use lobbyists provide two types of information that are not part of the threefold classification of information posited by the communications theory of lobbying: technical information (i.e., information about the technical aspects of a specific land use project) and activity information (i.e., information about what they have done to accommodate a project's opponents). Because the land use process is technical and complex, land use lobbyists often find themselves providing government decision makers with technical information designed to demonstrate that a specific land use project conforms to the law. As for activity information, my respondents told me that local government decision makers are much more likely to support a project if they believe that its proponents (including the lobbyist) have worked hard to accommodate its opponents and have listened carefully and thoughtfully to their concerns. So land use lobbyists provide activity information to these local government officials.

Lastly, Chapter 6 shows that procurement lobbyists rely heavily upon yet another type of information that is not part of the three-part classification of information yielded by the communications theory of lobbying – product information, which is information about a product's price and performance. Not surprisingly, government officials who make purchasing decisions are keenly interested in both of these things. In addition to product information, procurement lobbyists also regularly provide policy-analytic information to government decision makers. It is interesting that this information is often about the firm that sells the product or service in question, rather than about the product or service itself. Finally, the data indicate that procurement lobbyists also provide career-relevant information to government officials when they lobby. For example, they may provide legislators (or other elected officials) with information about how supporting the purchase of a certain item might serve them well come election time. Similarly, they may provide bureaucrats with information about how a specific product or service will help an agency solve its problems. To paraphrase one of my respondents, procurement lobbyists often appeal to bureaucrats' career ambitions by telling them that if they bring an exciting new technology or product or service to their bosses, they will "look good" and may eventually be promoted.

What Determines Whether or Not Lobbyists Win?

To a person, the lobbyists I spoke to said that there are times when they get what they want from government. In other words, lobbyists sometimes win. So what determines whether or not a lobbyist is successful in affecting what the government does? There is not a simple and straightforward answer to this question.[1] As Chapters 3–6 show, a number of factors affect a lobbyist's chances of success, and these factors vary by the type of lobbying a lobbyist engages in.

The data suggest that five factors in particular affect public policy lobbyists' ability to get what they want from government. First is how much is asked for. Public policy lobbyists are much more likely to get what they want when they do not ask for too much. Second is how much they do. The more they do, the more likely they are to win. Third is the ability to deploy good and credible policy-analytic information. Public policy lobbyists who have such information in support of their viewpoint are much more likely to win than lobbyists who do not. Fourth is whether they are playing defense rather than offense. Public policy lobbyists who are trying to stop something from happening have a much higher chance of winning than those who are trying to make something happen. Finally, there is the nature of the lobbyist's organization. Public policy lobbyists with a large membership or base of support that can be mobilized during a grassroots lobbying effort have a higher chance of winning than lobbyists without a large membership or base of support.

As for land use lobbyists, three factors in particular appear to affect their chances of winning. First is the disposition of the public. Land use lobbyists have a better chance of winning if the public is on their side than if it is not. Second is the disposition of the planning staff. They have a better chance of winning if the planning staff is on their side than if it is not. Finally is the ability to make a solid technical argument. Land use lobbyists have a better chance of winning if they are able to make an airtight technical argument in favor of their proposal.

Finally, five specific factors appear to determine procurement lobbyists' chances of winning. First is the extent of their connections. Procurement lobbyists have a better chance of winning if they have numerous connections than if they do not. Second is the nature of the product they are selling. Procurement lobbyists have a better chance of winning if they are selling a product that governments use often. Third is the track record of the product or service they are selling. They have a better chance of winning if it is a product or service that has an excellent track record with other government users. Fourth is their knowledge of the arcane procurement process. They have a better chance of winning if they know the procurement process inside and out than if they do not. Fifth is the ability to attach solutions to problems. They have a better chance of winning if they can convince government users that their product or service can help a government buyer solve a current problem.

In the end, the data suggest that the determinants of success differ greatly across the three kinds of lobbying. However, public policy lobbyists, land use lobbyists, and procurement lobbyists undoubtedly have one thing in common: They sometimes win, and they sometimes lose.

Summary
The most important findings are: (1) Lobbying takes place at all three levels of government, though local lobbying is decidedly different from state and national lobbying in that it primarily concerns land use. (2) Business firms dominate lobbying in the United States, though other types of organized interests lobby as well. (3) Virtually all lobbyists spend a great deal of time on nonlobbying activities, though the specific types of nonlobbying activities in which they engage depend upon what kind of lobbying they do. (4) Lobbyists target all three branches of government as well as the public, though the judiciary gets far less attention than the legislature, the executive branch, or the public. (5) Lobbyists have a variety of techniques at their disposal, but they rely most heavily upon meeting personally with legislators and/or their aides and meeting personally with executive agency personnel. (6) Meeting personally with legislators and/or their aides, meeting personally with executive agency personnel, and engaging in grassroots lobbying are the most effective lobbying techniques. (7) Lobbyists sometimes succeed in getting what they want, but the determinants of their success are to some extent dependent upon the kind of lobbying in which they engage.

FINAL THOUGHTS

In closing, I would like to offer final observations about lobbying and lobbyists in America. These observations constitute, for lack of a better phrase, "food for thought" as you think about what you have read in this book. Each flows directly from the data I presented in Chapters 3–6, and each raises important questions about the role of lobbyists and lobbying in American democracy. It is my hope that they will stimulate further thought about the subject, and perhaps even lead you to do your own research on lobbyists and lobbying.

Lobbying Is Often Devoid of Conflict

One of the things that struck me during my interviews with lobbyists was how seldom they mentioned conflict with other lobbyists. To be sure, conflict between lobbyists and between organized interests *does* exist. For example, anyone conversant in American public policy knows that when government officials in the United States consider restricting access to abortion, or adopting restrictive gun control policies, or adopting or repealing environmental regulations, they are faced with massive pressure from both sides of the issue.[2] Moreover, the data in Chapter 5 show that developers often face opposition from neighborhood associations and NIMBY groups when they lobby for specific land use proposals. Similarly, some procurement decisions engender conflict between vendors competing for the same lucrative government contract. But the data suggest that this state of affairs – in which lobbyists on opposing sides of a proposed or pending government decision square off against each other – is decidedly less common than many people think. Indeed, many land use, procurement, and public policy battles are characterized by little or no conflict between lobbyists.

How can this be? There are two primary answers. First, the data indicate that lobbyists and the organized interests they represent try to avoid conflict whenever possible, and many are good at it.[3] Land use lobbyists, for example, work hard to demobilize opposition to their projects long before they seek formal government permission to proceed. These lobbyists negotiate and compromise, and in some cases, barter with opponents to ensure that when it is time for government officials to make up their minds, they are faced with little or no opposition. Similarly, procurement lobbyists work hard to ensure that they are in the driver's seat to obtain government contracts well before the government actually publicizes its need for a product or service. And public policy lobbyists try hard to avoid conflict by making sure they do not ask for too much from government. These lobbyists know that asking for huge policy changes is a recipe for failure. As such, they tend to moderate their claims to improve their chances of success. The less public policy lobbyists ask for, the less likely they are to have opposition.

A second explanation for why lobbying is often devoid of conflict is that lobbyists often ask for things to which no one objects.[4] Governments in the United States do a *lot* of things: They regulate everything you can think of (at least to some degree), they spend literally trillions of dollars, and they purchase a massive assortment of goods and services. Because so much of what the government does is inscrutable to most people, lobbyists are often in the position of asking for things – for example, permits to engage in certain activities, small changes in the way zoning regulations are implemented, and contracts to provide certain goods or services – that no one objects to. Time and again my respondents told of instances in which they lobbied for things that other lobbyists simply did not care about.

In short, my interviews indicate that lobbyists of all kinds often (but by no means always) face little or no opposition from other lobbyists when they lobby. To many people this sounds bad. After all, if a lobbyist wants something and no one objects, the lobbyist will get what he or she wants, right? Well, it turns out that the answer to this question is "not necessarily." (I address this more fully in the next section.) But even if it were true that lobbyists always get what they want because no one objects to what they ask for, this would not necessarily be a bad thing. I say this because lobbyists often moderate their demands to avoid conflict with other lobbyists. What this means is that they often do not ask for all they want. Thus, when they get what they ask for, they are not necessarily getting all they would really like to get. You cannot conclude that lobbyists get everything they *want* just because they get everything they *ask for*.[5] To get an accurate picture of how influential a lobbyist is, you would have to look at what the lobbyist actually wants rather than what the lobbyist eventually asks for. And the data show that lobbyists often ask for far less than they truly want.

Lobbyists Are Often Exceedingly Cautious

While most people think of lobbyists as aggressive "go-getters" relentlessly pushing their selfish agendas on timorous government officials who eventually cave in to their unyielding pressure, the data paint a far different picture. After interviewing lobbyists for this book, the one word that comes to mind when I think about most (though certainly not all) lobbyists is *cautious*.[6] Far from being the freewheeling "loose cannons" of political lore, most lobbyists are careful to avoid asking for things that will ruffle large numbers of feathers or lead to radical changes in the direction of government. Again, this does not mean that lobbyists inevitably fail in their attempts to affect government decisions. In fact, exactly the opposite is true: Because many government decisions are made without substantial input from the public or opposing lobbyists, lobbyists often substantially affect what the government does. However, I am convinced that the cautious nature of most lobbyists means that in the United States, the impetus for big changes in government and politics comes not from lobbyists but from government officials and the citizens who elect them.[7]

Lobbyists know that the ultimate power over what government does lies in the hands of government officials. This is why they work so hard to influence what government officials do. Think about it: If lobbyists were as powerful as many people assume they are, they would spend little time lobbying government officials; instead they would simply snap their fingers and count on government officials to do their bidding. I say that lobbyists are cautious because they appear to respond to government decisions and attempt to modify them and/or adapt to them as much as they push new ideas and seek to determine the overall course of government. Again, this does not mean that lobbyists never get what they want from government. But it does mean that they seldom determine what government does on issues and matters of high salience and enormous importance. Moreover, it means that lobbyists seldom determine the overall general course of government.

After interviewing lobbyists for this book, I have come to the conclusion that lobbyists are the "detail men and women" of American politics. When it comes to determining the overall course of American government – that is, when it comes to determining if the government will be conservative or liberal or moderate, or will expand or contract or stay about the same size, or will spend more on fighter airplanes or less, or will adopt a unilateral foreign policy or a multilateral foreign policy, or will allow or disallow rapid unfettered development of undeveloped land, or will spend huge amounts of money on goods and services or small amounts – lobbyists are relatively insignificant. At all three levels of government, when it comes to the overall direction of politics and government, government officials and the public (primarily through elections) are the primary agents of influence. But when it comes to the *fine details* of government, lobbyists are much more influential. For example, when the government tilts in a decidedly conservative direction (as is the case as I write this book), it is because the public has demanded it and government officials have delivered it. However, often it is lobbyists who hammer out the details of how this conservatism will play out in specific government decisions.

In sum, the data indicate that lobbyists are much more cautious than the received wisdom suggests. They know that to win they cannot ask for too much. Caution, it seems, is a valuable attribute for lobbyists of all kinds.

Lobbying in America Is Dominated by Business Firms

I have said this before (and indeed, it is part of the conventional wisdom on lobbyists and lobbying I described in Chapter 2), but it bears repeating because it is so important: Business firms dominate lobbying in the United States. This insight is not novel, as scholars of lobbying and lobbyists have long known that the universe of organized interests in America is heavily skewed in favor of business interests. My data reiterate this important fact. For example, Chapters 5 and 6, respectively, clearly demonstrate that land use lobbying and procurement lobbying are largely the purview of business firms. In addition, even in the realm of public policy lobbying, where a greater variety of interests is represented, lobbyists for business firms and trade associations appear to be more plentiful and active than lobbyists for other types of organized interests. While it is the case that a much wider variety of organized interests is involved in public policy lobbying than in either land use or procurement lobbying, the data still suggest that business firms are disproportionately represented among public policy lobbyists.

The dominance of business lobbyists raises two important questions: (1) Why do business firms dominate lobbying in the United States? and (2) What difference does it make?

Why Do Business Firms Dominate Lobbying in the United States? Political scientists have long known what my data confirm: that business firms are disproportionately well represented by lobbyists. Why is this the case? The data I presented in Chapters 3–6 provide obvious answers. Let's start with Chapters 5 and 6, which show that business lobbyists outnumber nonbusiness lobbyists in land use and procurement politics because businesses that wish to either develop land or sell to government are essentially forced to hire lobbyists. For example, Chapter 5 shows that virtually every business in the United States that wishes to develop undeveloped land or build large-scale commercial, residential, or industrial projects must *by law* get explicit government permission to do so. To get government permission to develop land, business firms *must* interact with government officials and try to get them to sign off on their development plans. This is the very definition of lobbying. Similarly, Chapter 6 shows that virtually every business firm that wishes to sell goods or services to the government must convince government buyers that their wares are worth buying. This requires them to interact with government officials. Again, this is the very definition of lobbying.

As for public policy lobbyists, Chapters 3 and 4 show that most business firms in this country must comply with extensive regulations that govern how they can and cannot do business.[8] To *abide* by government rules and regulations, business firms must *be aware* of government rules and regulations. And while lobbying government is not absolutely necessary for businesses that wish to keep abreast of government policies, it certainly helps. Many business firms must be politically active to some degree simply to stay in business. While it is certainly the case that many business firms are not politically active, it is also the case that many are. Even small businesses with few employees must engage in some kind of compliance monitoring.

There is something paradoxical about the fact that many business firms – especially those firms that develop land or sell to government – are virtually forced to hire lobbyists. Some of the most outspoken critics of lobbying and lobbyists are people who believe that the government is too cozy with business firms. Many of these same critics support the notion that government programs and regulations are important safeguards against business dominance of American politics. One of the "warning signs" of business dominance cited by these critics is the enormous lobbying presence of business firms. The paradox here is that this very warning sign of business dominance is partially a consequence of the types of government rules, regulations, and programs that critics of business support. For example, the reason that business lobbyists dominate land use lobbying is that local governments regulate land use to such a great extent. This forces development firms to interact with local governments virtually every time they wish to develop land. Similarly, the reason business lobbyists dominate procurement politics is that governments in the United States spend hundreds of billions of dollars every year on goods and services to fulfill their mandates. If the government did not regulate land use, developers probably would not hire lobbyists; they would simply buy land and do with it as they pleased. Similarly, if governments in the United States did not do so many things and spend so much money, many business firms (specifically, the business firms that sell to government) would not hire lobbyists to help them get government contracts because there would be no government contracts to compete for. And if governments in the United States did not make so many public policy decisions, business firms would probably not direct as much energy toward affecting these public policy decisions.

In sum, one of the reasons that so much lobbying is conducted by business firms is that business firms are virtually forced, by dint of government decisions of various kinds, to engage in political activity.

What Difference Does It Make That Business Firms Dominate Lobbying in the United States? Does it make a difference that business lobbyists outnumber nonbusiness lobbyists to such a large degree? Unfortunately,

there is no easy answer.[9] In fact, the data point to an ambiguous conclusion. On the one hand, the data support the conclusion that the vast
number of business lobbyists active in American politics is a sign of business *weakness* rather than strength.[10] I say this because Chapters 3–6 show
unequivocally that business firms in this country are highly constrained
by government. In other words, business firms are not free to do whatever
they wish. Development firms, for example, cannot buy large tracts of land
and develop them as they please with no interference from government or
the public. Similarly, because of government regulations, health-care firms
cannot simply flout government regulations and sell patient information
willy-nilly to whoever is willing to pay for it. And business firms that sell
to government are not free to sell whatever they want to whomever they
want at whatever price they want. Business firms do not have free rein to
do as they please.[11]

On the other hand, the fact that business lobbyists so outnumber lobbyists for other types of organized interests surely means that business lobbyists have disproportionate power over government decisions.[12] Regardless
of why business firms lobby – that is, even if they lobby simply because
they must do so to get government permission to do business – the fact is
that business lobbyists are virtually always around when government decisions are made. Citizen group, labor union, and charity lobbyists, among
others, are *not* always around when governments make decisions. The data
show that government decisions of all kinds are made with disproportionate input from business lobbyists. Does this mean that business lobbyists
always get what they want? Of course not. But it does mean that the one
voice that is virtually always heard by government decision makers at all
levels of government, in all areas of government decision making, is the
voice of business. And this is no small thing.

Proving that business lobbyists have disproportionate influence over
government decisions is impossible. But the data provide hints that this
is the case. First, they suggest that resources are an important determinant of lobbyist success.[13] And there is no question that business firms
in this country have substantial resources to draw upon. Resources can
help business firms hire more lobbyists, see more government officials,
and, if necessary, mount expensive grassroots lobbying campaigns (if they
are trying to affect public policy decisions).[14] Second, the data show that
business lobbyists have a built-in advantage over other types of organized
interests by dint of their impact on the economy.[15] Chapters 3–6 show
that lobbyists of all kinds rely heavily upon policy-analytic information
when they lobby. This information often concerns the economic benefits

of a particular course of action. And no matter what a business lobbyist asks for, he or she can almost always make the argument that it is good for the economy. A developer that wishes to develop a pristine piece of land, for example, can always argue that no matter how much controversy surrounds the project, it will provide jobs for hundreds of people and will generate local tax revenue, thus helping the local economy. Similarly, a manufacturing firm that opposes a proposed government regulation to limit factory emissions can always argue that no matter how wonderful the regulation sounds, it will likely raise the costs of doing business, which in turn could lead to job losses and higher prices for consumers. And a procurement lobbyist for a business firm can always argue that buying a specific good or service from the company that he or she represents will help the business firm and thus help the overall economy. The data show that policy-analytic information is crucial to the success of lobbyists of all kinds. Business lobbyists can almost always present solid and convincing policy-analytic information to support their views.

In sum, the data do not allow us to answer once and for all the question of whether or not business predominance in lobbying communities translates into disproportionate business influence. On the one hand, the massive presence of business lobbyists cannot be seen as irrefutable evidence of business strength. On the other hand, this massive presence surely means that business lobbyists are seldom ignored.

Lobbyists Spend Considerable Time on Nonlobbying Activities

This, too, I have said before (and this, too, is part of the conventional wisdom on lobbyists and lobbying described in Chapter 2), but it bears repeating because it is so important: Lobbyists spend considerable time on activities other than lobbying, as shown in Chapters 3–6. This fact has a number of important implications. First, it means that the question of how much *influence* lobbyists wield is often irrelevant. Many times, lobbyists are not even trying to influence what government does, but rather are working to *keep up* with what government does. Second, it means that lobbyists tend to be *reactive*, rather than *proactive*. Polls show that many citizens are distrustful of organized interests and their lobbyists. They believe, for example, that government officials in the United States are at the beck and call of lobbyists who push their pet proposals down the throats of these reluctant or helpless officials. My data present a different story. Far from pushing their views on helpless public officials, lobbyists often react to government, rather than pushing for change. And the fact that lobbyists spend considerable time advising and counseling their clients (in the case of contract lobbyists) or the higher-ups in the organizations they work for (in the case of in-house lobbyists) means that lobbyists are not simply ciphers who channel the beliefs and values and policy positions of the people who pay them and hire them. Rather, lobbyists are autonomous actors who bring their own beliefs and values and policy positions to the table when they lobby. Rather than just doing what they are told, lobbyists draw upon their experience and their expertise to mold the goals and desires of the people they represent. In this sense, they are very powerful autonomous actors in American politics.[16]

The fact that lobbyists spend so much time on nonlobbying activities means that many citizens' views of lobbyists are skewed. While we tend to think of lobbyists as all-powerful rainmakers who relentlessly work on behalf of organized interests to get the government to do their bidding, the reality of lobbying is bit more mundane. The work of the typical lobbyist entails a lot of drudgery, a lot of research, and a lot of boredom. And often it is not even lobbying.

Lobbyists Rely Primarily on Personal Meetings

Table 2 showed that lobbyists use a large variety of techniques. However, Chapters 3–6 showed that although lobbyists of all kinds have a variety of techniques to choose from, most (though certainly not all) rely primarily upon two techniques – meeting personally with legislators and/or their aides and meeting personally with executive agency personnel.[17] (For land use lobbyists, you can add meeting personally with citizens to this list). In short, lobbyists of all kinds rely primarily upon the generic technique of meeting personally with government officials. Ultimately, despite advances in technology, changes in government, and fundamental changes in American society, lobbying is not that much different today than it was 50 or even 100 years ago. Lobbying is still primarily a personal business based on face-to-face contact. While media techniques and sophisticated electronic grassroots campaigns are unquestionably important weapons in the lobbyist's arsenal, the main weapon remains the personal, face-to-face meeting.

Meeting Personally: Still Effective after All These Years. Why do lobbyists rely so heavily upon meeting personally with government officials (and, in the case of land use lobbyists, citizens)? I addressed this question briefly previously, and for all three types of lobbyists the answer is basically the same: *because it works.*

Why is meeting personally so effective? The data indicate there are three basic answers. First, meeting personally with government officials or citizens allows for a very efficient exchange of information. My respondents told me that during personal meetings lobbyists can convey a lot of information in a relatively short period of time and be assured that the information is being received. Second, personal meetings with government officials (though not with citizens) are effective because, all things being equal, officials prefer doing things for people they know and like. This puts a premium on a lobbyist's ability to make a personal connection with a government official; and it is easier to make a personal connection with a government official in person than it is to make such a connection over the telephone or through written communication. Third, meeting personally with government officials and citizens alike affords a lobbyist the opportunity to *listen* as well as to talk. The data show that lobbyists of all kinds believe that their effectiveness rests partially on their ability to stay up-to-date on what government and, in some cases, citizens are doing. And meeting personally with government officials and citizens gives lobbyists lots of opportunities to hear from the horse's mouth what's going on.

The finding that so many lobbyists rely so heavily upon personal meetings has a number of implications. First, it means that people (like me) who study lobbying should perhaps focus more upon these personal meetings than they presently do. After interviewing lobbyists for this book, I am utterly convinced that the key to understanding most lobbying is understanding what happens at these personal meetings. This does not mean that the other techniques that lobbyists use are unimportant. But it does mean that a thorough understanding of all three kinds of lobbying requires us first and foremost to accept the fact that personal meetings are the bedrock of most lobbying campaigns. Focusing on other lobbying techniques, while not unwise, takes the spotlight away from the few things that almost all lobbyists do most of the time.

Second, it means that access to government decision makers remains absolutely crucial to lobbying success. Government officials are busy. My respondents were unanimous in the opinion that most government officials work hard, try hard, and are anything but indolent. As such, they do not have unlimited time to spend with lobbyists. However, because lobbying remains a personal business, a lobbyist's ability to get face time with government officials is critical to his or her success. Thus, access is crucial to lobbying success. How do lobbyists get access? One answer is *money*.[18] Money can buy access in two ways. To begin with, it can be contributed to candidates for office. According to my respondents, when candidates reach office they are much more likely to grant access to people who give them money than they are to people who do not. Of course, my respondents were quick to note that most government officials – especially elected officials – also tend to favor constituents when they decide whom to meet with. Thus, it is not the case that deep-pocketed lobbyists get access to government officials that ordinary citizens cannot. But things being equal, money helps determine who gets access to decision makers and who does not. Another way that money can buy access is that it can be used to hire a contract lobbyist with built-in connections. Many of my respondents told me that contract lobbyists – many of whom have extensive government experience – are valued primarily for their connections. In short, if an organized interest hires a well-connected contract lobbyist, it has instant access to the government officials whom the contract lobbyist knows. The fact that money can buy access means that organized interests with deep pockets have a higher chance of winning than organized interests that do not. It also means that on issues with little public participation, lobbyists are quite likely to exercise influence over government decision makers.

Many Lobbying Techniques Are Not Particularly Effective

The data suggest that some lobbying techniques are not particularly effective, no matter who uses them. Specifically, the data suggest two general conclusions. First, contributing money is an overrated technique of influence.[19] My respondents told me that in and of itself, contributing money is virtually worthless as a lobbying technique. Simply put, government officials do not often let money determine what they do. Contributing money can open the door, but meeting personally is the way lobbyists close the deal. Thus, while money is important, it is a means to an end rather than an effective technique in and of itself.

Second, some lobbying techniques – including direct democratic, several electoral, several grassroots, judicial lobbying, and even some executive branch techniques (e.g., trying to affect bureaucratic appointments, engaging in adjudication) – are not so much ineffective as they are inadequate. The data show that some lobbying techniques are more versatile than others. By this I mean that some lobbying techniques – especially meeting personally with government officials – "travel well" and can be utilized in a variety of contexts to present a variety of types of information to government officials, while other techniques are rather limited. For example, direct democratic techniques can be very effective. But the opportunities to use them are few and far between, and the types of government decisions on which they can be deployed are severely limited. Similarly, judicial lobbying techniques can be very effective. But the vast majority of government decisions never reach the courts, and so specializing in this type of lobbying severely limits a lobbyist's effectiveness. The data show that some techniques – while potentially valuable and occasionally effective – are simply irrelevant to the day-to-day lives of most lobbyists. This does not make them ineffective per se, but it does limit their effectiveness.

In the end, the data show that for most lobbyists, the answer to the effectiveness question comes down to personal meetings with government officials. Lobbyists everywhere rely heavily upon the time-honored technique of meeting personally with government officials to get what they want.

Lobbying = Providing Information

This is something that people who study lobbying have always known (and yes, it too is part of the conventional wisdom on lobbyists and lobbying), but it is worth reiterating because it is so important: Lobbying = providing information. The data I presented in Chapters 3–6 show that lobbying is, above all, about the provision of information. Information, it appears, is the lobbyist's stock in trade. For example, as the communications theory of lobbying predicts, all three kinds of lobbyists rely heavily upon policy-analytic information when they lobby. My data show that most government officials, no matter what kind of decision they are considering, want to do the right thing when they make decisions and are eager to receive information that either supports their view of the right thing or points them in the right direction. Policy-analytic information is very helpful in both respects. Moreover, as many respondents (especially land use lobbyists) told me, government officials are not experts on most issues. They *need* the information that lobbyists provide to help them make up their minds.

The data show that lobbyists of all kinds also regularly deploy career-relevant information when they lobby. Career-relevant information – about the implications of a particular course of action for a government official's prospects of keeping and/or advancing in his or her job – is particularly useful when lobbyists lobby elected officials, especially legislators. My respondents were unanimous in the opinion that most legislators desperately want to be reelected, and thus are desperate for information that points them toward a course of action that is either supported or not opposed by their constituents. Lobbyists rely heavily upon career-relevant information when they lobby legislators, but they also do so when they lobby bureaucrats. According to my respondents, though bureaucrats are not elected and so do not have constituents per se, they do consider certain people "their constituents" and are loath to upset them. Moreover, my respondents said that bureaucrats are sensitive to the fact that if they "screw up," they might be fodder for newspaper and television reports. Because they are anxious to avoid negative publicity, bureaucrats value information from lobbyists about how a particular course of action is viewed by the public.

As pointed out in Chapter 2, the communications theory of lobbying suggests that lobbyists rely partially on political information – about the status and prospect of a proposed or potential government decision – when they lobby. However, my data suggest that most lobbyists ply political information less than they ply policy-analytic and career-relevant information. In fact, the data suggest that in many cases, it is lobbyists who need political information from government officials, not government officials who need political information from lobbyists. Given that government officials often have the inside track on political information, this makes sense.

Other Types of Information. While the communications theory of lobbying is obviously accurate, my data suggest that it is incomplete. Specifically, the data indicate that there are three types of information on which lobbyists rely that are not part of the threefold classification of information that flows from the theory. First, in Chapter 6, I pointed out that procurement lobbyists rely heavily upon product information when they lobby. Second, as noted in Chapters 3 and 5, public policy lobbyists and land use lobbyists regularly deploy technical information when they lobby. And the data in Chapter 5 show that land use lobbyists often deploy what I call activity information when they lobby.

While the data support the general contention of the communications theory of lobbying that lobbyists rely heavily upon policy-analytic and career-relevant information, they also suggest that lobbyists rely upon other types as well, though less on political information.

For Many Lobbyists, What the Public Wants Matters a Lot

Finally, I conclude on an optimistic note. My respondents were remarkably consistent on the following point: *Government officials do not like to flout public opinion.* This may surprise you. After all, polls show that many Americans distrust their government and believe that government officials regularly ignore ordinary citizens and do things that benefit their friends and the "special interest groups" that give them money and provide them with gifts and favors.[20] But lobbyists – people who interact extensively with government officials every day – clearly believe that government officials do not ignore their constituents.[21] In one sense, it does not even matter if this belief is false. The fact is that lobbyists behave *as if it is true*. And this is important because it means that what the public wants is often on their minds when they lobby. It would be virtually unheard of, for example, for land use lobbyists to conclude early in a development project that they can ignore the public. Even if they have little reason to believe that public opposition to their project will arise, they must consider the possibility and must attempt to do something about it. Similarly, public policy lobbyists cannot afford to close their eyes to the wishes of the public. They know full well that mobilized citizens can trump them any time, any place, on any issue.

My interviews with lobbyists suggested to me that lobbyists generally have more faith in the public and our democratic system of government than most ordinary citizens do. Most lobbyists have *seen* the power of the public close-up and firsthand. Virtually all land use lobbyists have witnessed (often to their dismay) neighborhood and environmental groups rise up and stop controversial development projects. Similarly, all the public policy lobbyists I talked to said that at some point during their careers they had witnessed a public outcry over something that got the government's attention and shifted the course of government decisions. And procurement lobbyists know full well that government buyers cannot buy whatever they please with no regard for what the public wants. However, lobbyists also realize that most citizens are not particularly active in politics. Thus, they often get what they want because no one objects to what they ask for. In the end, because the public often ignores what goes on in government, lobbyists are able to exert substantial influence over government decisions. But for this, citizens have no one to blame but themselves and the leaders they elect.

The Classification System: Public Policy, Land Use, and Procurement Lobbying

In an attempt to make this book accessible to undergraduates and non-experts, I have avoided jargon whenever possible and stuck to the facts, rather than presenting an overarching theoretical scheme or conceptual framework. Nonetheless, the data I present here and my previous research on lobbying and lobbyists suggest that the threefold classification system of lobbying used in this book is more than simply a convenient organizational device. It is useful in and of itself in helping us understand lobbying and lobbyists.[1] It is useful primarily because it points up the fact that not all lobbying is the same. In other words, *there are important differences between (1) public policy lobbying, (2) land use lobbying, and (3) procurement lobbying.* In this brief appendix, I explain why I chose to divide lobbying into these three categories and how my threefold classification system can help us understand lobbying.

THE CLASSIFICATION SYSTEM

As I pointed out in Chapter 1, public policy lobbying is *the lobbying that accompanies government decisions (e.g., laws, rules, regulations, court decisions) made in response to societal demands for action on important issues of the day;* land use lobbying is *the lobbying that accompanies government decisions rendered in response to specific requests for permission to utilize land in a certain way;* and procurement lobbying is *the lobbying that accompanies government decisions concerning which specific goods and/or services the government will purchase.* Most actual cases of lobbying, I believe, can be placed into one of these three categories. Further, I believe that the key to understanding lobbying is understanding that it comes in these three basic forms, and that these forms are unique (though they have some things in common).

My classification system is useful not just because it provides a convenient way for me to organize this book, but also because it simplifies the
complex phenomenon of lobbying. In Chapters 3–6, I put my threefold
classification system to use by describing and explaining these three types
of lobbying.

Why This Classification System?

At first glance, my classification system may appear misguided. After all,
wouldn't a more conventional approach that distinguishes between *local
lobbying, state lobbying,* and *national lobbying* be more useful and appropriate? My answer to this question is a resounding, "No!" I say this for two
reasons. First of all, recent studies of lobbying have shown that local lobbying, state lobbying, and national lobbying are quite similar. For example,
studies show that state lobbying is not that much different from national
lobbying, and that local lobbying looks a lot like both state and national
lobbying.[2] Because local, state, and national lobbying are so similar, distin-
guishing among them does not really get us anywhere in understanding
the larger phenomenon of lobbying. There are, to be sure, differences
among them, but I have come to see them as relatively minor, especially
compared to the differences among public policy, procurement, and land
use lobbying. The second reason I reject the local/state/national lobbying
classification system is that lobbyists themselves appear to reject it. My
research (for this book and for other projects) indicates that many lobbyists are more likely to classify themselves according to the type(s) of
government decisions they attempt to influence than they are to classify themselves according to where they work. In other words, what
makes procurement lobbyists who work in Los Angeles different from
other lobbyists who work in Los Angeles, Nashville, or Washington is that
they lobby on procurement matters rather than public policy or land use
matters.

Another possible criticism of my classification system is that it wrongly
elevates land use and procurement lobbying to the level of public policy
lobbying. A criticism along these lines might go something like this:

> Everyone knows that public policy is important. Government decisions
> about income tax levels, gay and lesbian marriage rights, and whether
> or not to overthrow the dictatorial leader of a foreign country are very
> important. Government decisions about who gets a government contract
> to print up an official city map or whether or not an oil refinery gets
> government permission to expand its facilities are not very important.

The basic contention here is that while public policy lobbying is important, land use and procurement lobbying are not. As such, the argument goes, devoting valuable time and energy and effort to studying land use and procurement lobbying is silly; the focus should be on public policy lobbying.

This critique is implicit in many books and articles on lobbying. For example, most leading textbooks on lobbying say virtually nothing about either procurement or land use lobbying. The primary reason is that most people (including me until now) who study lobbying and lobbyists consider public policy lobbying much more important than land use and procurement lobbying. At first glance, this seems reasonable. After all, contentious high-profile policy battles certainly seem more important than clashes over who gets a government contract to print that map or whether or not that oil refinery gets permission for expansion. But at second glance, this assertion is hard to defend. Remember, this is a book about *lobbying and lobbyists*. To a lobbyist representing a business firm that prints maps and sells them to the government, procurement decisions about which printer to hire may literally be life-and-death matters. Similarly, to the owners of an oil refinery that seeks to expand its facilities, land use decisions are crucially important – arguably more so than government public policy decisions about whether or not to go to war or to sanction gay marriages. Thus, while public policy decisions may *seem* more important than procurement or land use decisions, they are not necessarily so. Moreover, lobbyists in the United States are not active solely on public policy issues. For these reasons and more, in this book I take an expansive view of lobbying and examine land use and procurement lobbying, as well as public policy lobbying.

Does the Classification System Work?

Now that you have read this book, you are in a good position to answer the following question: Does the threefold classification system I use here actually *work*? I believe that the answer is "Yes." (However, I would be remiss if I did not admit that I am biased on the matter). I say this because Chapters 3–6 demonstrate that there are indeed substantial differences among public policy, land use, and procurement lobbying. While the differences are manifold, as summarized at the end of Chapters 4–6, nine in particular stand out:

- *Public policy lobbying is unique in that it is practiced by a wide range (indeed, virtually the entire range) of types of organized interests.*

about lobbying in the United States. In fact, it became clear to me mid-way through my interviews that the "public policy" category I use is quite broad. It is so broad, in fact, that it encompasses lobbying on literally hundreds of issues, including issues as disparate as national defense, education, and immigration. Political scientists have long believed that there are different *kinds* of public policies, and some have even formulated policy typologies. I stand by my conclusion that public policy lobbying differs in predictable and important ways from both land use and procurement lobbying. Nonetheless, I concur that there are different kinds of public policies, and thus I believe that there are different kinds of public policy lobbying. Unfortunately, this substantial topic must, as they say, wait for another time – and another book.

APPENDIX B

Methodological Notes

In this brief methodological appendix I describe: (1) my data-gathering approach and (2) the way I selected my sample of respondents.

THE APPROACH: ELITE INTERVIEWING

Of the many ways to study lobbyists and lobbying, I employed *elite interviewing* as my principal method of inquiry. In this section, I discuss the pros and cons of elite interviewing and how I attempted to minimize problems associated with this method.

The Basic Approach

Elite interviewing is defined as "a specialized case of interviewing that focuses on a particular type of interviewee. Elite individuals are considered to be the influential, the prominent, and the well-informed people in an organization or community and are selected for interviews on the basis of their expertise in areas relevant to the research."[1]

I chose elite interviewing primarily because of the enormous amounts of data it produces. As mentioned in Chapter 1, ultimately I conducted a total of 34 interviews, 33 over the telephone, and 1 in person. I tape-recorded (with respondents' permission) and later transcribed 32 of the 33 telephone interviews. I transcribed the remaining 1 telephone interview and 1 in-person lobbyist interview on the spot.[2] In all, my interviews produced 248 single-spaced pages (more than 120,000 words) of interview transcripts.[3]

Elite Interviewing as a Methodology: Some Pitfalls
and How I Dealt with Them

Although the primary strength of elite interviewing is that it has the capacity to produce a surfeit of data, it is not without disadvantages. The most
obvious problem is that elite interview data are fraught with reliability and
validity problems.[4] In the most general sense, validity problems are those
that cause us to offer erroneous descriptions of the world, while reliability
"is a matter of whether a particular technique, applied repeatedly to the
same object, would yield the same result each time."[5]

To alleviate reliability and validity problems, I took six concrete steps.
First, before each interview, I engaged in what political methodol-
ogists Janet Buttolph Johnson and Richard A. Joslyn call "advance
preparation."[6] This entailed two specific activities, research on the topic
and research about my respondents. Before I conducted my interviews,
I researched lobbying, lobbyists, land use, government procurement, and
public policy. I did not set out to learn everything there was to know
about each of these topics, only as much as I needed to know to conduct
useful interviews. Next, I learned as much as I could about each respondent before his or her interview. Specifically, I searched the Internet as
well as newspaper and magazine databases to gather information about
each respondent. Of course, some respondents have higher profiles than
others, but in general I found some information about each interviewee.
The advantages of advance preparation are manifold:[7] (1) It "helps the
researcher to interpret and understand the significance of what is being
said, to recognize a remark that sheds new light on a topic, and to catch
inconsistencies between the interviewee's version and other versions of
events."[8] (2) It impresses the interviewee" with "the researcher's serious
interest in the topic."[9] (3) It "gives the researcher a basis for deciding what
questions to ask and in what order."[10] This last point is especially important here, because some sections of my survey were not appropriate for
some respondents.

The second step I took to alleviate reliability and validity problems was
to rely heavily upon what interest group scholar and veteran interviewer
Jeffrey Berry calls "probing." All of my interviews began with a survey
template comprising a small number of broad, open-ended questions.
However, this template was a mere starting point. During the course of
each interview I formulated probing follow-up questions when necessary. Probes are especially useful when respondents are not forthcom-
ing with information or when a respondent takes "the interviewer down

an unanticipated path."[11] In general, probing is simply asking follow-up questions to get as much information as possible. Probing is beneficial for several reasons: (1) It "allows the researcher to make decisions about what additional questions to ask" as the interview "session progresses."[12] In other words, probing allows a high level of flexibility in data gathering. (2) Probing allows the researcher to "gather more depth about the topic being discussed."[13] (3) Unlike closed-ended survey questions, for example, probing allows respondents to "tell the interviewer what's relevant and what's important rather than being restricted by the researchers' preconceived notions about what is important."[14]

Third, I protected each respondent's identity.[15] Before the interviews, I told respondents that none of their names, their organizations' names, or names of any individual or organization they mentioned during the interview would be revealed to anyone without their permission. I also told each respondent that if I used a direct quote I would not attribute it to any specific individual. After the rough draft of this book was completed, I also allowed respondents to examine the sections that relied on their input. I gave each respondent the opportunity to clarify anything he or she had said during the interview. In addition, I gave each respondent the chance during the interview to declare any statement "off the record" and therefore off limits to me. In short, I took a number of steps to make sure that my respondents would tell me the truth. Candor from respondents is absolutely essential in elite interviewing.[16]

Fourth, I tape-recorded my interviews whenever possible. I failed to record only two interviews – those with respondents no. 12 (who declined permission to be recorded) and no. 26 (whom I interviewed in person).[17] The advantage of tape recording is obvious: It allows for maximum data retrieval and accuracy. Of course, there is always the possibility that a respondent "held back" because his or her interview was being recorded. But in my judgment, respondents were quite forthright in their answers.

Fifth, I used multiple sources. In other words, I interviewed a *lot* of lobbyists. The advantage of multiple sources is that they allow the researcher to "test" what each respondent says by comparing it to what similar respondents say. Is a respondent telling the truth? Does his or her account of events seem plausible? These questions can be addressed by using multiple sources.[18] This is, admittedly, a crude way to discern how much stock to put in the words of each respondent. While my sample size is relatively small (compared to the sample sizes of some of the large-scale survey studies I mentioned in Chapter 2), it is large enough to ensure that one or two or three interviews did not have undue influence over the final results. In further defense of my relatively small number of interviews, I must resort to the old "breadth over depth" argument. While previous studies have tended to sacrifice depth for breadth, this study sacrifices breadth for depth.

Sixth, I conducted all the interviews myself. I did so because I wanted to be sure that each respondent was questioned in the same fashion. In general, interpreting data gathered from elite interviews is easier if there are not multiple interviewers.

In sum, I took these six concrete steps to gather accurate, valid, and reliable data.

THE SAMPLE OF RESPONDENTS

Choosing whom to interview was not a straightforward task. Most scholars of survey and interview research conclude that randomly selecting interviewees is the best way to ensure that data are accurate. But random selection was not an option here. Unfortunately, we have no way to determine the precise makeup of the lobbyist universe in the United States. For example, we do not know how many lobbyists are procurement, or land use, or public policy lobbyists. Therefore, I could not be sure that a random sample (especially if it was small, which it by necessity would be given the labor-intensive method I used here) would include representatives from each category of lobbyist.[19] Because I wished to learn about each category of lobbyists regardless of the number of lobbyists it contained (for example, I wanted to learn about procurement lobbyists even if they constitute only a small fraction of the population of lobbyists in the United States), I could not take the chance of using a random sample. Instead, I used a type of quota sample to locate lobbyists in all three categories.

The Nature of the Sample

Ultimately, I decided to utilize a type of quota sample. I began by conducting Internet searches for lobbyists in each category. For example, to locate procurement lobbyists I entered the terms *procurement lobbyist, procurement lobbying,* and *procurement* into the google.com Internet search engine, chose a page arbitrarily, and tried to identify specific procurement lobbyists. To locate public policy and land use lobbyists I used the same basic procedure. Most interviewees were chosen in this fashion. Six respondents, however, were not: They are: Lobbyist no. 6, who is a friend of a family member (though I did not know him before I interviewed him); Lobbyist no. 11, who was referred to me by Lobbyist no. 24; Lobbyist no. 14, who was referred to me by Lobbyist no. 22; Lobbyist no. 24, who is a former student of mine; Lobbyist no. 26, who is a Washington contract lobbyist introduced to me by a friend; and Lobbyist no. 34, who was also introduced to me by a friend.

Initially, I did not set a target number of interviews, though I did believe that I would need to interview approximately 100 lobbyists to learn everything I wanted to learn. It became clear early on, however, that 100 interviews would not be necessary. After 30 interviews, I concluded that a few more interviews were all I needed to get a good general portrait of the differences among land use, procurement, and public policy lobbyists. As mentioned in Chapter 1, I interviewed a total of 34 lobbyists. In the end, I followed the advice of qualitative research guru Steinar Kvale, who suggests that interviewers interview "as many subjects as necessary to find out what you need to know."[20] I am in no way implying that my interviews taught me everything there is to know about lobbyists. What I am saying is that by the time I finished, I was satisfied that I had collected enough data to limn a broad but accurate portrait of lobbyists in each category.

Making Contact. To locate each lobbyist, I attempted to make contact by e-mail, asking if he or she would be willing to participate in a study entitled "What Lobbyists Want from Government." If the lobbyist replied and expressed interest, I sent a follow-up message stating that I would telephone at a time and place of his or her choosing for an interview. After the interview time was set, I did so. If the lobbyist granted me permission, I tape-recorded the interview. The survey contained a series of basic background questions, as well as one section for each lobbying specialty – that is, one section on land use lobbying, one section on procurement lobbying, and one section on public policy lobbying. Each lobbyist answered the same set of background questions, as well as those questions that pertained to his or her lobbying specialty or specialties. I contacted a total of 63 lobbyists, 34 of whom agreed to participate, for a response rate of 54 percent.

A Nonrepresentative Sample. Table 1 (in Chapter 1) shows that my sample is far from representative. For example, the sample has a disproportionate number of federal government lobbyists and lobbyists who work for consulting, law, lobbying, or public relations firms. This, however, is not all that troubling because the key variable in this study is the type of government decision a lobbyist attempts to affect. In other words, given what I was attempting to learn, the overrepresentation of federal lobbyists and "outside" lobbyists is more or less irrelevant.

Table 1 also suggests that my sample has a disproportionate number of public policy lobbyists. The overrepresentation of these lobbyists is due primarily to the fact that many sample lobbyists dabble in public policy lobbying in addition to their primary focus. If we consider only the primary category in which sample lobbyists fit, the number in each category is as follows: 14 public policy lobbyists, 13 procurement lobbyists, and 7 land use lobbyists. This, too, seems a bit off-kilter, as the sample seems to underrepresent land use lobbyists. But it is probably reflective of the relative proportion of land use lobbyists in the United States, as they are active almost exclusively at the local level, whereas public policy and procurement lobbyists operate at all three levels of government.

Potential Problems. I am the first to acknowledge that my sampling method has not produced an ideal sample of lobbyists. In addition to the fact that contract lobbyists are overrepresented, my sampling technique possibly excluded from consideration a potentially large group of lobbyists for whom there is no contact or professional information available on the Internet. Are my findings generalizable? Possibly not. Perhaps a better term for my data would be what methodologist Martyn Denscombe calls "transferable." Transferability refers to:

> a process in which the researcher and the readers infer how the findings might relate to other situations. They literally "transfer" the research situation to other situations. The transferability of the findings relies on information being provided about the people, events, or data being studied – information that is sufficiently detailed to allow an informed judgement [*sic*] about how far and how well the findings map on to other situations.[21]

This said, at this point I have no reason to believe that the respondents I chose are radically different from others of their type. In other words, I believe that a great deal of my data *is* generalizable.

In sum, the sample I utilize here is a quota sample. Though it is far from perfect, I believe it allowed me to reach a number of conclusions about the nature of lobbying in the United States.

My basic research approach can best be described as what Clifford Geertz calls "thick description," by which "an account of a situation . . . manages to capture the many facets, the various angles and the multiple levels that comprise the complex reality of social life."[22] My effort at "thick description" is designed to provide the broad outlines of lobbying in the United States.

Notes

1. STUDYING LOBBYISTS AND LOBBYING

1. These vignettes are based on lobbyists I interviewed for this book. Their names have been changed to protect their anonymity.
2. In this book, I use the terms *bureaucrats* and *executive agency personnel* interchangeably.
3. For more information on my classification scheme, see Appendix A.
4. Frank R. Baumgartner and Beth L. Leech, *Basic Interests: The Importance of Groups in Politics and in Political Science* (Princeton, NJ: Princeton University Press, 1998), p. 33 (italics theirs).
5. Lester W. Milbrath, *The Washington Lobbyists* (Chicago: Rand McNally & Company, 1963); Robert H. Salisbury, "Washington Lobbyists: A Collective Portrait," in Allan J. Cigler and Burdett A. Loomis (eds.), *Interest Group Politics*, Second Edition, (Washington, DC: CQ Press, 1986), pp. 146–161.
6. Baumgartner and Leech, *Basic Interests*, p. 34.
7. Paul A. Sabatier, "The Need for Better Theories," in Paul A. Sabatier (ed.), *Theories of the Policy Process* (Boulder, CO: Westview Press, 1999), pp. 3–17, at p. 3.
8. Clive S. Thomas, "Introduction: The Study of Interest Groups," in Clive S. Thomas (ed.), *Research Guide to U.S. and International Interest Groups* (Westport, CT: Praeger Publishers, 2004), pp. 1–23, at p. 6.
9. Anthony J. Nownes, *Pressure and Power: Organized Interests in American Politics* (Boston: Houghton Mifflin Company, 2001), p. 8.
10. This definition comes from William P. Browne, *Groups, Interests, and U.S. Public Policy* (Washington, DC: Georgetown University Press, 1998), pp. 11–12.
11. Kay Lehman Schlozman and John T. Tierney, *Organized Interests and American Democracy* (New York: Harper and Row Publishers, 1986), see especially Chapter 4.
12. See, for example, Jack L. Walker, "The Origins and Maintenance of Interest Groups in America," *American Political Science Review* 77 (1983), 390–406; Robert H. Salisbury, "Interest Representation: The Dominance of Institutions," *American Political Science Review* 78 (1984), 64–76.
13. Thomas, "Introduction," p. 6.

2. LOBBYING AND LOBBYISTS IN THE UNITED STATES: A PRIMER

1. Kevin Phillips, *Arrogant Capital: Washington, Wall Street, and the Frustration of American Politics* (Boston: Little, Brown and Company, 1994), p. 33; John R. Wright, *Interest Groups and Congress: Lobbying, Contributions, and Influence* (Needham Heights, MA: Allyn and Bacon, 1996), p. 10.

2. Robert J. Hrebenar, *Interest Group Politics in America*, Third Edition (Armonk, NY: M. E. Sharpe, Inc., 1997), p. 17.

3. Nownes, *Pressure and Power*, p. 11.

4. For a directory (albeit incomplete) of business firms that engage in political activity, see Valerie S. Sheridan (ed.), *National Directory of Corporate Public Affairs 2004, Twenty-Second Edition* (Washington, DC: Columbia Books, Inc. 2004).

5. Nownes, *Pressure and Power*, p. 11. For information on trade associations active in the United States, see Buck Downs (ed.), *National Trade and Professional Associations of the United States, 2005* (Washington, DC: Columbia Books, Inc. 2005).

6. See "About Us," (Washington, DC: U.S. Chamber of Commerce, 2005). Electronic document accessed at http://www.uschamber.com/about/default on December 16, 2005. See also "Careers at the Nam" (Washington, DC: National Association of Manufacturers, 2005). Electronic document accessed at http://www.nam.org/s_nam/sec.asp?CID=201992&DID=232221 on December 16, 2005.

7. In fact, many business firms belong to more than one trade association.

8. Nownes, *Pressure and Power*, p. 13. For information on professional associations active in the United States, see Downs (ed.), *National Trade and Professional Associations of the United States, 2005.*

9. "About the ABA" (Chicago: American Bar Association, n.d.). Electronic document accessed at http://www.abanet.org/about/home.html on December 20, 2005. See also "Membership Eligibility" (Chicago, IL: American Medical Association, 2005). Electronic document accessed at http://www.ama-assn.org/ama/pub/category/12051.html on December 16, 2005.

10. "About APII" (Haddon Heights, NJ: Professional Association of Innkeepers, 2004). Electronic document accessed at http://www.paii.org/contactus.asp on December 21, 2005. See also "About the Association of Professional Chaplains" (Schaumburg, IL: Association of Professional Chaplains, 2005). Electronic document accessed at http://www.professionalchaplains.org/index.aspx?id=95&TierSlicer1_TSMenuTargetID=6&TierSlicer1_TSMenuTargetType=4&TierSlicer1_TSMenuID=1 on December 16, 2005.

11. Nownes, *Pressure and Power*, p. 13. For a directory (though incomplete) of citizen groups, see CQ Editors (eds.), *Public Interest Group Profiles, 2004–2005* (Washington, DC: CQ Press, 2004).

12. "50+: AARP Annual Report 2003" (Washington, DC: AARP, 2004). Electronic document accessed at http://assets.aarp.org/www.aarp.org_/articles/aboutaarp/AARPCorporateAR2003.pdf on December 12, 2005. See also "NRA.org" (Washington, DC: National Rifle Association, 2005). Electronic

document accessed at http://www.nra.org on December 16, 2005. See also "Inside Sierra Club" (San Francisco: Sierra Club, n.d.). Electronic document accessed at http://www.sierraclub.org/inside on December 16, 2005.

13. Nownes, *Pressure and Power,* p. 12. For a good directory of labor unions, see *Directory of Labor Unions* (n.p., n.d.). Electronic document accessed at http://www.unionism.com/director.htm on December 16, 2005.

14. "Who Are the Teamsters" (Washington, DC: International Brotherhood of Teamsters, 2004). Electronic document accessed at http://org.teamster.org/whoare.htm on December 16, 2005. See also "About AFSCME" (Washington, DC: American Federation of State, County and Municipal Employees, n.d.). Electronic document accessed at http://www.afscme.org/about/index.html on December 16, 2005.

15. "About Us," (Washington, DC: ALF-CIO, 2005). Electronic document accessed at http://aflcio.org/aboutus on December 16, 2005.

16. Nownes, *Pressure and Power*, pp. 14 and 15.

17. Ronald G. Shaiko, "Making the Connection: Organized Interests, Political Representation, and the Changing Rules of the Game in Washington Politics," in Paul S. Herrnson, Ronald G. Shaiko, and Clyde Wilcox (eds.), *The Interest Group Connection: Electioneering, Lobbying, and Policymaking in Washington,* Second Edition (Washington, DC: CQ Press, 2005), pp. 1–24, at p. 11.

18. Nownes, *Pressure and Power,* p. 14. For a history of think tanks in America, see James G. McGann, "Academics to Ideologues: A Brief History of the Public Policy Research Industry," *PS: Political Science and Politics* 25 (1992), 733–740.

19. "About AEI" (Washington, DC: American Enterprise Institute, 2005). Electronic document accessed at http://www.aei.org/about/filter.all/default.asp on December 16, 2005.

20. "About the Heritage Foundation" (Washington, DC: The Heritage Foundation, 2005). Electronic document accessed at http://www.heritage.org/about/ on December 16, 2005.

21. For information on charities that lobby, see the Web site for Center for Lobbying in the Public Interest at http://www.clpi.org/. Electronic document accessed on December 16, 2005.

22. See "Advocacy: Take Action Now" (Chicago: Alzheimer's Association, 2005). Electronic document accessed at http://www.alz.org/Advocacy/overview.asp on December 16, 2005.

23. See "Advocacy and Public Policy" (Washington, DC: American Cancer Society, Inc., 2005). Electronic document accessed at http://www.cancer.org/docroot/AA/content/AA_2_3_Advocacy_and_Public_Policy.asp?sitearea=AA on December 16, 2005.

24. Nownes, *Pressure and Power,* p. 15. For a nice discussion of university and college lobbying, see Constance Ewing Cook, *Lobbying for Higher Education: How Colleges and Universities Influence Federal Policy* (Nashville, TN: Vanderbilt University Press, 1998).

25. Alan Rosenthal, *The Third House: Lobbyists and Lobbying in the States*, Second Edition (Washington, DC: CQ Press, 2001), p. 148. The preeminent work on

coalitions is Kevin W. Hula, *Lobbying Together: Interest Group Coalitions in Legislative Politics* (Washington, DC: Georgetown University Press, 1999).

26. For information on the Tax Relief Coalition, see http://www.taxreliefcoalition.org/. Electronic document accessed on December 16, 2005. For information on the Sustainable Energy Coalition, see http://www.sustainableenergy.org/. Electronic document accessed on December 16, 2005.

27. Nownes, *Pressure and Power,* pp. 14–15.

28. For a brief discussion of such firms, see Shaiko, "Making the Connection," pp. 12–16.

29. You may have also noticed that I do not discuss political action committees (PACs) here. The reason is that many PACs are affiliated with other organizations.

30. To see current federal lobbying registration documents, visit the United States Senate's Office of Public Records Web site at http://sopr.senate.gov/. See also The Office of the Clerk of the House of Representative's Web site at http://clerk.house.gov/pd/. Electronic documents, both accessed on December 30, 2005.

31. On lobbying in local politics, see Glenn Abney and Thomas P. Lauth, "Interest Group Influence in City Policy-Making: The Views of Administrators," *Western Political Quarterly* 38 (1985), 148–161; Christopher A. Cooper and Anthony J. Nownes, "Citizen Groups in Big City Politics," *State and Local Government Review* 35 (2003), 102–111; Robert Jay Dilger, *Neighborhood Politics: Residential Community Associations in American Governance* (New York: New York University Press, 1992); David R. Elkins, "The Structure and Context of the Urban Growth Coalition: The View from the Chamber of Commerce," *Policy Studies Journal* 23 (Winter 1995), 583–600. On lobbying in the states, see Virginia Gray and David Lowery, *The Population Ecology of Interest Representation: Lobbying Communities in the American States* (Ann Arbor: The University of Michigan Press, 1996); Ronald J. Hrebenar and Clive S. Thomas (eds.), *Interest Group Politics in the Southern States* (Tuscaloosa: University of Alabama Press, 2002); Ronald J. Hrebenar and Clive S. Thomas (eds.), *Interest Group Politics in the Northeastern States* (University Park: The Pennsylvania State University Press, 1993); Anthony J. Nownes and Patricia Freeman, "Interest Group Activity in the States," *Journal of Politics* 60 (1998), 86–112; Rosenthal, *The Third House.*

32. Joseph A. Dunn, *New York Temporary State Commission on Lobbying: 2004 Annual Report* (New York: New York Temporary State Commission on Lobbying, 2004). Electronic document accessed at http://www.nylobby.state.ny.us/annreport/03artext.html on December 16, 2005. *2004 Annual Report to the Governor and the General Assembly* (Nashville: Tennessee Registry of Election Finance, 2005). Electronic document accessed at http://64.233.161.104/search?q=cache:43J7Z0qpHPcJ:www.state.tn.us/tref/forms/ar2004.pdf+number+of+registered+lobbyists+2004&hl=en on December 16, 2005. "Number of Lobbyists and Lobbyist Agents, 2004," (Lansing: State of

Michigan, 2004). Electronic document accessed at http://www.michigan
.gov/documents/L-Number_of_L_and_L_Agents-info_sheet_04_108724_7.pdf
on December 16, 2005.

33. W. Michael Cox and Richard Alm, "The Fruits of Free Trade," *The Insider*
(Washington, DC: The Heritage Foundation, 2003), pp. 3–6, at p. 4.
Electronic document accessed at http://www.heritage.org/about/community/
insider/2003/aug03/fruits.pdf. on December 16, 2005.

34. "2004 Lobbying Registrations," (Los Angeles: Los Angeles City Ethics
Commission, 2005). Electronic document accessed at http://ethics.lacity
.org/EFS2003/index.cfm?fuseaction=lobreports.firmbylobbyist&year=2004
on December 16, 2005.

35. There was some overlap in these two groups of registered lobbyists. See "Individual Lobbyist Registered with Los Angeles County," (Los Angeles: County
of Los Angeles, 2005). Electronic document accessed at http://bos.co.la.ca.us/
lobbyist/reglob.htm on December 16, 2005.

36. See "Registered Lobbyist, 2004" (Anchorage, AK: Municipality of Anchorage, 2004). Electronic document accessed at http://www.muni.org/iceimages/
Assembly2/2004_lobbyist_1-24-05.pdf on December 16, 2005. See also "Registered Lobbyists Index, 2004," (Nashville: The Metropolitan Government
of Nashville and Davidson County, Tennessee, 2004). This document is no
longer available online, but an updated document is. See "Registered Lobbyists Index, 2005" (Nashville: The Metropolitan Government of Nashville
and Davidson County, Tennessee, 2005). Electronic document accessed
at http://www.nashville.gov/mc/lobbyist_index_2005.htm on December 19,
2005.

37. Cooper and Nownes, "Citizen Groups in Big City Politics," p. 107; Thomas L.
Gais and Jack L. Walker, Jr., "Pathways to Influence in American Politics,"
in Jack L. Walker, Jr. (ed.), *Mobilizing Interest Groups in America: Patrons, Professions and Social Movements* (Ann Arbor: The University of Michigan Press,
1991), pp. 103–121; Ken Kollman, *Outside Lobbying: Public Opinion and Interest Group Strategies* (Princeton, NJ: Princeton University Press, 1998), Chapter
2; Nownes and Freeman, "Interest Group Activity in the States," p. 92; Kay
Lehman Schlozman and John T. Tierney, "More of the Same: Washington
Pressure Group Activity in a Decade of Change," *Journal of Politics* 45 (1983),
357.

38. This list is not meant to be definitive. Clearly, there are more lobbying techniques than the ones listed in Table 2. Nonetheless, these are the techniques
that studies indicate are the most common.

39. For one of the best treatments of legislative lobbying, see Wright, *Interest Groups
and Congress*. See also Marie Hojnacki and David C. Kimball, "Organized Interests and the Decision of Whom to Lobby in Congress," *American Political Science
Review* 92 (1998), 775–790; Kevin M. Leyden, "Interest Group Resources and
Testimony at Congressional Hearings," *Legislative Studies Quarterly* 20 (1995),
431–439; Bruce C. Wolpe and Bertam J. Levine, *Lobbying Congress: How the*

System Works, Second Edition (Washington, DC: Congressional Quarterly Inc., 1996).

40. For more information on the value of legislative hearings to both lobbyists and legislators, see Wright, *Interest Groups and Congress*, pp. 40–43.

41. Rosenthal, *The Third House*, pp. 111–114.

42. At the federal and state levels of government, there is a strict separation of powers between the legislature and the chief executive (as well as the executive bureaucracy). In some localities, however, this is not the case.

43. For details on executive agency lobbying, see Steven J. Balla and John R. Wright, "Interest Groups, Advisory Committees, and Congressional Control of the Bureaucracy," *American Journal of Political Science* 45 (2001), 799–812; Daniel P. Carpenter, "Groups, the Media, Agency Waiting Costs, and FDA Drug Approval," *American Journal of Political Science* 46 (2002), 490–505; Scott R. Furlong, "Exploring Interest Group Participation in Executive Policymaking," in Herrnson et al., *The Interest Group Connection*, Second Edition, pp. 282–297; Marissa Martino Golden, "Interest Groups in the Rule-Making Process: Who Participates? Whose Voices Get Heard?" *Journal of Public Administration Research and Theory* 8 (1998), 245–270; Cornelius M. Kerwin, *Rulemaking: How Government Agencies Write Law and Make Policy* (Washington, DC: CQ Press, 1994), Chapter 5. Surprisingly little research has been done on state and local executive branch lobbying.

44. For information on lobbying chief executives, see Mark A. Peterson, "The Presidency and Organized Interests: White House Patterns of Interest Group Liaison," *American Political Science Review* 86 (1992), 612–625; Joseph A. Pika, "Opening Doors for Kindred Souls: The White House Office of Public Liaison," in Allan J. Cigler and Burdett A. Loomis (eds.), *Interest Group Politics*, Third Edition, (Washington, DC: CQ Press, 1991), pp. 277–298. Relatively little research has been conducted on lobbying governors and local chief executives.

45. Kathryn Dunn Tenpas, "Lobbying the Executive Branch: Outside-In and Inside-Out," in Herrnson et al., *The Interest Group Connection*, Second Edition, pp. 249–257.

46. Tenpas, "Lobbying the Executive Branch," pp. 252–253.

47. See Furlong, "Exploring Interest Group Participation in Executive Policymaking," p. 289.

48. Wright, *Interest Groups and Congress*, p. 52.

49. See Suzanne J. Piotrowski and David H. Rosenbloom, "The Legal-Institutional Framework for Interest Group Participation in Federal Administrative Policymaking," in Herrnson et al., *The Interest Group Connection*, Second Edition, pp. 258–281.

50. For more information on judicial branch lobbying, see Gregory A. Caldeira and John R. Wright, "Amici Curiae before the Supreme Court: Who Participates, When, and How Much?" *Journal of Politics* 52 (1990), 782–806; Gregory A. Caldeira and John R. Wright, "Organized Interests and Agenda Setting in the U.S. Supreme Court," *American Political Science Review* 82 (1988),

1109–1127; Lee Epstein, "Exploring the Participation of Organized Interests in State Court Litigation," *Political Research Quarterly* 47 (1994), 335–351; Joseph F. Kobylka, "A Court-Created Context for Group Litigation: Libertarian Groups and Obscenity," *Journal of Politics* 49 (1987), 1061–1078; Susan M. Olson, "Interest-Group Litigation in Federal District Court: Beyond the Political Disadvantage Theory," *Journal of Politics* 52 (1990), 854–882.

51. In truth, there is a variety of ways that organized interests engage in litigation. For more information, see Karen O'Connor, "Lobbying the Justices or Lobbying for Justice? The Role of Organized Interests in the Judicial Process," in Herrnson et al., *The Interest Group Connection*, Second Edition, pp. 319–340.

52. Jeffrey M. Berry, *The Interest Group Society*, Third Edition (New York: Longman, 1997), p. 175.

53. For details on the Court's ruling, see *Brown v. Board of Education*, 347 U.S. 483 (1954). Electronic document accessed at http://caselaw.lp.findlaw.com/scripts/getcase.pl?court=US&vol=347&invol=483 on December 16, 2005.

54. O'Connor, "Lobbying the Justices or Lobbying for Justice? The Role of Organized Interests in the Judicial Process," pp. 329–331.

55. Berry, *The Interest Group Society*, p. 116.

56. Clyde Wilcox and Dong-Young Kim, "Continuity and Change in the Congressional Connection," in Herrnson et al., *The Interest Group Connection*, Second Edition, pp. 129–140.

57. Wilcox and Kim, "Continuity and Change in the Congressional Connection," p. 137.

58. Nownes, *Pressure and Power*, p. 171. The terms *initiative* and *referendum* are sometimes used interchangeably and sometimes not. In some places, referenda are special kinds of initiatives that are first passed by the legislature and then must be approved by the public to take effect. For more information on the differences between referenda and initiatives, see "Initiatives, Referendum and Recall," (Denver: National Conference of State Legislatures, 2005). Electronic document accessed at http://www.ncsl.org/programs/legman/elect/initiat.htm on December 16, 2005.

59. For more information on direct democratic lobbying techniques, see Robert M. Alexander, *Rolling the Dice with State Initiatives: Interest Group Involvement in Ballot Campaigns* (Westport, CT: Praeger Publishers, 2002); Elisabeth R. Gerber, *The Populist Paradox: Interest Group Influence and the Promise of Direct Legislation* (Princeton, NJ: Princeton University Press, 1999).

60. I do not have space here to summarize the laws and regulations that govern organized interest contributions. These laws and regulations vary between levels of government and from place to place. For more information on electoral lobbying, see Robert Biersack, Paul S. Herrnson, and Clyde Wilcox (eds.), *After the Revolution: PACs, Lobbies, and The Republican Congress* (Boston, Allyn and Bacon, 1999); M. Margaret Conway, Joanne Connor Green, and Marian Currinder, "Interest Group Money in Elections," in Allan J. Cigler and Burdett A. Loomis (eds.), *Interest Group Politics*, Sixth Edition (Washington, DC:

CQ Press, 2002), pp. 117–140; Gary C. Jacobson, "The Effect of the AFL-CIO's 'Voter Education' Campaigns on the 1996 House Elections," *Journal of Politics* 61 (1999), 185–194; Timothy B. Krebs, "Urban Interests and Campaign Contributions: Evidence from Los Angeles," *Journal of Urban Affairs* 27 (2005), 165–176; David Magleby (ed.), *Election Advocacy: Soft Money and Issue Advocacy in the 2000 Congressional Elections* (Provo, UT: Brigham Young University Press, 2000); Mark J. Rozell, Clyde Wilcox, and David Madland, *Interest Groups in American Campaigns: The New Face of Electioneering,* Second Edition (Washington, DC: CQ Press, 2006); David Schultz (ed.), *Money, Politics, and Campaign Finance Reform Law in the States* (Durham, NC: Carolina Academic Press, 2002).

61. The rules governing in-kind contributions are complicated and varied as well.
62. Paul S. Herrnson, "Interest Groups and Campaigns: The Electoral Connection," in Herrnson et al., *The Interest Group Connection,* Second Edition, pp. 25–48, at p. 33 (italics his). Dr. Herrnson notes that there are several different ways that organized interests (again, usually through their PACs) try to help or hurt candidates.
63. For more information on election issue advocacy, see Robert Biersack and Marianne H. Viray, "Interest Groups and Federal Campaign Finance: The Beginning of a New Era," in Herrnson et al., *The Interest Group Connection,* Second Edition, pp. 49–74, at pp. 57–59; Magleby, *Election Advocacy*; Mark J. Rozell and Clyde Wilcox, *Interest Groups in American Campaigns: The New Face of Electioneering* (Washington, DC: CQ Press, 1999), p. 113.
64. For information on the electoral activities of conservative Christian organizations, see John C. Green, Mark J. Rozell, and Clyde Wilcox (eds.), *The Christian Right in American Politics: Marching to the Millennium* (Washington, DC: Georgetown University Press, 2003); John C. Green, Mark J. Rozell, and Clyde Wilcox (eds.), *Prayers in the Precincts: The Christian Right in the 1998 Elections* (Washington, DC: Georgetown University Press, 2000); James L. Guth, Lyman A. Kellstedt, John C. Green, and Corwin E. Smidt, "A Distant Thunder? Religious Mobilization in the 2000 Elections," in Cigler and Loomis, *Interest Group Politics,* Sixth Edition, pp. 161–184.
65. "2004 Sierra Club Endorsements" (San Francisco: Sierra Club, 2004). Electronic document accessed at http://www.sierraclub.org/endorsements/2004/ on December 16, 2005.
66. This definition is paraphrased from Nownes, *Pressure and Power,* p. 147, and is based upon the definition found in Rozell and Wilcox, *Interest Groups in American Campaigns,* p. 126.
67. "2004 Christian Coalition Voter Guide" (Washington, DC: Christian Coalition of America, 2004). Electronic document accessed at http://www.cc.org/voterguides2004/national.pdf on December 16, 2005.
68. This is especially true in light of the Bipartisan Campaign Reform Act of 2002 (BCRA), which changed federal campaign finance law substantially. For details on the BCRA, see "Bipartisan Campaign Reform Act of 2002,"

(Washington, DC: Federal Election Commission, n.d.). Electronic document accessed at http://www.fec.gov/pages/bcra/bcra_update.shtml on December 16, 2005.

69. The preeminent study of organized interest coalitions is Hula, *Lobbying Together*. For an interesting and informative case study, see Kevin W. Hula, "Dolly Goes to Washington: Coalitions, Cloning, and Trust," in Herrnson et al., *The Interest Group Connection*, Second Edition, pp. 229–248.

70. Kollman, *Outside Lobbying;* Nownes and Freeman, "Interest Group Activity in the States," pp. 91–92; Darrell M. West and Burdett A. Loomis, *The Sound of Money: How Political Interests Get What They Want* (New York: W. W. Norton and Company, 1998).

71. Several studies, however, have established the effectiveness of specific lobbying techniques (without addressing the larger question of which techniques are most and least effective). For example, on the effectiveness of entering into coalitions, see Hula, *Lobbying Together*. On the effectiveness of contributing money to candidates, see Matthew C. Fellowes and Patrick J. Wolf, "Funding Mechanisms and Policy Instruments: How Business Campaign Contributions Influence Congressional Votes," *Political Research Quarterly* 57 (2004), 315–324. See also Christine DeGregorio, "Assets and Access: Linking Lobbyists and Lawmakers in Congress," in Paul S. Herrnson, Ronald G. Shaiko, and Clyde Wilcox (eds.), *The Interest Group Connection: Electioneering, Lobbying, and Policymaking in Washington* (Chatham, NJ: Chatham House Publishers, Inc. 1998), pp. 137–153; Richard L. Hall and Frank W. Wayman, "Buying Time: Moneyed Interests and the Mobilization of Bias in Congressional Committees," *American Political Science Review* 84 (1990), 797–820; Dennis P. Quinn and Robert Y. Shapiro, "Business Political Power: The Case of Taxation," *American Political Science Review* 85 (1991), 851–874; John R. Wright, "PACs, Contributions, and Roll Calls: An Organizational Perspective," *American Political Science Review* 79 (1985), 400–414. On the effectiveness of grassroots lobbying, see Jeffrey M. Berry, *Lobbying for the People: The Political Behavior of Public Interest Groups* (Princeton, NJ: Princeton University Press, 1977), Chapter 8; James G. Gimpel, "Grassroots Organizations and Equilibrium Cycles in Group Mobilization and Access," in Herrnson et al., *The Interest Group Connection*, pp. 100–115; Kelly Patterson, "The Political Firepower of the National Rifle Association," in Cigler and Loomis, *Interest Group Politics*, Fifth Edition, pp. 119–142; West and Loomis, *The Sound of Money*.

72. Berry, *Lobbying for the People*, Chapter 8.

73. Milbrath, *The Washington Lobbyists*, Chapters 11 and 12.

74. Clive S. Thomas, "Interest Group Power and Influence," in Thomas, *Research Guide to U.S. and International Interest Groups*, pp. 192–196, at p. 192.

75. See Baumgartner and Leech, *Basic Interests*, Chapter 8.

76. Wright, *Interest Groups and Congress*. See also Kevin M. Esterling, *The Political Economy of Expertise: Information and Efficiency in American National Politics* (Ann Arbor: The University of Michigan Press, 2004).

77. Wright, *Interest Groups and Congress*, p. 82.

78. Ibid.
79. Ibid., p. 75.
80. Ibid., p. 88.
81. For example, see Raymond A. Bauer, Ithiel de Sola Pool, and Lewis Anthony Dexter, *American Business and Public Policy: The Politics of Foreign Trade*, Second Edition (Chicago: Aldine Atherton, Inc., 1972); Kollman, *Outside Lobbying*, Chapter 1; John Mark Hansen, *Gaining Access: Congress and the Farm Lobby, 1919–1981* (Chicago, The University of Chicago Press, 1991), Chapter 1; Milbrath, *The Washington Lobbyists*, especially Chapter 15.
82. Frank R. Baumgartner and Beth L. Leech, "Interest Niches and Policy Bandwagons: Patterns of Interest Group Involvement in National Politics," *Journal of Politics* 63 (2001), 1191–1213. See also Baumgartner and Leech, *Basic Interests*, Chapter 5.
83. Virginia Gray and David Lowery, "The Institutionalization of State Communities of Organized Interests," *Political Research Quarterly* 54 (2001), 265–284; Gray and Lowery, "The Demography of Interest Organization Communities."
84. On the high level of lobbying activity by business interests in local politics, see Abney and Lauth, "Interest Group Influence in City Policy-Making"; Paul Schumaker and Russell W. Getter, "Structural Sources of Unequal Responsiveness to Group Demands in American Cities," *Western Political Quarterly* 36 (1983), 7–29. It is interesting that despite the substantial presence of business interests, both studies show that neighborhood groups are the preeminent lobbying organizations active in local politics.
85. Berry, *The Interest Group Society*, p. 68 (italics mine).
86. Ibid. Berry actually uses the Chamber of Commerce as an example. I chose to use a different example to show that the logic works across a variety of group contexts.
87. See Mancur Olson, *The Logic of Collective Action: Public Goods and the Theory of Groups* (Cambridge, MA: Harvard University Press, 1971).
88. Something else to keep in mind when explaining why institutions are so well represented by lobbyists is that many institutions (especially business firms) lobby for *private goods* rather than collective goods. Private goods are *goods that if attained by an organized interest accrue solely to that organized interest*. An example of a private good would be an exclusive government contract to provide a city with asphalt to fill in potholes. The contract may be worth thousands of dollars, and all of this money benefits the company that wins the contract and no one else. The free-rider problem does not apply to organized interests seeking private goods.
89. John P. Heinz, Edward O. Laumann, Robert L. Nelson, and Robert H. Salisbury, *The Hollow Core: Private Interests in National Policy Making* (Cambridge, MA: Harvard University Press, 1993), Chapters 3 and 4; Nownes and Freeman, "Interest Group Activity in the States," pp. 94–96; Rosenthal, *The Third House*, pp. 65–71; Robert H. Salisbury, "The Paradox of Interest Groups in Washington – More Groups, Less Clout," in Anthony King (ed.), *The New American Political System*,

Second Version (Washington, DC: The AEI Press, 1990), pp. 203–229, at pp. 225–228.

90. Salisbury, "The Paradox of Interest Groups in Washington – More Groups, Less Clout," p. 225. See also Elizabeth A. Capell and Clive S. Thomas, "The Role of Lobbyists," in Thomas, *Research Guide to U.S. and International Interest Groups,* pp. 154–160; Richard A. Harris, "Politicized Management: The Changing Face of Business in American Politics," in Richard A. Harris and Sidney M. Milkis (eds.), *Remaking American Politics* (Boulder, CO: Westview Press, 1989), pp. 261–286; Heinz et al., *The Hollow Core*; Nownes and Freeman, "Interest Group Activity in the States"; Rosenthal, *The Third House.*

91. Rogan Kersh, "Corporate Lobbyists as Political Actors: A View from the Field," in Cigler and Loomis, *Interest Group Politics,* Sixth Edition, pp. 225–248, at pp. 241–242.

92. Ibid., pp. 236–237.

93. Ibid., p. 237.

94. Actually, Kersh finds that lobbyists spend over half of their time on activities that he calls "combination" activities – activities that encompass more than one specific activity. Explaining issues, however, is the most common activity besides combination activities.

95. Kersh, "Corporate Lobbyists as Political Actors," p. 236.

96. Ibid., p. 237.

97. Ibid.

98. See especially Robert A. Dahl, *Who Governs? Democracy and Power in an American City* (New Haven, CT: Yale University Press, 1961); David B. Truman, *The Governmental Process: Political Interests and Public Opinion* (New York: Alfred A. Knopf, 1951).

99. David Lowery and Holly Brasher, *Organized Interests and American Government* (Boston: McGraw Hill, 2004), p. 18.

100. See, for example, Browne, *Groups, Interests, and U.S. Public Policy,* Chapter 7; Heinz et al., *The Hollow Core,* Chapter 11.

101. See William P. Browne, "Organized Interests and Their Issue Niches: A Search for Pluralism in a Policy Domain," *Journal of Politics* 52 (1990), 477–509.

102. Heinz et al., *The Hollow Core,* p. 351.

103. Clive S. Thomas, "Lobbyists: Definitions, Types, and Varying Designations," in Thomas, *Research Guide to U.S. and International Interest Groups,* pp. 151–154, at p. 152. See also Salisbury, "Washington Lobbyists," p. 154.

104. Rosenthal, *The Third House,* pp. 102–107; Wolpe and Levine, *Lobbying Congress,* p. 13.

105. Milbrath, *The Washington Lobbyists,* Chapter 5; Rosenthal, *The Third House,* Chapter 2; Salisbury, "Washington Lobbyists," pp. 151–153.

106. Among the factors that appear to affect which techniques a lobbyist chooses to use are the following: First is the type of organization(s) for which the lobbyist works (e.g., whether or not it is for a business organized interest). See Gais and Walker, "Pathways to Influence in American Politics"; Kollman,

Outside Lobbying, Chapter 2. The second factor is what a lobbyist's opponents are doing (e.g., how hard the opponents are lobbying against him or her). See David Austen-Smith and John R. Wright, "Counteractive Lobbying," *American Journal of Political Science* 38 (1994), 25–44; Thomas T. Holyoke, "Choosing Battlegrounds: Interest Group Lobbying across Multiple Venues," *Political Research Quarterly* 56 (2003), 325–336. Third is the beliefs and dispositions of potential lobbying targets (e.g., whether a specific government decision maker normally agrees with the lobbyist or not). See Austen-Smith and Wright, "Counteractive Lobbying"; Arthur T. Denzau and Michael C. Munger, "Legislators and Interest Groups: How Unorganized Interests get Represented," *American Political Science Review* 80 (1986), 89–106; Hojnacki and Kimball, "Organized Interests and the Decision of Whom to Lobby in Congress"; John R. Wright, "Contributions, Lobbying, and Committee Voting in the U.S. House of Representatives," *American Political Science Review* 84 (1990), 417–438. Fourth is a lobbyist's past experiences (e.g., whether or not the lobbyist has had success lobbying a particular venue or government official in the past). See Frank R. Baumgartner and Bryan D. Jones, *Agendas and Instability in American Politics* (Chicago: The University of Chicago Press, 1993), Chapter 2; Thomas G. Hansford, "Lobbying Strategies, Venue Selection, and Organized Interest Involvement at the U.S. Supreme Court," *American Politics Research* 32 (2004), 170–197; Olson, "Interest-Group Litigation in Federal District Court." Fifth is the scope and nature of a lobbyist's personal relationships with government officials (e.g., who the lobbyist knows). See Scott Ainsworth, "Regulating Lobbyists and Interest Group Influence," *Journal of Politics* 55 (1993), 41–56; Scott H. Ainsworth, "The Role of Legislators in the Determination of Interest Group Influence," *Legislative Studies Quarterly* 22 (1997), 517–533. Sixth is a lobbyist's professional status (i.e., whether he or she is a contract lobbyist or an in-house lobbyist). See Rosenthal, *The Third House,* pp. 38–39.

3. PUBLIC POLICY LOBBYING, PART ONE

1. James E. Anderson, *Public Policymaking,* Fourth Edition, (Boston: Houghton Mifflin, Company, 2000), p. 4.
2. Ibid., p. 5.
3. Ibid.
4. This is a hybrid definition that combines elements of several definitions I found online. See "Definitions of **law** on the Web" (n.p., n.d.). Electronic document accessed at http://www.google.com/search?hl=en&lr=&rls=GGLD, GGLD:2003-33,GGLD:en&oi=defmore&q=define:law on December 16, 2005.
5. "Glossary of Terms," (Columbus: State of Ohio General Assembly, 2005). Electronic document accessed at http://www.legislature.state.oh.us/glossary.cfm on December 20, 2005.
6. Norman J. Ornstein, Thomas E. Mann, and Michael J. Malbin, *Vital Statistics on Congress, 2001–2002* (Washington, DC: The AEI Press, 2002), p. 149.

7. Gary L. Galemore, *Presidential Vetoes, 1789–Present: A Summary Overview* (Washington, DC: Congressional Research Service, 2003). Electronic document accessed at http://64.233.161.104/search?q=cache:3LM_sOb8HooJ:lugar.senate.gov/CRS%2520reports/Presidential_Vetoes_1789-Present_A_Summary_Overview.pdf+number+of+vetoes+overridden&hl=en on December 16, 2005.

8. Actually, in some local governments, the chief executive is part of the legislature. In "weak mayor" systems, for example, mayors are essentially members of the legislative body who do not have the broad array of administrative powers that governors and presidents do. In "strong mayor" systems, however, mayors are somewhat similar to the president and governors.

9. As Chapter 5 illustrates, *local* bureaucratic agencies make important land use decisions as well as public policy decisions.

10. For more information on delegation of power to bureaucratic agencies, see James Fesler and Donald Kettl, *The Politics of the Administrative Process* (Chatham, NJ: Chatham House Publishers, 1991); Charles Goodsell, *The Case for Bureaucracy: A Public Administration Polemic,* Second Edition (Chatham, NJ: Chatham House Publishers, 1985).

11. This example comes from Michael S. Greve, "Power without Responsibility: How Congress Abuses the People through Delegation – book reviews," *Reason* (January, 1995). Electronic document accessed on-line at http://www.findarticles.com/p/articles/mi_m1568/is_n8_v26/ai_16530812 on December 16, 2005.

12. This definition borrows heavily from the State of California's definition of *regulation*. See "California Code of Regulations, Frequently Asked Questions" (Sacramento: State of California, n.d.). Electronic document accessed at http://www.calregs.com/faq.htm on December 16, 2005.

13. Robert Crowe, "Gay Couples Face Hurdles as Judges Interpret Law," *Houston Chronicle,* June 25, 2004. Electronic document accessed at http://www.hrc.org/Template.cfm?Section=Home&CONTENTID=20390&TEMPLATE=/Content Management/ContentDisplay.cfm on December 19, 2005.

14. This is not exactly the case, as the federal government has commissioned a number of studies to learn about global warming and has urged industry to cut down on certain emissions. But as of this writing, the federal government has not adopted any large-scale policies designed to combat global warming.

15. John W. Kingdon, *Agendas, Alternatives, and Public Policies* (Boston: Little, Brown and Company, 1984), p. 4.

16. One public policy lobbyist, Lobbyist no. 26, is a freelance contract lobbyist.

17. Salisbury, "The Paradox of Interest Groups in Washington," pp. 225–228.

18. "State Legislative Monitoring," (Arlington, VA: Stateside Associates, n.d.). Electronic document accessed at http://www.stateside.com/intelligence/state.shtml on December 19, 2005.

19. "Regulatory Services," (Arlington, VA: Stateside Associates, n.d.). Electronic document accessed at http://www.stateside.com/intelligence/regulatory.shtml on December 19, 2005.

20. Economics majors and more advanced political science students may recognize that the relationship between a lobbyist and his or her boss is a principal–agent relationship. In such a relationship, one party, the principal (in this case, the boss) hires an agent (in this case, the lobbyist) to perform tasks on his or her behalf. Problems arise because the principal cannot be sure (because the agent cannot be observed 24 hours a day) that the agent is performing the way the principal wishes. One way for a principal to keep tabs on the agent is through monitoring, which is what I am talking about here. For more information on the lobbyist as agent, see Kersh, "Corporate Lobbyists as Political Actors."

4. PUBLIC POLICY LOBBYING, PART TWO

1. See, for example, Kollman, *Outside Lobbying*, p. 35; Nownes and Freeman, "Interest Group Activity in the States," p. 92; Schlozman and Tierney, "More of the Same," p. 357.
2. Kollman, *Outside Lobbying*, Chapter 2; Nownes and Freeman, "Interest Group Activity in the States," p. 92; Schlozman and Tierney, "More of the Same," p. 357.
3. Some local legislatures do not have an independent executive.
4. Peterson, "The Presidency and Organized Interests"; Rosenthal, *The Third House*, pp. 11–12.
5. There is surprisingly little research on the role of bureaucratic agencies in local public policymaking. For information on what local bureaucrats do, see Robert E. England, "City Managers and the Urban Bureaucracy," in John P. Pelissero (ed.), *Cities, Politics, and Policy: A Comparative Analysis* (Washington, DC: CQ Press, 2003), pp. 196–216.
6. "Environmental Permitting Handbook," (Nashville: State of Tennessee, Department of Environment and Conservation, n.d.). Electronic document accessed at http://www.state.tn.us/environment/permits accessed on December 19, 2005.
7. See, for example, the classics: John W. Kingdon, *Congressmen's Voting Decisions*, Second Edition (New York: Harper and Row, 1981); David R. Mayhew, *Congress: The Electoral Connection* (New Haven, CT: Yale University Press, 1974).
8. The additional lobbyist who mentioned grassroots lobbying, Lobbyist no. 8, neglected to tell me what kind of grassroots lobbying techniques he uses.
9. This phrase was coined by organized interest expert Jeffrey Berry. For details, see Berry, *The Interest Group Society*, p. 117.
10. Two studies that demonstrate this are Kingdon, *Congressmen's Voting Decisions*, and Mayhew, *Congress*.
11. This does not mean that the others do not contribute money. I did not explicitly ask my respondents whether or not they make monetary contributions. Instead, I let the respondents speak freely about their lobbying activities, and only six mentioned monetary contributions.

12. Though monetary contributions sometimes flow from PACs or individuals to elected officials who are not legislators – chief executives, for example – almost all research on the influence of money on elected officials' behavior has been conducted on legislators. Thus, the studies I cite here focus on legislators, rather than other kinds of elected officials.

13. See, for example, R. Kenneth Godwin, *One Billion Dollars of Influence: The Direct Marketing of Politics* (Chatham, NJ: Chatham House Publishers, Inc., 1988); Stephen Moore, Sidney M. Wolfe, Deborah Lindes, and Clifford E. Douglas, "Epidemiology of Failed Tobacco Control Legislation," *Journal of the American Medical Association* 272 (1994), 1171–1175; Quinn and Shapiro, "Business Political Power."

14. See, for example, Janet M. Grenzke, "PACs and the Congressional Supermarket: The Currency is Complex," *American Journal of Political Science* 33 (1989), 1–24; Wright, "PACs, Contributions, and Roll Calls"; Wright, "Contributions, Lobbying, and Committee Voting in the U.S. House of Representatives."

15. Rosenthal, *The Third House*, pp. 136–140.

16. See Hall and Wayman, "Buying Time"; Wright, "Contributions, Lobbying, and Committee Voting in the U.S. House of Representatives."

17. Because bureaucrats do not run for office, they are ineligible to receive monetary contributions. Federal judges and many state judges also do not run for office, and are thus also ineligible to receive contributions.

18. "Woody Allen Quotes," (n.p.: BrainyMedia, Inc., 2005). Electronic document accessed at http://www.brainyquote.com/quotes/authors/w/woody_allen .html on December 19, 2005.

19. See, for example, Thomas E. Patterson, *The Vanishing Voter: Public Involvement in an Age of Uncertainty* (New York: Vintage Books, 2003); Martin P. Wattenberg, *Where Have All the Voters Gone?* (Cambridge, MA: Harvard University Press, 2002).

20. See, for example, West and Loomis, *The Sound of Money*.

5. LAND USE LOBBYING

1. I obtained information on Paramahansa Yogananda from the following sources: No Author, "Self-Realization Fellowship," (Charlottesville, VA: The Religious Movements Homepage Project, 1998). Electronic document accessed at http://religiousmovements.lib.virginia.edu/nrms/SelfReal.html on December 19, 2005. "The Life of Paramahansa Yogananda," (Los Angeles: Self-Realization Fellowship, 2000). Electronic document accessed at http://www.yogananda-srf.org/py-life/index.html on December 19, 2005. "Paramhansa Yogananda," (Portland, OR: Extra Gentle Yoga, n.d.). Electronic document accessed at http://www.extragentleyoga.com/Master.htm on December 19, 2005. Kristen Holland, "Yogi's Movement Still Growing 50 Years after Death," *Dallas Morning News*, March 9, 2002. Electronic document accessed at http://www.rickross.com/reference/selfreal/selfreal5.html on December 19, 2005.

2. For information on the SRF's current activities, see the Self-Realization Fellowship home page at http://www.yogananda-srf.org/. Electronic document accessed on December 30, 2005.

3. See Ron Russell, "Return of the Swami," *Los Angeles New Times*, July 1, 1999. Electronic document accessed at http://www.rickross.com/reference/selfreal/selfreal2.html on December 19, 2005. Ron Russell, "A Mountain of Discontent," *Los Angeles New Times*, June 1, 2000. Electronic document accessed at http://www.rickross.com/reference/selfreal/selfreal1.html on December 19, 2005.

4. Paul E. Peterson, *City Limits* (Chicago: The University of Chicago Press, 1981), p. 25.

5. Stuart Meck, Paul Wack, and Michelle J. Zimet, "Zoning and Subdivision Regulations," in Charles J. Hoch, Linda C. Dalton, and Frank S. So (eds.), *The Practice of Local Government Planning*, Third Edition (Washington, DC: The International City/County Management Association, 2000), pp. 343–374, at p. 346.

6. I use the terms *governing body* and *local legislative body* and *local legislature* interchangeably throughout this chapter.

7. Arnold Fleischmann, "Politics, Administration, and Local Land-Use Regulation: Analyzing Zoning as a Policy Process," *Public Administration Review* 49 (1989), 337–344, at p. 337.

8. Meck et al., "Zoning and Subdivision Regulations," p. 350.

9. Ibid.

10. This definition comes from the home page of Henderson County, North Carolina. See "Frequently Asked Questions about the Comprehensive Plan," (Hendersonville: Henderson County, North Carolina, n.d.) Electronic document accessed at http://www.hendersoncountync.org/planning/ccp/FAQ.html on December 19, 2005.

11. For more information on comprehensive plans, see "A Citizen's Guide to Planning," (Sacramento, CA: Governor's Office of Planning and Research, 2001), pp. 3–5.

12. "The Conditional Use Permit," (Sacramento, CA: Governor's Office of Planning and Research, 1997). Electronic document accessed at http://ceres.ca.gov/planning/cup/condition.htm on December 19, 2005.

13. These categories are my own and do not reflect the full range of land use decisions.

14. Eric Damian Kelly, "Zoning," in Frank S. So and Judith Getzels (eds.), *The Practice of Local Government Planning*, Second Edition (Washington, DC: The International City Management Association, 1988), pp. 251–284, at p. 257.

15. Ibid., p. 258.

16. These phrases and ones like them appear in zoning ordinances throughout the country.

17. "Pierce County Planning and Land Services: Zoning Code Quick Answers," (Pierce County, WA: Pierce County, 2005). Electronic document accessed at http://www.co.pierce.wa.us/text/services/home/property/pals/regs/zoning.htm on December 19, 2005.

18. Ibid.
19. "Glossary of Terms" (Various locations: Crye-Leike Realtors, 2004). Electronic document accessed at http://www.crye-leike.com/commercial/glossary.php on December 19, 2005.
20. Katherine Barnard, "Zoning Variances: A Citizen's Guide to Westport's Permit Process" (Westport: The Town of Westport, CT, 1999). Electronic document accessed at http://www.ci.westport.ct.us/publication/forms/forms/variance_guide.pdf on December 19, 2005.
21. It is worth noting, however, that the process by which a developer wins approval for a comprehensive plan amendment is quite similar to the process by which a developer wins approval for a rezoning.
22. See, for example, Michael E. Kraft, and Bruce B. Clary, "Citizen Participation and the NIMBY Syndrome: Public Response to Radioactive Waste Disposal," *Western Political Quarterly* 44 (1991), 299–328; Berry G. Rabe, *Beyond NIMBY: Hazardous Waste Siting in Canada and the United States* (Washington, DC: The Brookings Institution, 1994); Eric R. A. N. Smith and Marisela Marquez, "The Other Side of the NIMBY Syndrome," *Society and Natural Resources* 13 (2000), 273–280.
23. Robert H. Nelson, an expert on neighborhood associations, estimates that there are more than 200,000 neighborhood associations in the United States. See p. 30 of Robert H. Nelson, "The Rise of Private Neighborhood Associations: A Constitutional Revolution in Local Government," a paper prepared for presentation at the Lincoln Institute of Land Policy conference entitled "The Property Tax, Land Use and Land Use Regulation," January 13–15, 2002, Scottsdale, Arizona. For more information on neighborhood associations and other local organized interests involved in land use politics, see Hugh Butcher, *Community Groups in Action: Case Studies and Analysis* (Boston: Routledge and Kegan Paul, 1980); Dilger, *Neighborhood Politics*; John R. Logan and Gordana Rabrenovic, "Neighborhood Associations: Their Issues, Their Allies, and Their Opponents," *Urban Affairs Quarterly* 26 (1990), 68–94; Robert C. Lowry, "All Hazardous Waste Politics Is Local: Grass-Roots Advocacy and Public Participation in Siting and Cleanup Decisions" *Policy Studies Journal* 26 (1998), 748–759; David J. O'Brien, *Neighborhood Organization and Interest-Group Processes* (Princeton, NJ: Princeton University Press, 1975); Willett Kempton, Dorothy C. Holland, Katherine Bunting-Howarth, Christopher Payne, and Erin Hannan, "Local Environmental Groups: A Systematic Enumeration in Two Geographical Areas," *Rural Sociology* 66 (2001), 557–578.
24. Henderson, Nevada, is a midsize city outside of Las Vegas. It was the fastest-growing city in the United States from 1990 to 1998, and remains among the five fastest growing as of this writing.
25. A buffer is a small strip of land – often one with trees and/or grass – that separates a development or project from some other structure or a road.
26. Of these types of organized interests, the data suggest that churches, universities and colleges, and hospitals are most active in land use politics because they own land.

27. See, for example, Fleischmann "Politics, Administration, and Local Land use Regulation."
28. Wright, *Interest Groups and Congress*, p. 88.

6. PROCUREMENT LOBBYING

1. Danielle Brian, "Economic Impacts of the National Security Build-up: Government Procurement Practices," Council on Foreign Relations speech, Project on Government Oversight. Electronic document accessed at http://www.pogo.org/p/contracts/co-021101-reform.html on December 19, 2005.
2. Tanya N. Ballard, "Lawmaker Wants More Inquiries into Charge Card Abuses," *GovExec.com* (Washington, DC: National Journal Group, Inc., 2002). Electronic document accessed at http://www.govexec.com/dailyfed/1002/100802t1.htm on December 19, 2005.
3. Khi V. Thai, "Public Procurement Re-Examined," *Journal of Public Procurement* 1 (2001), 9–50, at p. 21.
4. Steven J. Kelman, "Contracting," in Lester M. Salamon (ed.), *The Tools of Government: A Guide to the New Governance*, (New York: Oxford University Press, 2002), pp. 282–318, at p. 288.
5. Although in many states the budget process is somewhat similar to the federal budget process, at the local level, it varies from place to place, and in some cases looks quite different from the federal process. The biggest difference exists in cities with city managers rather than strong mayors. In city manager cities, the city manager generally prepares the proposed budget and submits it to the legislature.
6. Kelman, "Contracting," p. 289 (italics his).
7. Scott A. Stanberry, *Federal Contracting Made Easy* (Vienna, VA: Management Concepts, 2001), p. 19. The text of the FAR is available online at http://www.arnet.gov. Electronic document accessed on January 2, 2006.
8. Susan A. MacManus, with the assistance of Steven A. Watson and Donna Camp-Blair, *Doing Business with Government: Federal, State, Local, and Foreign Government Purchasing Practices for Every Business and Public Institution* (New York: Paragon House Publishers, 1992), pp 50–54.
9. Kelman, "Contracting," p. 290.
10. Another key choice in contracting is whether to use a "cost-reimbursement" contract or a "fixed-price" contract. As the name implies, in a fixed-price contract, a government entity agrees to pay a contractor an "agreed-upon cost for a specific unit of a good or service." In contrast, in a cost-reimbursement contract, a government entity agrees to reimburse a contractor for justifiable direct and indirect costs and to provide a certain specified profit. For details, see McManus, et al., *Doing Business with Government*, p. 54.
11. Kelman, "Contracting," p. 296.
12. MacManus et al., *Doing Business with Government*, p. 42.

13. A variant of competitive sealed bidding, often used by the Department of Defense, is what political scientist Susan McManus calls "two-step formal advertising and bidding." In the first step, the government entity issues an IFB, then evaluates each vendor's technical capacities without considering price. After acceptable vendors have been identified, the government accepts formal bids and uses price as the determining factor. See Susan A. MacManus et al., *Doing Business with Government*, p. 47.

14. *Women Business Owners: Selling to the Federal Government* (Washington, DC: Small Business Administration, 1995). Electronic document accessed at http://www.sba.gov/gopher/Government-Contracting/Sell/sellall.txt on December 19, 2005.

15. Kelman, "Contracting," p. 299.

16. Ibid.

17. FAR 48 CFR §42.1501. Accessed online at http://www.arnet.gov/far/current/html/Subpart%2042_15.html on December 19, 2005.

18. "Best Value Purchasing," (Frankfort: Finance and Administration, State of Kentucky, 1999), p. 7. Electronic document accessed at http://www.state.ky.us/agencies/adm/leadership/bestvalue/sld007.htm on December 19, 2005.

19. Kelman, "Contracting," p. 300.

20. John R. Bartle, and Ronnie LaCourse Korosec, "Procurement and Contracting in State Government, 2000," (Syracuse, NY: The Government Performance Project at the Campbell Public Affairs Institute at Syracuse University, 2001), pp. 13–14. Electronic document accessed at http://www.maxwell.syr.edu/gpp/pdfs/ProcurementContracting_in_State_Government.pdf on March 28, 2006.

21. "Women Business Owners."

22. Kelman, "Contracting," p. 303.

23. Ibid., p. 304.

24. "Women Business Owners."

25. FAR 13.002. Electronic document accessed at http://farsite.hill.af.mil/reghtml/regs/far2afmcfars/fardfars/far/13.htm on December 19, 2005.

26. There are numerous other simplified acquisition procedures, but I do not discuss them all in this book.

27. "Wal-Mart Stores Inc." (Yahoo Finance, Industry Center, 2005). Electronic document accessed at http://finance.yahoo.com/q?s=WMT&d=t on December 19, 2005.

28. One respondent, Lobbyist no. 34 is no longer a lobbyist but was formerly a contract procurement lobbyist.

29. This is not the company's real name.

30. Some agencies, especially for large and complex procurements, issue RFQs (requests for qualifications) before they issue RFPs. This is especially common at the local level. Lobbyists may be involved in this process as well, helping clients prepare documents to prove they are qualified.

31. I changed the nature of the actual product in question at the respondent's request.

32. This is a pseudonym used at the respondent's request.
33. In the interest of full disclosure, I wish to note that this quote came from an e-mail message that Lobbyist no. 16 sent me after our initial telephone interview. I thanked him by e-mail after our conversation, and he responded at length.
34. Stanberry, *Federal Contracting Made Easy*, p. 198.
35. I was asked by Lobbyist no. 33 not to divulge the precise details of the product in question.
36. Lobbyist no. 33 was quick to note that this is "not the way it usually works."
37. I must caution, however, that grassroots procurement lobbying is not unheard of. Large government contractors – defense firms, in particular – often advertise their wares on radio, television, and even on public transportation. The goal of such lobbying is not to reach the public at large, but rather to reach procurement personnel who ultimately make procurement decisions. Journalist Ellen McCarthy of the *Washington Post* is one of the few people who has studied this phenomenon. See Ellen McCarthy, "Contractors Take Message to Their People," *Washington Post*, November 28, 2005, p. D1. Electronic document accessed at http://www.washingtonpost.com/wp-dyn/content/article/2005/11/27/AR2005112700758.html?nav=rss_technology/techpolicy on December 16, 2005.
38. In many cases, procurement lobbyists do not actually demonstrate the products they sell, but rather leave this task to the company's representatives.
39. Wright, *Interest Groups and Congress*, p. 88.
40. Thai, "Public Procurement Re-Examined," p. 25.
41. "Federal Procurement Resources for Minority- and Woman-Owned Businesses" (Vienna, VA: Fairfax County Economic Development Authority, 2003). Electronic document accessed at http://www.fairfaxcountyeda.org/publications/minority_procurement.pdf, on December 19, 2005.
42. FAR, Part 25. Electronic document accessed at http://www.arnet.gov/far/current/html/FARTOCP25.html on December 19, 2005. There are numerous exceptions to the Buy American Act.

7. RECAP AND FINAL THOUGHTS

1. The best evidence for this is Heinz et al., *The Hollow Core*, Chapter 11.
2. Numerous scholars of the "neo-pluralist" school have concluded that conflict among organized interests is far from rare during public policy battles. See especially Thomas L. Gais, Mark A. Peterson, and Jack L. Walker, "Interest Groups, Iron Triangles and Representative Institutions in American National Government," *British Journal of Political Science* 14 (1984), 161–185; Hank C. Jenkins-Smith, Gilbert K. St. Clair, and Brian Woods, "Explaining Change in Policy Subsystems: Analysis of Coalition Stability and Defection over Time," *American Journal of Political Science* 35 (1991), 851–880.
3. This is one of the primary insights offered by organized-interest expert William P. Browne. See Browne, "Organized Interests and Their Issue Niches." See also Baumgartner and Leech, "Interest Niches and Policy Bandwagons"; James Q.

Wilson, *Political Organizations* (New York: Basic Books, Inc. Publishers, 1973), pp. 263–267.

4. Business firms, in particular, often ask for things to which no one objects. For details, see Mark A. Smith, *American Business and Political Power: Public Opinion, Elections, and Democracy* (Chicago: The University of Chicago Press, 2000), especially Chapter 2. See also R. Kenneth Godwin and Barry J. Seldon, "What Corporations Really Want from Government: The Public Provision of Private Goods," in Cigler and Loomis, *Interest Group Politics*, Sixth Edition, pp. 205–224.

5. On not asking for everything you want, see Rosenthal, *The Third House*, p. 181.

6. For more on the cautious nature of lobbyists and organized interests, see Wilson, *Political Organizations*, pp. 263–267.

7. For more on the power of ordinary citizens, see Smith, *American Business and Political Power*, Chapter 5. See also the provocative Peter F. Nardulli, *Popular Efficacy in the Democratic Era: A Reexamination of Electoral Accountability in the United States, 1828–2000* (Princeton, NJ: Princeton University Press, 2005).

8. For an excellent discussion of how regulation has led to more business lobbying, see Harris, "Politicized Management." See also William P. Browne, "Exchange Theory and the Institutional Impetus for Interest Group Formation," in Cigler and Loomis, *Interest Group Politics*, Sixth Edition, pp. 313–329; David Plotke, "The Political Mobilization of Business," in Mark P. Petracca (ed.), *The Politics of Interests: Interest Groups Transformed* (Boulder, CO: Westview Press, 1992), pp. 175–198.

9. Indeed, this question has been debated for decades. For details on the ongoing debate, see Graham K. Wilson, "Thirty Years of Business and Politics," paper presented at the IPSA Research Group on Business and Politics, May 2002, London, England. See also David M. Hart, "'Business' Is Not an Interest Group: On the Study of Companies in American National Politics," *Annual Review of Political Science* 7 (2004), 47–69.

10. For more on the idea that numbers do not always translate into power, see Gary Mucciaroni, *Reversals of Fortune: Public Policy and Private Interests* (Washington, DC: The Brookings Institution, 1995).

11. There are many studies that document the fact that businesses are far from omnipotent. Here are a few: Martha A. Derthick, *Up in Smoke: From Legislation to Litigation in Tobacco Politics* (Washington, DC: CQ Press, 2002); James T. Hamilton, "Testing for Environmental Racism: Prejudice, Profits, Political Power?" *Journal of Policy Analysis and Management* 14 (1995), 107–132; Andrew S. McFarland, "Interest Groups and Political Time: Cycles in America," *British Journal of Political Science* 21 (1991), 257–284; Neil J. Mitchell, *The Conspicuous Corporation: Business, Public Policy, and Representative Democracy* (Ann Arbor: The University of Michigan Press, 1997).

12. Two classic studies of the disproportionate resources and thus power of business organized interests are Robert A. Dahl, *Democracy and Its Critics* (New Haven, CT: Yale University Press, 1989) and Charles E. Lindblom, *Politics and Markets: The World's Political-Economic Systems* (New York: Basic Books Inc., Publishers, 1977).

13. While my data clearly suggest this is the case, the literature is somewhat ambiguous on this point. See especially Heinz et al., *The Hollow Core*, Chapter 11.
14. For more on this, see West and Loomis, *The Sound of Money*.
15. See Fred Block, *Revising State Theory: Essays in Politics and Postindustrialism* (Philadelphia: Temple University Press, 1987); Jacob S. Hacker, and Paul Pierson, "Business Power and Social Policy: Employers and the Formation of the American Welfare State," *Politics and Society* 30 (2002), 277–325; Lindblom, *Politics and Markets*.
16. Political scientist Rogan Kersh makes this same argument in Kersh, "Corporate Lobbyists as Political Actors."
17. Studies that emphasize the efficacy and use of personal meetings include Berry, *Lobbying for the People*; Jeffrey H. Birnbaum, *The Lobbyists: How Influence Peddlers Get Their Way in Washington* (New York: Times Books, 1992); Milbrath, *The Washington Lobbyists*; Rosenthal, *The Third House*, Chapter 6.
18. Several studies support the notion that money buys access. For example, see David B. Magleby and Candice J. Nelson, *The Money Chase: Congressional Campaign Finance Reform* (Washington, DC: The Brookings Institution, 1990); Larry J. Sabato, *Paying for Elections: The Campaign Finance Thicket* (New York: Priority Press Publications, 1989); Frank J. Sorauf, *Inside Campaign Finance: Myths and Realities* (New Haven, CT: Yale University Press, 1992).
19. Of course, monetary contributions *can* have an impact. But most studies suggest that the influence of money is contingent. For a very brief overview of PAC studies, see Ronald J. Hrebenar, "Political Action Committees (PACs)," in Thomas, *Research Guide to U.S. and International Interest Groups*, pp. 147–149.
20. See, for example, data on public opinion concerning whose interests the government serves, on the National Election Studies homepage at http://www.umich.edu/~nes/nesguide/nesguide/toptable/tab5a_2.htm. Electronic document accessed on January 2, 2006.
21. On the importance of public opinion to lobbyists and organized interests, see Ken Kollman, "Interest Groups and Public Opinion," in Thomas, *Research Guide to U.S. and International Interest Groups*, pp. 89–91; Kollman, *Outside Lobbying*; Arthur Lupia, "Busy Voters, Agenda Control, and the Power of Information," *American Political Science Review* 86 (1992), 390–403.

APPENDIX A. THE CLASSIFICATION SYSTEM

1. On the use of classification schemes in general, see Kenneth D. Bailey, *Typologies and Taxonomies: An Introduction to Classification Techniques* (Thousand Oaks, CA: Sage Publications, 1994).
2. See note 31, Chapter 2, for sources.

APPENDIX B. METHODOLOGICAL NOTES

1. Catherine Marshall and Gretchen B. Rossman, *Designing Qualitative Research*, Second Edition (Thousand Oaks, CA: Sage Publications, 1995), p. 83.

2. I recorded my telephone interviews only after having received explicit permission from respondents. One respondent did not wish to be recorded, and so I transcribed his interview on the spot.

3. I am indebted to my research assistant, Krissy Gladders, who transcribed most of the tapes.

4. Jeffrey M. Berry, "Validity and Reliability Issues In Elite Interviewing," (Medford, MA: Tufts University, Department of Political Science, n.d.). Electronic document accessed at http://ase.tufts.edu/polsci/faculty/berry/paper-validity.asp on December 20, 2005.

5. Earl Babbie, *The Practice of Social Research*, Eighth Edition (Belmont, CA: Wadsworth Publishing Company, 1998), p. 129.

6. Janet Buttolph Johnson and H. T. Reynolds, *Political Science Research Methods*, Fifth Edition (Washington, DC: CQ Press, 2005), p. 272.

7. Ibid., pp. 272–273.

8. Ibid., p. 272.

9. Ibid.

10. Ibid.

11. Berry, "Validity and Reliability Issues In Elite Interviewing."

12. Ibid.

13. Ibid.

14. Ibid.

15. For the first several interviews, I read the informed consent statement over the telephone just before the interview. For all subsequent interviews, I e-mailed a copy of the informed consent form to respondents before the interview.

16. Berry, "Validity and Reliability Issues In Elite Interviewing." See also Kenneth Goldstein, "Getting in the Door: Sampling and Completing Elite Interviews," *PS: Political Science and Politics* 35 (2002), 669–672.

17. Lobbyist no. 26 agreed to be recorded. However, early on in our interview, I decided that he was speaking slowly enough that I could take accurate notes, and so I turned off the recorder. I should also note that Lobbyist no. 26 was the first person I interviewed, and thus acted as a sort of pretest for the survey.

18. Berry, "Validity and Reliability Issues In Elite Interviewing."

19. Besides, I do not have a list of the entire population of lobbyists, which would be necessary for a truly random sample.

20. Steinar Kvale, *InterViews: An Introduction to Qualitative Research Interviewing* (Thousand Oaks, CA: Sage Publications, 1996), p. 101.

21. Martyn Denscombe, *Ground Rules for Good Research: A 10 point Guide for Social Researchers* (Buckingham, UK: Open University Press, 2002), pp. 149–150.

22. Ibid.

Index